God

www.**penguin**.co.uk

By Reza Aslan

BOOKS

God: A Human History

Zealot: The Life and Times of Jesus of Nazareth

*Beyond Fundamentalism: Confronting Religious
Extremism in the Age of Globalization*
(originally published as *How to Win a Cosmic War:
God, Globalization, and the End of the War on Terror*)

*No god but God: The Origins, Evolution,
and Future of Islam*

EDITED COLLECTIONS

*Tablet & Pen: Literary Landscapes from
the Modern Middle East*

*Muslims and Jews in America: Commonalities,
Contentions, and Complexities*
(with Aaron J. Hahn Tapper)

God

A Human History

REZA ASLAN

BANTAM PRESS

LONDON · TORONTO · SYDNEY · AUCKLAND · JOHANNESBURG

TRANSWORLD PUBLISHERS
61–63 Uxbridge Road, London W5 5SA
www.penguin.co.uk

Transworld is part of the Penguin Random House group of companies
whose addresses can be found at global.penguinrandomhouse.com

First published in Great Britain in 2017 by Bantam Press
an imprint of Transworld Publishers

A CIP catalogue record for this book
is available from the British Library.

ISBNs
9780593079829 (hb)
9780593079836 (tpb)

Typeset in Sabon
Printed and bound by Clays Ltd, Bungay, Suffolk

Penguin Random House is committed to a sustainable
future for our business, our readers and our planet. This book
is made from Forest Stewardship Council® certified paper.

1 3 5 7 9 10 8 6 4 2

FOR MY SONS,

Cyrus, Jaspar, and Asa, as they embark

on their own spiritual journeys

Contents

x CONTENTS

Part Three

What Is God?

In Our Image

WHEN I WAS A CHILD, I thought God was a large, powerful old man who lived in the sky—a bigger, stronger version of my father, but with magical powers. I imagined him handsome and grizzled, his long gray hair draped over his broad shoulders. He sat on a throne enwrapped by clouds. When he spoke, his voice boomed through the heavens, especially when he was angry. And he was often angry. But he was also warm and loving, merciful and kind. He laughed when he was happy and cried when he was sad.

I'm not sure where this image of God came from. I may have glimpsed it somewhere, painted on stained glass or printed in a book. It could be that I was born with it. Studies have shown that young children, no matter where they are from or how religious they may be, have a difficult time distinguishing between humans and God in terms of action or agency. When asked to imagine God, they invariably describe a human being with superhuman abilities.[1]

As I grew older, I left behind most of my childish views. Yet the image of God remained. I was not raised in a particularly religious household, but I was always fascinated by religion and spirituality. My head teemed with half-formed theories about what God was, where he came from, and what he looked like (curiously, he still resembled my father). I didn't want to simply know about God; I wanted to experience God, to feel his presence in my life. Yet when I tried, I couldn't help but imagine a great chasm opening up between us, with God on one side, me on the other, and no way for either of us to cross over.

In my teens, I converted from the tepid Islam of my Iranian parents to the zealous Christianity of my American friends. All at once, that childhood urge to think of God as a powerful human being crystallized into the worship of Jesus Christ as literally "God made flesh." At first, the experience felt like scratching an itch I had had my entire life. For years, I'd been searching for a way to bridge the chasm between me and God. Now, here was a religion that claimed there was no chasm. If I wanted to know what God was like, all I had to do was imagine the most perfect human being.

It made a certain amount of sense. What better way to remove the barrier between human beings and God than by making God a human being? As the famed German philosopher Ludwig Feuerbach said, in accounting for the enormous success of Christianity's conception of God, "only a being who comprises in himself the whole man can satisfy the whole man."[2]

I first read that Feuerbach quote in college, just around the time I decided to embark on a lifelong quest to study the religions of the world. What Feuerbach seemed to be saying is that the near-universal appeal of a God who looks, and thinks, and feels, and acts just like us is rooted in our deep-seated need to experience the divine as a reflection of ourselves. That truth hit me like a clap of thunder. Is that why I was drawn to Christianity as a kid? Had I been constructing my image of God all this time as a mirror reflecting back to me my own traits and emotions?

The possibility left me feeling bitter and disillusioned. Seeking a more expansive conception of God, I abandoned Christianity and returned to Islam, drawn by the religion's radical iconoclasm: the belief that God cannot be confined by any image, human or otherwise. I quickly recognized, however, that Islam's refusal to depict God in human form did not translate into a refusal to think of God in human terms. Muslims are just as likely as other people of faith to ascribe to God their own virtues and vices, their own feelings and flaws. They have little choice in the matter. Few of us do.

It turns out that this compulsion to humanize the divine is hardwired in our brains, which is why it has become a central feature in almost every religious tradition the world has known. The very process through which the concept of God arose in human evolution compels us, consciously or not, to fashion God in our own image. In fact, the entire history of human spirituality can be viewed as one long, interconnected, ever-evolving, and remarkably cohesive effort to make sense of the divine by giving it our emotions and our personalities, by ascribing to it our traits and our desires, by providing it with our strengths and our weaknesses, even our own bodies—in short, by making God *us*. What I mean to say is that, more often than not, whether we are aware of it or not, and regardless of whether we're believers or not, what the vast majority of us think about when we think about God is a divine version of ourselves: a human being but with superhuman powers.[3]

This is not to claim that there is no such thing as God, or that what we call God is wholly a human invention. Both of these statements may very well be true, but that is not the concern of this book. I have no interest in trying to prove the existence or nonexistence of God for the simple reason that no proof exists either way. Faith is a choice; anyone who says otherwise is trying to convert you. You either choose to believe that there is something beyond the material realm—something real, something *knowable*—or you don't. If, like me, you do, then you must ask yourself another question: Do you wish to experience this thing? Do you wish to commune with it? To *know* it? If so, then it may help to have a language with which to express what is fundamentally an inexpressible experience.

That is where religion comes in. Beyond the myths and rituals, the temples and cathedrals, the dos and don'ts that have, for millennia, separated humanity into different and often competing camps of belief, religion is little more than a "language" made up of symbols and metaphors that allows believers to communicate, to one another and to themselves, the ineffable experience of faith. It's just that, throughout the history of religions, there has been one symbol that has stood out as universal and supreme— one grand metaphor for God from which practically every other symbol and metaphor in nearly all the world's religions has been derived: *us;* the human being.

This concept, which I call "the humanized God," was embedded in our consciousness the moment the idea of God first occurred to us. It led to our earliest theorizing about the nature of the universe and our role in it. It informed our first physical representations of the world beyond ours. Belief in humanized gods guided us as hunter-gatherers, and then, tens of thousands of years later, led us to swap our spears for plows and begin planting instead. Our first temples were built by people who thought of the gods as superhuman beings—as were our first religions. The Mesopotamians, the Egyptians, the Greeks, the Romans, the Indians, the Persians, the Hebrews, the Arabs, all devised their theistic systems in human terms and with human imagery. The same holds true for nontheistic traditions, such as Jainism or Buddhism, both of which conceive of the spirits and devas that populate their theologies as superhuman beings who are, like their human counterparts, bound by the laws of karma.[4]

Even those contemporary Jews, Christians, and Muslims who strive so hard to profess theologically "correct" beliefs about a sole, singular God who is incorporeal or infallible, ever-present or all-knowing, seem compelled to envision God in human form and to speak of God in human terms. Studies performed by a range of psychologists and cognitive scientists have shown that the most devout believers, when forced to communicate their thoughts about God, overwhelmingly treat God as though they were talking about some person they might have met on the street.[5]

Think about the way believers so often describe God as good or loving, cruel or jealous, forgiving or kind. These are, of course, human attributes. Yet this insistence on using human emotions to describe something that is—whatever else it is—utterly *nonhuman* only further demonstrates our existential need to project our humanity onto God, to bestow upon God not just all that is worthy in human nature—our capacity for boundless love, our empathy and eagerness to show compassion, our thirst for justice—but all that is vile in it: our aggression and greed, our bias and bigotry, our penchant for extreme acts of violence.

There are, as one can imagine, certain consequences to this natural impulse to humanize the divine. For when we endow God with human attributes, we essentially *divinize* those attributes, so that everything good or bad about our religions is merely a reflection of everything that is good or bad about us. Our desires become God's desires, but without boundaries. Our actions become God's actions, but without consequence. We create a superhuman being endowed with human traits, but without human limitations. We fashion our religions and cultures, our societies and governments, according to our own human urges, all the while convincing ourselves that those urges are God's.

That, more than anything else, explains why, throughout human history, religion has been a force both for boundless good and for unspeakable evil; why the same faith in the same God inspires love and compassion in one believer, hatred and violence in another; why two people can approach the same scripture at the same time and come away with two radically opposing interpretations of it. Indeed, most of the religious conflicts that continue to roil our world arise from our innate, unconscious desire to make ourselves the apotheosis of what God is and what God wants, whom God loves and whom God hates.

It took many more years for me to realize that the conception of God I was looking for was simply too expansive to be defined by any one religious tradition, that the only way I could truly experience the divine was to *dehumanize* God in my spiritual consciousness.

And so this book is more than just a history of how we have humanized God. It is also an appeal to stop foisting our human compulsions upon the divine, and to develop a more *pantheistic* view of God. At the very least it is a reminder that, whether you believe in one God or many gods or no god at all, it is we who have fashioned God in our image, not the other way around. And in that truth lies the key to a more mature, more peaceful, more *primal* form of spirituality.

Part One

The Embodied Soul

Chapter One

Adam and Eve in Eden

IN THE BEGINNING was the void. Darkness. Chaos. A vast sea of emptiness without shape or substance. No sky, no earth, no waters parted. No gods made manifest nor names pronounced. No fates decreed until . . . a flash, some light, and a sudden expansion of space and time, of energy and matter, of atoms and molecules—the building blocks of a hundred billion galaxies, each studded with a hundred billion stars.

Near one of these stars, a particle of dust, a micrometer in size, collides with another and, through hundreds of millions of years of accretion, it begins to whirl, gathering mass, forming a crust, creating oceans and land and, unexpectedly, *life:* simple, then complex; slithering, then walking.

Millennia pass as glaciers advance and retreat over the surface of the earth. The ice caps melt and the seas rise. Sheets of continental ice soften and slide over the low hills and valleys of Europe and Asia, transforming vast forests into treeless plains. And into this refuge step the incunabula of our species—the "historical" Adam and Eve, if you will: *Homo sapiens,* "the wise human."

Tall, straight-limbed, and powerfully built, with broad noses and unsloped foreheads, Adam and Eve began their evolution between 300,000 and 200,000 B.C.E. as the final branch in the human family tree. Their ancestors trudged out of Africa roughly 100,000 years ago, at a time when the Sahara was not the empty barren it is today but a land of generous lakes and lush vegetation. They crossed the Arabian Peninsula in waves, fanning north across the Central Asian steppes, east into the Indian subcontinent, across the sea to Australia, and west over the Balkans, until they reached southern Spain and the edge of Europe.

Along the way, they encountered earlier species of migrating humans: the upright *Homo erectus,* who had made a similar journey into Europe hundreds of thousands of years earlier; the hearty *Homo denisova,* who roamed the plains of Siberia and east Asia; the barrel-chested *Homo neanderthalensis*—the Neanderthal— whom *Homo sapiens* either annihilated or absorbed (no one knows for sure).[1]

Adam is a hunter, so when you picture him, picture a javelin at his side, a mammoth's fur split and draped across his shoulders. His transformation from prey to predator has left behind a genetic imprint, an instinct for the hunt. He can track an animal over seasons, patiently waiting for the right moment to strike in a blur of violence. When he kills, he does not tear into the meat and devour it on the spot. He brings it back to his shelter to share with his community. Huddled under a broad canopy made of animal hide and framed by mammoth bones, he cooks his food in stone-ringed hearths and stores the leftovers in pits dug deep in the permafrost.

Eve, too, is a hunter, though her weapon of choice is not a javelin but a net, which she has spent months, perhaps years, weaving out of delicate plant fibers. Crouched on the forest floor in the dim early light, she carefully sets her snares along the mossy surface and waits patiently for a hapless rabbit or fox to step into them. Meanwhile her children scour the woods for edible plants, unearthing fungi and roots, scooping up reptiles and large insects to bring back to camp. When it comes to feeding the community, everyone has a role.[2]

The tools Adam and Eve carry are made of flint and stone, but these are not simple gadgets gathered from the ground and easily discarded. They are part of a permanent repertoire: durable and intricately cast; made, not found. Adam and Eve take their tools with them from shelter to shelter and trade them occasionally for better tools, or for trinkets made of ivory or antler, pendants made of bone and teeth and mollusk shells. Such things are precious to them; they set them apart from the rest of their community. When one of them dies and is buried in the ground, these objects will be buried, too, so the deceased can continue to enjoy them in the life to come.[3]

There will be a life to come, of that Adam and Eve are certain. Why else bother with burial? They have no practical reason to bury the dead. It is far easier to expose the bodies, to let them decay out in the open or be stripped clean by the birds. Yet they insist on interring the bodies of their friends and family, on shielding them from the ravages of nature, on according them a measure of respect. They will, for example, deliberately pose the corpse, stretching it out or curling it into fetal position, orienting it toward the east to meet the rising sun. They may scalp or flay the skull, reinter it in a secondary burial, or remove it entirely for display, complete with artificial eyes to simulate a gaze. They may even crack the skull open, scoop out the brain, and devour it.

The body itself they will dust with blood-red ochre (the color a symbol for life) before laying it on a bed of flowers and ornamenting it with necklaces, shells, animal bones, or tools—objects that were dear to the dead; objects he or she may need in the next life. They will light fires around the body and make offerings to it. They will even place stones on the mound to mark the grave so they can find it again and revisit it for years to come.[4]

The assumption is that Adam and Eve do these things because they believe the dead are not really dead but merely in another realm, one that the living can access through dreams and visions. The body may rot but something of the self persists, something distinct and separate from the body—a *soul,* for lack of a better word.[5]

Where they got this idea we do not know. But it is essential to their awareness of themselves. Adam and Eve seem to know *intuitively* that they are embodied souls. It is a belief so primal and innate, so deep-rooted and widespread, that it must be considered nothing less than the hallmark of the human experience. Indeed, Adam and Eve share this belief with their forebears, the Neanderthal and *Homo erectus.* They, too, appear to have practiced various forms of ritual burial, meaning that they, too, may have conceived of the soul as separate from the body.[6]

If the soul is separate from the body, it can survive the body. And if the soul survives the body, then the visible world must teem with the souls of everyone who has ever lived and died. For Adam and Eve, these souls are perceptible; they exist in numberless forms. Disembodied, they become *spirits* with the power to inhabit all things—the birds, the trees, the mountains, the sun, the moon. All of these pulse with life; they are *animated.*

A day will come when these spirits will be fully humanized, given names and mythologies, transformed into supernatural beings, and worshiped and prayed to as gods.

But we are not there yet.

Still, it is no great leap for Adam and Eve to conclude that their souls—the thing that makes them *them*—are not so different in form or substance from the souls of those around them, the souls of those before them, the spirits of the trees, and the spirits in the mountains. Whatever they are, whatever makes up their essence, they share with all creation. They are part of a whole.

This belief is called *animism*—the attribution of a spiritual essence, or "soul," to all objects, human or not—and it is very likely humanity's earliest expression of anything that could be termed *religion*.[7]

OUR PRIMITIVE ANCESTORS, Adam and Eve, are primitive only with regard to their tools and technology. Their brains are as large and developed as ours. They are capable of abstract thoughts and possess the language to share those thoughts with each other. They speak like us. They think like us. They imagine and create, communicate and reason like us. They are, quite simply, *us*: full and complete human beings.

As full and complete human beings, they can be critical and experimental. They can use analogical reasoning to posit complex theories about the nature of reality. They can form coherent beliefs based on those theories. And they can preserve their beliefs, passing them down from generation to generation.

In fact, nearly everywhere *Homo sapiens* went, they left behind an imprint of these beliefs for us to uncover. Some of these are in the form of open-air monuments, most of which were swept away over time. Others are inhumed in burial mounds that, even tens of thousands of years later, display unambiguous signs of ritual activity. But nowhere do we come into closer contact with our ancient ancestors—nowhere do they come more fully into focus as *human*—than inside the spectacularly painted caves that dot the landscape of Europe and Asia like footprints marking the path of their migration.[8]

As far as we can tell, fundamental to Adam and Eve's belief system is the notion that the cosmos is tiered. The earth is a middle ground layered between the dome of the sky and the shallow bowl of the underworld. The upper realms can be reached only in dreams and altered states, and usually only by a *shaman*— someone who acts as an intermediary between the spiritual and material worlds. But the lower realms can be accessed by anyone, simply by burrowing deep into the earth—by crawling, sometimes for a mile or more, through caves and grottos to paint, etch, and sculpt their beliefs directly upon the rock wall, which acts as a "membrane" connecting their world to the world beyond.[9]

These painted caves can be found as far afield as Australia and on the islands of Indonesia. They appear across the Caucasus— from the Kapova cave in the southern Ural Mountains in Russia, to the Cuciulat cave in western Romania, and all along Siberia's upper Lena River valley. Some of the oldest and most stunningly well-preserved samples of prehistoric rock art can be found in the mountainous regions of Western Europe. In northern Spain, a large red disk painted on a cave wall in El Castillo can be traced to approximately 41,000 years ago, just around the time that *Homo sapiens* first arrived in the region. Southern France is perforated with such caves—from Font de Gaume and Les Combarelles in the Vézère valley, to Chauvet, Lascaux, and the Volp caves in the foothills of the Pyrenees.[10]

The Volp caves in particular provide a unique glimpse into the purpose and function of these subterranean sanctuaries. The caves consist of three interconnected caverns carved out of limestone by the persistence of the Volp River: *Enlène* to the east, *Le Tuc d'Audoubert* to the west, and in the center *Les Trois-Frères*, named after the three French brothers who accidentally discovered the caves in 1912.

The three caves were first studied by the French archaeologist and priest Henri Breuil, known as Abbé Breuil, who meticulously copied by hand the trove of images he found inside. His renderings opened a window into a dim past, allowing us to reconstruct a plausible interpretation of the astonishing spiritual journey that our prehistoric ancestors might have taken here tens of thousands of years ago.[11]

That journey begins about five hundred feet from the entrance of the first cave in the Volp complex—Enlène—in a small antechamber now called the Salle des Morts. It is important to note that Adam and Eve do not live in these caves; they are not "cavemen." Most painted caves are hard to reach and unfit for human habitation. Entering them is like passing through liminal space, like crossing a threshold between the visible and supersensible worlds. Some caves show evidence of prolonged activity, and others contain a sort of anteroom where archaeological evidence suggests worshippers may have gathered to eat and sleep. But these are not dwelling places; this is sacred space, which explains why the images found inside them are often placed at great distances from the cave's entrance, requiring a perilous journey through labyrinthine passages to view.

In the Volp caves, the Salle des Morts serves as a kind of staging ground, a place where Adam and Eve can prepare themselves for the experience to come. Here, they are enveloped in the suffocating stench of burning bone. There are sunken hearths all along the chamber floor, blazing with piles of animal bone. Bone is obviously a strong combustible, but that is not why it is burned here. There is, after all, no shortage of wood in the foothills of the Pyrenees; wood is far more plentiful than bone, and far easier to procure.

Yet animal bones are believed to possess a mediating power—they are inside the flesh but not of the flesh. That is why they are so often collected, polished, and worn as ornaments. It is why they are carved into talismans intricately engraved with images of bison, reindeer, or fish—animals that rarely correspond to the bones themselves. Sometimes the bones are inserted directly into the clefts and crevices of the cave walls, perhaps as a form of prayer, a means of conveying messages to the spirit realm.

Burning animal bone in these hearths is likely a means of absorbing the essence of the animal. The overpowering aroma of smoldering bone and marrow in such a confined space acts as a kind of incense meant to consecrate those gathered here. Picture Adam and Eve sitting in this antechamber for hours at a time, swathed in smoke, swaying with their kin to the pounding rhythm of animal-hide drums, the tinny echo of flutes carved from vulture bones, and the ting of xylophones constructed from polished flint blades—all of which have been discovered in and around caves like these—until they achieve the sanctified state necessary to continue on their journey.[12]

Adam and Eve do not amble aimlessly through these caves. Each chamber, each niche, each fissure and corridor and recess has a specific purpose—all deliberately designed to induce an ecstatic experience. This is a carefully controlled affair, so that moving through the nooks and passages, absorbing the images cast on the walls, the floors, the ceilings elicits a particular emotional response, somewhat akin to following the Stages of the Cross in a medieval church.

First, they must get on their hands and knees and crawl through a two-hundred-foot passage that links Enlène to the second cave in the complex, Les Trois-Frères. Now they enter a wholly new realm, one marked by something that is so obviously missing from the first cave that it cannot possibly be a coincidence. For it is in this second cave that Adam and Eve first encounter the rock art that so indelibly defines their spiritual life.

The main passage in Les Trois-Frères forks into two narrow paths. The path to the left leads to a long chamber marked by row upon row of black and red dots of various sizes. Such dots represent the earliest form of cave painting; in some caves they've been dated to more than 40,000 years ago. No one really knows what the dots mean. They may be a recording of spirit visions. They may represent male and female symbols. What is fairly certain, however, is that the dots are not randomly scattered along the walls. On the contrary, they are often painted in a clearly perceptible pattern that is repeated from chamber to chamber. That suggests the dots may be a form of communication or instruction, a kind of code relaying some vital information to the supplicants as they continue journeying deeper into the bowels of the earth.[13]

The path to the right of the main passage in Les Trois-Frères veers toward another small, dark room popularly called the Galerie des Mains. The walls here are splotched not with dots, but with handprints—dozens of them. This is by far the most ubiquitous and instantly recognizable form of rock art in existence. The oldest handprints go back some 39,000 years and can be found not only in Europe and Asia, but also in Australia, Borneo, Mexico, Peru, Argentina, the Saharan desert, and even the United States. The prints are made either by dipping the hand into wet pigment and pressing it against the cave wall, or by placing the hand directly upon the wall and spraying ochre around it through a hollowed-out bone to create a negative shadow. The ochre itself has a sacred function; the blood-red paint serves as a bridge between the material and spiritual worlds.[14]

What's remarkable about these handprints is that they are almost never left on smooth, easy-to-access areas, as one would expect. Instead, they congregate around certain topographical

features: on top of or near fissures and cracks, inside concave
depressions or between stalagmite flows, on high ceilings or in
otherwise difficult-to-reach spaces. Some of the prints are shaped
in such a way that the fingers appear to be gripping the rock. Others have fingers either bent or missing. Several of the prints are
clearly made by the same hand, yet different fingers are missing
from one stencil to the next, suggesting that, like the black and
red dots, the handprints may also be an ancient form of symbolic
communication—a kind of primitive "sign language." Indeed,
the uncanny similarities among handprints found on opposite
sides of the globe may indicate that this practice shares a common origin, one that predates the migration of *Homo sapiens* out
of Africa nearly 100,000 years ago. It may be that the humans who
made the handprints in Indonesia and those who made them in
Western Europe were speaking the same symbolic language.

Negative and positive handprints found in Cueva de las Manos,
Santa Cruz, Argentina (c. 15,000 to 11,000 B.C.E.)
Mariano / CC-BY-SA-3.0 / Wikimedia Commons

Intriguingly, scholars now believe that the majority of hand-prints found in the caves of Europe and Asia belong to women. This puts the lie to the notion that these caves, and the rituals involved in them, were primarily a male affair. It may be the case that access to certain chambers or activities was restricted, perhaps to those engaging in some rite or initiation. But the sanctuaries themselves seem to have received all members of the community: male or female, young and old.[15]

By the faint light of a flickering flame, Adam and Eve carefully make their way through this chamber by touch, feeling every fluctuation in the walls—their undulations, their warm and cool spots—looking for just the right place to leave their own hand-prints. This is a long and intimate process, requiring a close familiarity with the rock surface. Only after leaving their marks are they ready to continue their journey into the very heart of the cave: a small, cramped room tucked away in a perilously sloped, nearly inaccessible corner of the complex that Breuil dubbed *the Sanctuary*.

Here the walls practically pulse with brightly colored images of animals, both drawn and incised into the rock. There are hundreds of them, superimposed one on top of the other, frozen in a frenzy of activity: bison and bears and horses, reindeer and mammoths, stags, ibexes, and a few creatures that are mysterious and unidentifiable—some too fantastical to be real, others that muddle the boundary between human and animal.

It is not exactly correct to call these drawings "images." They are, like the dots and the handprints, symbols reflecting our ancient ancestors' animistic belief that all living things are interconnected, that they all share in the same universal spirit. It is for this reason that one rarely sees the animals' environment depicted in these caves. Often, the beasts are drawn in a kinetic blur suggesting motion. But there is no grass or trees or shrubs or streams for them to move upon; there is no "ground" at all. The animals seem to float in space, upside down, at odd, impossible angles. They are hallucinatory, devoid of context, *unreal*.[16]

The common assumption is that these rock paintings are meant to be a kind of "hunting magic," a charm to assist the hunter in bagging his prey. Yet the animals depicted inside the caves are, for the most part, not representative of the animals that roam outside the caves. Archaeological digs have shown that there is little correspondence between the species displayed on the walls and those that supplied the artists' diet. Rarely are the animals shown as hunted or captured or suffering or in pain. There is hardly ever any sign of violence at all in these caves. Some of the animals are crisscrossed with sharp lines that are usually interpreted as spears or arrows piercing their flanks. But a closer look at the images suggests that these lines are not *entering* the animal's body; they are *emanating* from it. The lines appear to represent the animal's aura or spirit—its *soul*. As the French anthropologist Claude Lévi-Strauss observed, primitive humans chose the animals they cast upon the rock not because they were "good to eat" but because they were "good to think."[17]

Adam and Eve enter these caves not to paint the world they know. What would be the point of that? They are here to imagine the world that exists beyond theirs. In fact, they do not so much draw pictures of bison and bears on the rock as they *release* those pictures from it. Standing in the dim light of a narrow passageway, scanning the cave wall with their eyes, caressing it with their hands, they wait for the image to be projected back to them. A curve in the rock becomes an antelope's thigh. A fissure or a crack serves as the starting point for a reindeer's antler. Sometimes, all it takes is a little addition—a slash of paint here, a deep groove there—to transform the natural shape of the rock into a mammoth or an ibex. Whatever the subject, their task is not to draw the image, but to complete it.

The drawings are often tucked between pillars or otherwise placed in a position that allows them to be viewed only from certain angles and only by a handful of people at a time, indicating that the cave—not just the images projected upon it, but the cave itself—was intended to be part of the spiritual experience. The cave becomes a *mythogram;* it is meant to be *read,* the way one reads scripture.[18]

If the Volp caves are a form of scripture, then Adam and Eve are about to reach its keynote, the moment when the mystery of all they have so far experienced will be revealed in a spectacular climax.

At the far end of the Sanctuary is a tunnel so narrow it can accommodate only one or two people at a time. To enter it, they must inch their way forward on their hands and knees as the tunnel curves upward onto a narrow ledge just a few feet from the cave floor. Once at the top, they can straighten up and shuffle along the ledge, their backs to the wall, clinging to the rock face to keep from falling. After a few yards, the ledge grows wider, allowing them to turn their bodies and finally face the wall. Only then, as they lift their eyes toward the ceiling, can they see the crowning image of the complex—an image so awe-inspiring, so jaw-dropping, that it practically defies description.

It is a man—that much is certain. But it is something more. It has the legs and feet of a human being, but the ears of a stag and the eyes of an owl. A long, bushy beard falls from its chin to its chest. Two beautifully wrought antlers jut from its head. Its hands resemble the paws of a bear. Its muscular torso and thighs belong to an antelope or a gazelle. Thrust back between its hind legs is a large, semierect penis, which curves upward, almost grazing the

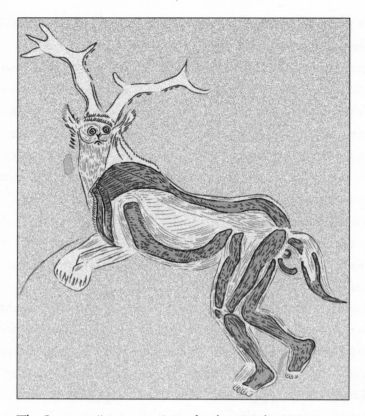

The Sorcerer (interpretation of a drawing by Henri Breuil). Les Trois-Frères, Montesquieu-Avantès, France (c. 18,000 to 16,000 B.C.E.) *Copyright © David Lindroth, Inc.*

bristling horsetail that protrudes from its buttocks. The figure is drawn in what appears to be mid-dance; its frame is lunging leftward. But it is facing the viewer, its owl eyes lined in black and open wide, the pupils small and white, and centered in perpetual focus.

The figure is unique in these caves in that it is both painted and engraved; it has been repeatedly modified, redrawn and repainted, perhaps for thousands of years. There are faint traces of color on the nose and forehead. In some places the details are superb. You can see the kneecap on its left leg. In others, it is slapdash. The front paws, in particular, look rushed and unfinished. The entire figure is about two and a half feet tall, far larger than any other image in the room. Whatever it is, it dominates the chamber, floating above the darkness.

When Henri Breuil first saw the figure a century ago, he was dumbstruck. Clearly this was a cult image meant for veneration, perhaps even worship. A single, dominant humanoid figure set apart like this is unheard of in such caves. Its location in the chamber, elevated high above eye level, makes it seem as though it is presiding over the tangle of animals collected in the Sanctuary. At first, Breuil assumed that the figure was a shaman dressed in the costume of some kind of hybrid animal. He christened it "the Sorcerer," and the name stuck.[19]

Breuil's initial interpretation of the figure is understandable. In ancient communities, shamans were thought to have one foot in this world and one foot in the next. They had the ability to enter altered states (often with the aid of hallucinogens) whereby they could shed their bodies and journey into the spirit world to bring back messages from the beyond, usually with the help of an animal guide.[20]

This connection with animals is why Breuil assumed the human-animal Sorcerer was a shaman, perhaps caught in midtransformation, shedding his body to journey into the other world. At least seventy other human-animal hybrid figures have been discovered in caves across Europe and Asia, and most of them are also assumed to represent shamans. In the Chauvet cave in France, a half-man/half-bison is etched onto a teardrop-shaped rock that hangs from the ceiling; his body folds over the unmistakable image of a vagina covered in thick black pubic hair drawn along the apex of the rock. On the walls of Lascaux there is an image of one man with a horse's head and another with the head of a bird lying down before a charging bull. Not far from where the Sorcerer looms in the Volp caves is the much smaller figure of a bison with human arms and legs playing what appears to be a flute attached to his nostrils.[21]

Yet these hybrid images do not represent shamans any more than the animal images represent actual animals. Like the dots and the handprints and practically everything else in such caves, these hybrid figures are *symbols* meant to represent "the other world"—the world beyond the material realm.

Even Breuil recognized there was something unique about the Sorcerer. After all, this was no mere human-animal hybrid, but rather a collage of species merged to create a single, active, animated being unlike anything else discovered in any painted cave. And so, after some consideration, he changed his mind about what he had discovered, concluding that this strange hypnagogic creature staring back at him from on high was not in fact a shaman. It was, as he wrote in his notebook, the earliest image ever found of God.[22]

Chapter Two

The Lord of Beasts

THE GOD BREUIL believed he had encountered in the Volp caves is one that scholars of religion had known about for years. It is an ancient deity, perhaps one of the first ever conceived, thought to be the master of animals, ruler and guardian of the forests. It can be beseeched with prayers to guide the hunter to his prey and placated with offerings should its anger be stoked and the animals disappear. To it belong the souls of all animals; it alone has the power to release them into the wild, and after they are hunted and killed, it alone can collect their souls back to itself. It is known as the Lord of Beasts.[1]

The Lord of Beasts is not just one of the oldest gods in religious history; it is also one of the most widely transmitted. Some version of the deity exists in nearly every part of the world—from Eurasia to North America to Mesoamerica. Its image can be found on Mesopotamian stone vessels dating to the end of the fourth millennium B.C.E. An ivory and flint knife made in Egypt sometime around 3450 B.C.E.—long before the rise of the pharaohs—has engraved on its handle a figure representing the Lord of Beasts grasping a lion in each hand. In the Indus Valley, the Lord of Beasts has been associated with both the Zoroastrian god Ahura Mazda and the Hindu deity Shiva, especially in his incarnation as Pashupati, or Lord of All Animals. Enkidu, the hirsute hero in the Babylonian *Epic of Gilgamesh*—one of the world's first written myths—is a Lord of Beasts figure, as is Hermes, and sometimes Pan, the half-goat, half-man god of nature, in Greek mythology.

Even the Hebrew god Yahweh is occasionally presented as the Lord of Beasts in the Bible. The book of Job depicts Yahweh boasting of the power to let the wild ass go free, of compelling the ostrich to leave its eggs on the earth so they can be gathered by men, and of ordering the wild ox to let itself be harnessed with ropes and set to harrow the valleys at man's command (Job 39). In the modern world, certain Wicca devotees and neopagan adherents worship the Lord of Beasts as the Horned God, a mythological being found in Celtic mythology.

How did this peculiar prehistoric deity, conceived by the Paleolithic mind tens of thousands of years ago, spread to Mesopotamia and Egypt, to Iran and India, to the Greeks and the Hebrews, to witches in America and neopagans in Europe? More to the point, how did our prehistoric ancestors evolve from a state of primitive animism to the kind of sophisticated belief system that would result in the creation of the Lord of Beasts in the first place?

Such questions have vexed theologians and scientists alike for centuries. What was it that spurred ancient humans to believe in "spiritual beings"? Did the religious impulse give us an advantage in our quest for dominance over every other species on earth? Was *Homo sapiens* the first species to exhibit religious belief, or could evidence of such belief be found in earlier species of humans?

What most scholars agree upon is that the religious impulse

Ivory and flint knife handle depicting the
Lord of Beasts, found in Egypt (c. 3450 B.C.E.)
Rama / CC BY-SA 2.0 FR / Wikimedia Commons

reaches deep into our Paleolithic past. But just how deep remains
a matter of fierce debate. The Paleolithic era is formally divided
into three periods: the Lower Paleolithic Period, between 2.5 million and 200,000 years ago, when *Homo sapiens* first appeared on
the scene; the Middle Paleolithic Period, between 200,000 and
40,000 years ago, when the first examples of cave paintings can be
found; and the Upper Paleolithic Period, between 40,000 and
10,000 years ago, when we start to see the blossoming of full-
fledged religious expression, including evidence of complex ritualistic behavior.

Not surprisingly, the majority of the religious artifacts discov-

ered so far—including the Sorcerer, which has been dated to between 18,000 and 16,000 years ago—comes from the Upper
Paleolithic Period. Yet new discoveries and improved dating pro-
cedures are constantly forcing us to reexamine our assumptions
about just how far back in human evolution religious expression
can be traced. For instance, in the remote islands of Indonesia,
researchers recently discovered painted caves that are almost as
old as those of El Castillo in Spain (painted approximately 41,000
years ago), but which contain not abstract symbols, as in the
Spanish cave, but clearly identifiable animal figures such as the
bulbous-bodied babirusa, or pig-deer. The presence of such advanced images on the other side of the world indicates that the
practice of cave painting may be far older than we thought, perhaps by tens of thousands of years.[2]

This view has been bolstered by a newly discovered cave in
Malaga, Spain, marked with what appears to be a procession of
seals descending a stalactite column. Remarkably, the seal drawings have been carbon-dated to somewhere between 43,500 and
42,300 years ago, meaning they were created not by *Homo sapiens,* who had yet to arrive in Europe, but by Neanderthals. In 2016
an even older Neanderthal cave was discovered near France's
Aveyron valley, this one containing an "altar" constructed from
broken stalagmites that were purposefully arranged on the cave
floor in two concentric rings—a sort of Paleolithic Stonehenge.
Initial carbon testing of the rings shows that the structure was
made more than 176,000 years ago, at the tail end of the Lower
Paleolithic Period.[3]

Indeed, many scholars now believe we should be looking beyond
even our Neanderthal cousins for evidence of prehistoric religious
expression. Archaeologists in the Golan Heights recently discovered a lump of rock, about one and a half inches tall, that had been
carved into an idol with the distinct shape of a large-breasted, pos-

Neanderthal stone rings in the shape of an altar, found in Bruniquel
cave, Aveyron, France (c. 176,500 B.P.)
Luc-Henri FAGE / CC BY-SA 4.0 / Wikimedia Commons

sibly pregnant woman. Called the Berekhat Ram Venus, the idol
is estimated to be at least 300,000 years old; that's before our species even existed. And while the oldest ritual burial sites containing
Homo sapiens can be dated to around 100,000 years ago, far older
grave sites have been unearthed that bear the unmistakable signs of
sacramental behavior, including a *Homo erectus* site in China that
may date as far back as half a million years.[4]

Even so, the problem with relying solely on these kinds of archaeological finds to date how far back in time religious expression may have existed is that beliefs do not fossilize. Ideas cannot
be buried in the ground and later unearthed. When confronted
with evidence of ritual behavior in a cave or a burial site, it would
be foolish for us to assume that such behavior arose suddenly and
synchronously with the belief that spurred it. Early humans maintained certain beliefs about the nature of the universe and their

place in it long before they began etching those beliefs onto the walls of their caves. Our ancestors, Adam and Eve, were not walking around in a nihilistic fog from which they suddenly snapped like prophets racked by revelation. Rather, Adam and Eve inherited their belief system much in the way they inherited their hunting prowess or their cognitive and linguistic skills: gradually, and over the course of hundreds of thousands of years of mental and spiritual evolution. When they enter the Volp caves, what they experience there, deep underground, is both the blooming of thousands of years of religious thought and the seeding of thousands of years to come. Everything they know is based on prior knowledge. Everything they create is the result of previous creations.

All of this is to say that if we are going to trace the origin of the religious impulse to its genesis, we must go beyond the discovery of material evidence. We must look deep into our evolutionary past, all the way back to the very moment we became human.

THE SCIENTIFIC DEBATE over the origins of religion began in earnest in the nineteenth century. It was a pursuit nurtured by the post-Enlightenment conviction that all queries—even those concerning the divine—could be answered through reasoned analysis and scientific scrutiny. This was the era of Charles Darwin and evolutionary theory. Concepts such as "natural selection" and "survival of the fittest"—the idea that certain adaptive traits can give an organism a better chance of surviving its habitat, and thus of passing on those traits to its offspring—were already widely adopted in the field of biology. They were increasingly being used to explain economic and political behavior as well (sometimes with devastating consequences). Why not, then, use Darwin to explain religion?

What remains undeniable is that religious belief is so widespread that it must be considered an elemental part of the human experience. We are *Homo religiosus,* not in our desire for creeds or institutions, nor in our commitments to specific gods and theologies, but in our existential striving toward *transcendence:* toward that which lies beyond the manifest world. If the propensity for religious belief is inherent in our species, then, scholars reasoned, it must be a product of human evolution. There must be some adaptive advantage to it. Otherwise there would be no reason for religion to exist.

Among the first to seriously tackle this problem was the mid-nineteenth-century English anthropologist Edward Burnett Tylor. For Tylor, the source of the religious impulse and the behaviors that arose from it lay within humanity's baffling, enigmatic belief in the soul as separate from the body—a belief that has, in one form or another, emerged in every society, in every culture, and throughout time. How did such an idea arise? Tylor wondered. What could possibly have convinced our ancient ancestors that they were eternal souls trapped in mortal bodies?

Tylor's hypothesis, outlined in his magisterial study *Primitive Culture,* was that the idea of the soul as an "animating, separable, surviving entity, the vehicle of individual personal existence," could only have occurred to us while we were asleep. "My own view," he wrote, "is that nothing but dreams and visions could have ever put into men's minds such an idea as that of souls being ethereal images of bodies."[5]

Imagine Adam huddled in his mammoth fur, finishing his meal by the light of a dying fire. He falls asleep and, in his dreams, he travels to another world—a world at once real and unfamiliar, a world whose edges are soft with reverie. Say he runs into a dead relative in his dream—a father or sister. How, Tylor asked, would he interpret their continued presence? Would he not simply assume that they weren't actually dead? That they exist in another realm as tangible and true as this one? Would Adam not then conclude that the souls of the dead could exist as spirits long after the destruction of the body? And, recognizing this, would he perhaps return to the grave of his father or sister and plead with their spirits to help him with the hunt, to make it stop raining, to heal his children? This, Tylor concluded, is how religion must have begun.

Few of Tylor's fellow anthropologists agreed with his dream hypothesis. Max Müller, Tylor's German counterpart, believed that humanity's first religious experiences were the result of encounters with nature. It is not what Adam envisions in his sleep, Müller suggested, but rather what he sees when he is awake that fuels his religious imagination. After all, Adam lives in a vast, incomprehensible world, teeming with mysteries he cannot possibly explain. He beholds oceans without end; he walks through forests so tall they scrape the sky, so old his ancestors told stories about them; he watches the sun forever chase the moon across the vault of heaven; and he knows that he had no role in creating these things. And so he assumes someone else—some*thing* else—must have created them for him.

The British ethnologist Robert Marett termed this feeling of wonderment *supernaturalism:* "the attitude of mind dictated by awe of the mysterious." Marett argued that ancient humans believed in an invisible force, a kind of "universal soul" that lay just behind the visible world. He called this force *mana,* an old Polynesian word meaning "power."[6]

Mana represents the impersonal, immaterial, supernatural force that, according to Marett, "takes abode in all inanimate and animate objects." The recognition of mana's presence in the oceans and trees, the sun and the moon, compelled ancient humans to begin worshiping those things—or rather, the thing within those things. Eventually, the impersonal mana evolved into personal souls. Each soul, released from a body, became a spirit. Some of those spirits passed into rocks or stones or bits of bone, transforming them into totems, talismans, and idols that were actively worshiped. Other spirits became individualized gods whom people could beseech for help, each serving a particular function (a god of rain, a god of the hunt, and so on). And then, in Marett's telling, after many years of spiritual development, these individualized gods evolved into the one omnipotent, universal God—a common conclusion among late nineteenth- and early twentieth-century scholars like Marett, Tylor, and Müller, who viewed humanity's move toward monotheism as the inevitable march from pagan savagery to Christian enlightenment.

Whether it was in dreams, or in the encounter with nature, or in speculations about departed ancestors, what all of these explanations have in common is the assumption that religion arose in human evolution to answer unanswerable questions and to help early humans manage a threatening and unpredictable world. It is an explanation for religious experience that remains popular to this day.

There's no doubt that for a great many people, religion helps make sense of a mystifying and volatile existence. The question is what, if any, adaptive advantage that would have provided primitive human beings in their early development. How exactly does offering soothing yet ever-shifting answers to the mysteries of the universe support the survival of the species?

Some scholars have argued that through ritual practice, certain feelings can be activated that could conceivably provide a primitive "believer" with the ability to, for example, control his fears and thus be more successful than a "nonbeliever" in hunting prey. But even if it were true that possessing supernatural beliefs could lead to physical or psychological benefits that increase evolutionary fitness (and that is highly doubtful), there is no reason to presume that *not* having such beliefs would *decrease* evolutionary fitness. Running headlong toward a bison because you do not fear death could just as likely sink as boost your chances of evolutionary survival.[7]

Regardless, for this theory to hold true, one would have to prove that there are certain emotions peculiar to religious expression, or that all religious expressions trigger similar emotions— neither of which is the case. One can experience the same sense of awe, the same sense of comfort, the same sense of fearlessness that so many people feel in response to religion in almost any nonreligious circumstance, and many religions do not engender such feelings at all. Despite common perception, there is simply no evidence for the existence of any emotion that is unique to religion—not even transcendence—and thus no reason to conclude that religious feelings are uniquely beneficial to human survival.[8]

If the religious impulse cannot be adequately explained by appealing to the individual's quest for meaning, perhaps we should look instead to its role in constructing and maintaining our sense of community. This was the central thesis of the nineteenth century's foremost sociologists, including the man who essentially fathered the discipline: Émile Durkheim.

Durkheim specifically rejected the idea that religion arose to assist primitive humans in seeking answers to the mystery of existence. In fact, Durkheim rejected the idea that religion has to do with the supernatural at all. For Durkheim, religion is "an eminently social thing," which is why, for it to have endured as a social construct in our early development, it must have been firmly planted in the *real:* not fanciful mythologies or wild speculations, not figments of the imagination or mystical beliefs, but real objects and experiences.[9]

Dreams are not real. Mana is not real. Spirits are not real.

What are real, Durkheim maintained, are the concrete actions of a community bound together by blood and kinship and working as one to adapt and survive in a hostile environment. The origins of the religious impulse, therefore, must be grounded in social life, in the rites and rituals that help a community form a collective consciousness.

Our ancestor Adam is not huddled near that dying fire by himself, after all. He is surrounded by a community. The meat he consumes is shared by everyone; he had help in stalking the prey, in cornering and spearing it, in cleaning and butchering it. The hunt is itself a sort of spiritual exercise, complete with rigidly defined rituals passed down through generations. Every action the hunters take is prescribed—from the carving of their spears to the movement of their bodies through the forest as they track their prey. Through it all, these hunters maintain a sense of mystical solidarity with their weapons, which are sacralized and charged with the spiritual power necessary to transform otherwise mundane objects—rocks and sticks and bone—into instruments that ensure the survival of the community. Survival is no small thing, of course, so it makes sense that such everyday objects as spears or knives could gradually come to be regarded as sacred, not because of any inherent power they possess, but because of their *usefulness*. For Durkheim, a thing becomes sacred solely through the ways in which an individual acts upon it.

The same logic holds for the collective actions of the hunters. It may make strategic sense for hunters to circle a beast and attack it together, and that may be why the practice was developed and handed down. But it is not difficult to imagine how the very concept of a circle of hunters could give rise to a religious ritual.

Let's say that before the hunt begins, Adam and his fellow hunters gather in a tight circle, hands clasped, simulating in the safety of their own environment the perils of the hunt. Perhaps they stack the bones of a previous kill in the middle of the circle and focus their intentions upon it. Maybe they eventually replace the bones with a living beast, which would be marked in some way, set apart and sacrificed in the hope that its blood will beget blood. Before they sacrifice the beast, they might make an appeal to its spirit to go out and help them find their prey. In this way, a mythology slowly arises about the hunt, about sacrifice—about the need to shed blood for the appeasement of the spirits, the need for the assistance of the gods and perhaps even for the forgiveness of sins. And so, little by little, what began as nothing more than a simple hunting trip (something *real*) transforms into a spiritual activity (something *supernatural*), thereby paving the way for belief in such things as individual souls and divine spirits.

Durkheim's theory that religion arose as a kind of social adhesive, a means of fostering cohesion and maintaining solidarity among primitive societies, remains the most widely held explanation for the origins of the religious impulse. Evolutionarily speaking, it makes a certain amount of sense to assume that by banding together around a common set of symbols and participating in a shared ritual experience, our ancient ancestors were able to enhance their collective viability and thus increase their chances of survival in a savagely competitive world.

The trouble with this line of reasoning, however, is that there is nothing intrinsically unifying or cohesive about religion. Religion certainly has the power to bring disparate people together. But it is just as efficient a dividing force as it is a uniting one. Religion engenders both inclusion and exclusion. It spawns as much conflict in society as it does cohesion. It benefits some members of a community more than—and often at the expense of—others. It delegitimizes as much as it legitimizes.[10]

More to the point, the theory of social cohesion is dependent upon the idea that religion is the primary, most dominant source of attachment among prehistoric communities. That is emphatically not the case. Kinship is a stronger and far more primal tool for social cohesion in our human evolution. Our Paleolithic ancestors lived in small-scale communities—an extended family sharing a shelter. Their sense of solidarity was engendered first and foremost by birth and blood, not by symbols and rituals. To argue that religion arose in human evolution because it gave "believing" communities an adaptive advantage over "nonbelieving" communities would require the existence in religion of some uniquely cohesive power that it simply does not possess. There can be no doubt that its communal properties have allowed religion to survive throughout human history. But whether those communal properties helped religiously inclined humans to survive is questionable.

Even as the anthropological and sociological explanations for the role of religious belief in human evolution were being debated, another new discipline of the nineteenth century, psychoanalysis, joined the fray. The two most famous pioneering theorists in the field, Sigmund Freud and Carl Jung, both sought to locate the origins of the religious impulse within the human psyche, in the blurred space between our conscious and unconscious minds. Indeed, both men equated the soul with the psyche. Unlike Jung, however, who had a generally positive view of religion and sought chiefly to "psychologize" traditional religious concepts like the soul, Freud considered religion to be a neurosis: a mental disorder that fosters belief in invisible, impossible things and leads to compulsive actions and obsessive conduct.[11]

Religious belief, Freud wrote in *The Future of an Illusion*, is "born from man's need to make his helplessness tolerable." Freud believed the religious impulse arose from an innate desire in primitive man to create a "father figure," though a perfectly good and all-powerful one. Human beings worship gods for the same reason a child idolizes his father: We need love and protection; we want comfort from our deepest and darkest fears.

In Freud's view, our ancestor Adam has no interest in dreams or nature or rites or ceremonies. His chief desire is to indulge his animal instinct. He wants to have sex with his mother and his sisters. He wants to kill and consume his father. But because he recognizes the social and psychic costs of doing these things, he represses his libido, inventing religion as a means of lessening the guilt that arises from the desire to disavow his basic human nature.

Freud wasn't alone in grounding the religious impulse in fear or violence. More than a century before Freud, the Scottish philosopher David Hume wrote that "the primary religion of mankind arises chiefly from an anxious fear." A century after Freud, the French philosopher René Girard theorized that religion arose among primitive peoples to mitigate violence by focusing that violence upon a ritual sacrifice—a "scapegoat," as he termed it. More generally, Freud's assumption that religious ideas are "illusions, fulfillments of the oldest, strongest and most urgent wishes of mankind" is merely an echo of his German predecessor Karl Marx, who famously called religion "the opiate of the people," and Ludwig Feuerbach, who defined God as "the feeling of want," which springs forth from our hearts. "What man is in need of . . . that is God," Feuerbach wrote in *The Essence of Christianity*.[12]

Almost everything Freud wrote about the origins of the religious impulse has been debunked. But his perception of religion as "wish fulfillment" has had a lasting impact on modern critics of religion, many of whom would enthusiastically agree that religion's primary purpose in human evolution is to alleviate discontent, to lessen suffering and anxiety, and to allay fears of the unknown. Yet this, too, is an overly simplistic and deeply flawed explanation for the religious impulse.

Let's assume for a moment that there is an adaptive advantage to having our anxieties assuaged and our guilt allayed, though there is no scientific reason to think so. Under no circumstances could religion be considered *intrinsically* a source of comfort. Quite the contrary. Religion perpetrates as much anxiety and guilt in people's lives as it alleviates. As the great American anthropologist Clifford Geertz wrote, "Religion has probably disturbed men as much as it has cheered them."[13]

Religion often involves wrathful, capricious spirits whose pleasure requires backbreaking physical and psychological effort from worshippers. Evolutionarily speaking, it requires actions that carry enormous costs in terms of energy and resources—both of which would be better spent on survival and reproduction.[14]

A variation of Freud's theory holds that religion's primary purpose in human evolution is to motivate altruistic behavior, to control primitive populations and keep them from tearing each other apart. In other words, the only thing stopping Adam from rising from his seat by the fire, stabbing his neighbor in the chest, and taking his meat from him is his belief that the spirits of his ancestors are watching him. They act as divine lawgivers compelling him to act morally or risk punishment. By promising a reward in the afterlife, religion compels him to restrain or alter his actions in some manner and so mitigates the social effects of selfishness among individuals in a group.[15]

It is certainly true that religion can enhance altruistic behavior between individuals (though it is equally adept at promoting selfishness). The question is whether religion has a unique moral effect on society. The cognitive scientist Paul Bloom has conducted years of research on how religion and religious belief affect moral views. His conclusion is that there is little evidence that "the world's religions have an important effect on our moral lives." In fact, study after study has demonstrated that the good and bad moral effects of religion are no more or less powerful than the good and bad moral effects of any other social practice.[16]

Even if, for the sake of argument, one concedes that religion can mitigate the social effects of selfish behavior in a group, that still does not adequately explain how or why religion evolved in the first place. What we call "religious morality" played no role in the spiritual lives of primitive peoples. Belief in a "divine law-giver" who determines good and bad behavior is barely five thousand years old; belief in a heavenly reward for such behavior is even newer.

The gods of the ancient world were rarely conceived of as "moral"; they were above the trifling concerns of human morality. The gods of Mesopotamia and Egypt were savage and brutal; their primary interest in human beings was as slaves to their whims. The Greek gods were capricious, vain, entitled beings who toyed with humanity for sport. Yahweh is a jealous god who regularly demands the wholesale slaughter of every man, woman, and child who does not worship him alone. Allah is a martial deity who prescribes an array of draconian punishments—in this life and the next—to those who oppose him. How are these gods, who are at best beyond morality and at worst simply immoral, supposed to serve as the source of moral behavior among humans?

In the end, what all of these seemingly sensible, commonly accepted theories on the origins of the religious impulse have in common is that they are concerned with what religion *does* rather than where religion came from, how it arose, or why. Despite everything we think we know, the evidence indicates that religion does not make people good or bad. It does not naturally police behavior or foster cooperation in society. It does not enhance altruism any more or less effectively than any other social mechanism. It is no more or less powerful in creating moral behavior. It

does not inherently drive cooperation in society. It does not increase advantage over competing groups. It does not necessarily
soothe the mind or comfort the soul. It does not automatically
lessen anxiety or improve reproductive success. It does not promote survival of the fittest.[17]

To quote the anthropologist Scott Atran, religion is "materi-
ally expensive and unrelentingly counterfactual and even counterintuitive. Religious practice is costly in terms of material sacrifice
(at least one's prayer time), emotional expenditure (inciting fears
and hopes), and cognitive effort (maintaining both factual and
counterintuitive networks of beliefs)." And so, as Paul Bloom
concludes, "religious belief is an unlikely candidate for a biological adaptation."[18]

But if that is true—if there is no adaptive advantage to the religious impulse and therefore no direct evolutionary reason for it
to exist—then why did religion arise? What spurred our ancient
ancestors' animism, their primal belief in themselves as embodied
souls? If Adam's religious impulse is not the product of his fears
or his search for meaning, if it isn't tied to his environment or his
anxiety, if it plays no significant role in helping him adapt and
survive, how can it be an evolutionary trait at all?

The answer, it would seem, is that it's not. That, at least, is the
consensus of a new crop of scholars who, over the last few decades, have begun applying a distinctly cognitive approach to the
problem of religion's origins. Faced with the evolutionary puzzle
that is the universality of supernatural beliefs, these scientists
have come up with an innovative answer. Religion, they say, is *not*
an evolutionary adaptation; religion is the accidental byproduct
of some other *preexisting* evolutionary adaptation.

Chapter Three

The Face in the Tree

Eve's day begins early—far earlier than Adam's. Before the sun rises and the forest floor is flooded with light, she will rouse her children and lead them into the woods to check the traps she set the night before. While the children climb the trees to gather fruits and nuts and any birds' eggs they may find in abandoned nests, Eve will club and collect her captured prey. Afterward, the family will wade knee-deep in the nearby river for crabs and mollusks and anything else edible they can find in the water. They may get lucky and come across a fallen beast, its body decomposed and stripped of meat by the birds of prey. No matter. They will collect the bones, break them, and scoop out the marrow to bring back to camp.

Through these actions, Eve and her children provide the bulk of the family's food. It may take a week for Adam to chase down a bison. Eve can bring that much food home every few days. After all, there is as much fat and protein in a pound of nuts as there is in a pound of meat—and nuts do not fight back. Our Paleolithic ancestors were primarily hunters, but what kept them alive was scavenging and foraging—and that was primarily the work of women and children.

Now imagine that as Eve and her children begin to trudge back to camp in the early morning darkness, she suddenly sees, out of the corner of her eye, a face staring back at her through the trees. She freezes. Her muscles stiffen. Her blood vessels constrict. Her heart rate accelerates. Adrenaline floods her body. She is ready to pounce or flee.

Then she looks again and realizes that what she thought was a face was actually knots on the trunk of a tree. Her muscles relax. Her heart rate drops. She lets out her breath and continues on her journey through the woods.

Cognitive theorists have a term for what Eve just experienced. They call it her Hypersensitive Agency Detection Device, or HADD. This is a biological process that arose deep in our evolutionary past, all the way back in the days when hominids were still stooped and hairy. In its simplest terms, HADD leads us to detect human *agency*, and hence a human *cause*, behind any unexplained event: a distant sound in the woods, a flash of light in the sky, a tendril of fog slithering along the ground. HADD explains why we assume every bump in the night is caused by someone doing the bumping.

Our innate willingness to attribute human agency to natural phenomena can have clear evolutionary advantages. What if it hadn't been a tree that Eve saw? What if it had been a bear? Isn't it better to err on the side of caution? There is no harm in mistaking a tree for a predator, but there certainly would be in mistaking a predator for a tree. Better to guess wrong than to be eaten.

It is obvious, in the above example, how HADD could promote Eve's survival. Yet according to a group of cognitive scientists who study religion, what Eve experienced in those dark woods is more than just an involuntary reaction to a potential threat. It is the basis for our belief in God: the true evolutionary origin of the religious impulse.

The cognitive science of religion begins with a simple premise: *Religion is first and foremost a neurological phenomenon.* The religious impulse, in other words, is ultimately a function of complex electrochemical reactions in the brain. Of course, this fact on its own is not a compelling observation, and it certainly does not diminish or delegitimize the religious impulse. Every impulse— *every impulse without exception*—is generated by complex electrochemical reactions in the brain. Why would the religious impulse be any different? Knowing the neural mechanics of the religious impulse does not undermine the legitimacy of religious belief any more than knowing the chemical process of romantic attraction makes the feeling any less real or the object of our affection any less worthy. As Michael J. Murray, one of the leading thinkers in the field, notes, "The mere fact that we have beliefs that spring from mental tools selected for by natural selection is, all by itself, totally irrelevant to the justification of the beliefs that spring from them."[1]

Nevertheless, if it is true that religion is a neurological phenomenon, then perhaps we should be searching for the origins of the religious impulse where that impulse actually resides: *in the brain.*

LET US RETURN for a moment to Eve's tree. In the dim light of early morning, Eve's cognitive bias toward agency convinced her, if only for an instant, that the tree was a predator. But imagine that Eve comes back to the tree later that day and, while inching closer to it, realizes to her astonishment that the tree trunk does in fact look as if it has a face. This is where another of her cognitive processes, called Theory of Mind, takes over.

Theory of Mind is an executive function of the brain that is activated the moment we attain the ability to view and understand other people the way we view and understand ourselves: as separate and distinct individuals who feel the same basic feelings, who think the same kinds of thoughts, who have the same *essence* as we do. Theory of Mind not only obliges us to think of others in the same terms we use to think of ourselves. It encourages us to use ourselves as the primary model for how we conceive of everyone else.

Think about it: If the only consciousness I'm aware of is my own, then I have no choice but to use myself as the model for my understanding of the universe. My perception of the internal states of other human beings is based on my own internal state.

What's surprising about Theory of Mind, however, is that it also compels me to perceive nonhumans who exhibit human traits in the same way that I perceive humans. So, for instance, if I am confronted by a bipedal entity with what looks like a head and a face, I think, "This being looks like me." If it looks like me, Theory of Mind leads me to think it must *be* like me. And so, instinctively, I ascribe my human thoughts and emotions to the human-looking thing.[2]

This is the reason why children treat certain toys as alive, possessing personality and will. Give a small child a model car and she will perceive the headlights as eyes and the grille as a mouth. She will automatically play with it as though it were a living thing and not a hunk of molded plastic. Even as she is consciously aware of the distinction between animate and inanimate, living and nonliving, she will nevertheless attribute life to the toy. She will give it *agency*.[3]

And here we get to the cognitive connection that, according to some theorists, links Theory of Mind, HADD, and the origins of the religious impulse.

We know that essential to Eve's consciousness of herself is the belief that she has a soul, and that her soul is separate from her body. Her body is present and tangible; her soul is invisible and immaterial. Put aside for a moment how Eve came up with this idea. What's important is that because Eve believes she has a soul separate from her body, Theory of Mind leads her to believe that everyone else must have one as well. But because Theory of Mind makes Eve prone to view nonhumans who exhibit human traits in the same way she views actual humans, she is just as likely to attribute a soul to certain inanimate things. Put another way, if the tree has a "face," as Eve does, it must, like Eve, also have a "soul."

Just as a child does with a toy car, Eve imparts agency and intention to the tree—consciously and in the cold light of day. She gives the tree a *spirit*. Perhaps she takes out a flint knife and accentuates the face in the trunk. She does not draw the face. As with the images in the cave, Eve merely releases the face that she perceives is already there. She transforms the tree into a totem: an object of worship. She may bring it offerings. She may even start praying to it for help in netting her prey. Thus religion is born, albeit by accident.

It's not really a religion, however, until Eve's beliefs are adopted by her community. It's one thing for Eve to develop a personal religious experience with the tree based on her own unique observation. It's something else to convince others to share her experience. HADD and Theory of Mind may explain how a specific religious belief can arise. But they do not explain how such a belief can then be successfully transmitted from believer to believer, culture to culture, century to century. Why do some religious beliefs—for instance, belief in a god who controls the beasts of the wild—survive and spread from generation to generation, while others are abandoned and forgotten?

The answer may once again lie with the brain. According to the cognitive anthropologist Pascal Boyer, our brains allow only certain types of beliefs to "stick." His research shows that we are more likely to absorb, retain, and share an idea if that idea is *slightly* anomalous. If an idea violates one or two basic, intuitive assumptions about a thing, it has a far stronger chance of being recalled and transmitted.[4]

Say Eve takes Adam back to her tree and shows him the face she carved into it (or, rather, released from it). Eve's Theory of Mind has endowed the tree with a soul like hers, giving her a unique spiritual connection to it. But for Adam to adopt Eve's experience of the tree and spread it to others—for the tree to be memorable and worth believing in—it needs some minimally counterintuitive physical or psychological property that breaches the boundaries of what Adam understands to be the tree's basic template. Put another way, the tree needs one or two attributes that violate, in some small way, the ontological category "tree."[5]

Perhaps Eve tells Adam not only that the tree has a face but that, late one night while visiting it, she thought she heard the tree speak. By violating just one of the natural attributes Adam expects from a tree—*It speaks!*—Eve has now made it more likely that Adam will remember her story and pass it on, even if he himself did not hear the tree speak. If, however, Eve violates too many of the tree's known properties—*It speaks! And it walks around! And it can become invisible!*—the concept becomes too difficult for Adam to conceptualize and therefore less likely for him to believe in and transmit to others. To make Eve's experience of the tree something her entire community can accept as its own requires her to make only a slight alteration to the tree's nature—

one that is simple, easy to comprehend, easy to transmit, and, most important, *useful*.

This last point bears repeating. Whatever slight alteration Eve applies to her sacred tree must, above all else, render it more useful than it would be in its natural state. A tree that becomes invisible or walks around is not useful. A tree that speaks, however, could be supremely useful. It could communicate to Eve and her kin information about the nonmaterial world. It could answer questions, provide vital knowledge about the past, even prophesy the future.

If Eve tells Adam that her tree has the ability to speak, Adam would be more likely to find the anomalous tree useful. He would be more likely to believe in it himself. He would be more likely to tell members of their community about it, and they, too, would be more likely to find it useful and worth believing in. Together Adam and Eve might construct an entire mythology around the talking tree, along with accompanying rituals that spread to their group. These myths and rituals could then spread to other communities who might also find the idea of a talking tree to be useful and who might, as a consequence, adopt and adapt the concept to their own particular cultures.

Thus we have the Greek historian Herodotus writing in the fifth century B.C.E. about the sacred forest of Dedona, whose trees spoke with human voices and had the gift of prophecy. Five hundred years later, the ancient Persian epic *Shahnameh*, or Book of Kings, tells of an encounter that took place between Alexander the Great and a talking tree that predicts Alexander's untimely death. "Neither your mother, nor your family, nor the veiled women of your land will see your face again," the tree tells the young world conqueror.

Three hundred years after that, Marco Polo wrote of coming

across the Tree of the Sun and Moon in India, which had two trunks, one that spoke in the daytime with a male voice, the other at night with the voice of a woman. In the book of Genesis, the biblical patriarch Abraham twice encounters his god at oracular trees, once near Nablus at the Oak of Moreh (Genesis 12:6), and again in Hebron at the Oaks of Mamre (Genesis 18:1). Throughout much of Europe, the concept of talking trees has for millennia been vital to Celtic and Druid spirituality, and it continues to be so among modern adherents of Druidry and neopaganism. There are even talking trees in *The Wizard of Oz*. And let us not forget the majestic Ents of J.R.R. Tolkien's Middle-earth. Thus, a slightly anomalous yet exceedingly useful concept that arose at some point in the distant past is transformed into a successful and widely transmitted belief able to penetrate countless cultures and civilizations, even as it maintains its original essence.[6]

A similar transmission process must have occurred with the Lord of Beasts. Ontological categories like "human" and "animal" carry with them certain clearly defined expectations. Simply violate one or two of those expectations in a minimally counterintuitive way (a human who communicates with animals), then make the new creation useful (a human-animal hybrid that provides us with the food we need to survive), and what you have is a belief durable enough to evolve from its origins as an ancient mental abstraction, to the Sorcerer some 18,000 years ago, to the book of Genesis some 2,500 years ago, all the way to neopagans today. In this way, a specific god is born and remains active in human culture through the millennia.

As we shall see, in the history of religion there is one particular anomaly—one minimally counterintuitive concept—that has outshone all others, resulting in what is unquestionably the single most successful, most memorable, most meaningful, most *useful*

Ballachulish figure of a goddess carved from alder
wood with quartzite pebbles for eyes, found in
Inverness-shire, Scotland (c. 600 B.C.E.)
Copyright © National Museums of Scotland

religious belief ever conceived of by human beings. That is the
concept of the "god-man"—a human being who is slightly altered
in some way, who exhibits heightened physical or mental abilities,
who may be invisible, or in all places at all times, who knows the
past and the future, who knows *everything*. A human being who
is, in other words, a *god*. But that must wait for a later chapter in
our story.[7]

For now, we are left with the intriguing theory, suggested by the cognitive science of religion, that human beings possess certain mental processes, developed through millions of years of evolution, that can, under the right circumstances, lead us to assign agency to inanimate objects, to endow those objects with a soul or spirit, and then to successfully transmit beliefs stemming from those objects to other cultures and other generations. It is a compelling explanation for the origin of the religious impulse—one that, unlike previous explanations, can be accounted for by natural selection.

There is, however, a problem.

As persuasive as the cognitive theory of religion may be, it fails to answer our initial question: Why does Eve think she has a soul in the first place? HADD may explain why Eve stops in her tracks when she sees the tree and why she thinks it has a face. Theory of Mind may explain why she would ascribe her own soul to the tree, giving it an animating spirit and transforming it into an object of worship that could then be passed on to her community. These cognitive processes have the ability to fortify and encourage already held belief systems. But they cannot, by themselves, *create* belief. For Eve to make the colossal leap from detecting agency to formulating religious belief requires that she be already predisposed to such thinking. Otherwise, she would simply assume she had encountered an interesting-looking tree and move on.[8]

After all, Eve's default cognitive response to the tree is that it's a tree. For her to override her initial, routine perception of the tree, Eve would need an *equally plausible* alternative explanation for it. But there are only two ways in which Eve could view a "supernatural" explanation as equally plausible: Either someone else would have to coerce her into believing the tree is more than just a tree (and where did that person conceive of the idea?), or she would have to form the belief on her own based on her essential knowledge of herself as an embodied soul. Either way, we are back where we began, with the problem that Edward Burnett Tylor homed in on two hundred years ago: Where did the idea of the soul come from?[9]

The truthful answer is that we don't know. What seems clear, however, is that belief in the soul may be humanity's *first* belief. Indeed, if the cognitive theory of religion is correct, belief in the soul is what led to belief in God. The origin of the religious impulse, in other words, is not rooted in our quest for meaning or our fear of the unknown. It is not born of our involuntary reactions to the natural world. It is not an accidental consequence of the complex workings of our brains. It is the result of something far more primal and difficult to explain: our ingrained, intuitive, and wholly experiential belief that we are, whatever else we are, embodied souls.

Our quest in the following chapters is neither to prove nor to disprove the existence of the soul (there is no proof either way). Rather, it is to demonstrate how this universal belief in the existence of the soul led to the concept of an active, engaged, divine presence that underlies all of creation; how that divine presence was gradually personalized, given names and backstories, endowed with human traits and emotions, and cast into a thousand different forms, each with its own personality and purpose; and how, after many years and with great difficulty, those forms gave way to the single divine personality we know today as God.

Part Two

The Humanized God

Chapter Four

Spears into Plows

THE GARDEN OF EDEN lies somewhere in southeastern Turkey, near the prehistoric city of Urfa (modern-day Şanlıurfa), a few miles north of the Syrian border. Or at least that is what the residents of the city believe.

According to the Bible, after God made Adam, he planted a garden "in the east" and placed him within it. He then made a river flow out of the garden, dividing it into four branches, two of which are known today as the Tigris and the Euphrates. Out of the soil, God made to grow every species of tree—those that were pleasant to the sight, and those that were good for food—and bade Adam to eat whatever fruit he desired (save one, of course). He then filled the garden with every animal of the field and every bird of the air, giving Adam dominion over all living things.

Together with his companion, Eve, Adam basked in this paradise, free from work and struggle. They had no need to till the soil, to sow or reap—no need for labor at all.

But when Adam and Eve disobeyed God and ate from the Tree

of Knowledge of Good and Evil, they were cast out of Eden forever, forced to survive through toil and hardship. The ground itself was cursed. The produce dried up, along with the soil of the
earth. The bounty turned into thorns and thistles, driving Adam
and his descendants to subsist by the sweat of their brow every
day for the rest of their lives until they returned to the dust from
which they were made.

There is no actual Garden of Eden, of course. As with so much
in our ancient scriptures, the story is meant to be read as *myth*.
But myths are not "false," in the way we understand the word
today. The significance of a myth rests not in any truth claims it
makes but in its ability to convey a particular perception of the
world. The function of a myth is not to explain how things are,
but *why* things are the way they are. The ancient Hebrews did not
organize time into seven-day weeks with the seventh day for rest
because that was how long it took God to create the world. Rather,
they claimed God took six days to create the world and the following day to rest because that is how they *already* organized
time.

The story of the Garden of Eden, like the numerous flood narratives of the Ancient Near East or the tales of gods who die and
return to life, represents a special class of myth called "folk memory." These are universal myths predicated on the collective memory of a particular culture or society (regardless of how chimerical
that memory may be) and passed down orally from generation to
generation. They can be found in some form in almost every religion and among nearly all cultures.

Embedded in the myth of the Garden of Eden is a collective
memory of an era long ago when human beings were free from
toil and struggle, when there was no need to slog day and night
over the land. An era, in other words, before the rise of agricul-

ture, when our ancient ancestors Adam and Eve were, to put it less biblically, *hunter-gatherers.*

And that is how the ancient city of Urfa has come to be regarded in the collective memory of its inhabitants as the location of the Garden of Eden. Believers will point to the fact that, like the biblical Eden, Urfa is nestled between four rivers, including the Tigris and Euphrates, and that it, too, is located in what the Bible terms "the east"—that is, west of ancient Assyria. However, the main reason so many people around the world believe that this city rests upon the ruins of Eden has less to do with Urfa's location than it does with what lies just ten miles to the northeast, atop a high mountain ridge called Göbekli Tepe, or Potbellied Hill. For buried there, just beneath a man-made mound on the very tip of the highest peak overlooking a desolate plateau, are the remains of what is widely recognized to be the earliest religious temple ever constructed—"the Temple of Eden," as Klaus Schmidt, the chief archaeologist of the site, playfully calls it.

The temple is comprised of twenty or more large enclosures built of mortar and stone. Some of these are circular; others are oblong. A few of them spiral like galaxies. The entire temple complex stretches a thousand feet long and a thousand feet wide. Tucked in the center of each stone enclosure are two matching megalithic T-shaped pillars, some of which stand more than sixteen feet high and weigh as much as ten tons. The central pillars are engraved with images of ferocious beasts and lethal creatures: lions, leopards, and vultures; scorpions, spiders, and snakes— nothing like the dreamy, docile animals found in the painted caves of the Paleolithic era. Alongside these beasts are intricately wrought geometric figures and abstract symbols carved up and down the pillars. The prevailing theory is that they represent a kind of symbolic language—a far more ancient equivalent of

Artist's rendition of the construction of Göbekli Tepe (c. 12,500 to 10,000 B.C.E.)   *Fernando G. Baptista/National Geographic Creative*

Egyptian hieroglyphics—though we lack the key to decipher them.

What makes the temple truly extraordinary, however, is that it was built at the end of the last Ice Age, between 14,000 and 12,000 years ago. That's at least six thousand years before Stonehenge and seven thousand years before the first Egyptian pyramids. It is so old it predates the rise of agriculture, meaning that this enormous, intricately designed monument was constructed by semi-nomadic Stone Age hunter-gatherers wearing animal skins who had yet to invent the wheel.

Even more startling is the fact that there is no evidence that anyone ever lived at the site. No homes or hearths have been unearthed anywhere near Göbekli Tepe. There is no obvious water source; the nearest freshwater stream is located many miles away. The only possible explanation for the lack of amenities is that this was a sacred place designated exclusively for the performance of religious ceremonies.

People would have journeyed from villages scattered within as much as a hundred-mile radius to participate in whatever rituals took place here. They would have been from different tribes. They would have claimed different gods. And yet somehow this disparate assemblage of Paleolithic peoples had managed to put aside their differences and focus their devotion on a common, unifying symbol. The archaeological work being done at Göbekli Tepe by Schmidt and others has given us an idea of what that unifying symbol may have been. It is the supreme symbol of human spirituality, born from the raw material of our cognitive processes, rendered in our earliest attempts to express our conception of the divine, and transmitted successfully into nearly every religion and culture the world has ever known. That symbol is the "humanized god"—the god made in our image—and it sits at the center of each and every one of the stone enclosures in the Temple of Eden.

The matching T-shaped pillars that dominate the temple structure are more than blocks of stone. Look closely and you can see that the pillars have arms carved into their sides. The arms come together at the front of each pillar, just above what might be a belt or loincloth. Some of the pillars appear to be wearing jewelry. The small blocks that cap the pillars and complete the T shape are widely assumed by researchers to be heads. All of this suggests that these are not merely pillars; they are abstract humanoid figures.

The figures are faceless; no eyes, nose, or mouth has been carved into them, but that is not because their creators lacked the skill. One need only look at the exquisite detail of some of the animal carvings at Göbekli Tepe to recognize what master artisans they were; a leopard carved into the side of one pillar is so detailed you can see its ribs. No one doubts that the temple's

T-shaped pillar at Göbekli Tepe with human hands and belt (c. 12,500 to 10,000 B.C.E.)   *Vincent J. Musi/National Geographic Creative*

builders could have carved the central pillars into more well-defined human beings if they had wanted to do so. But they chose to represent them in a deliberately abstract fashion, which suggests they did not intend the pillars to represent actual humans, but rather supreme beings in human form.

We do not know whether the humanized gods at Göbekli Tepe represent a pantheon of individual, personalized gods or are merely an expression of anonymous deities. The answer may lie in the unique set of glyphs etched into each pillar. The glyphs could be a form of identification. They could be the name of that particular god or a description of the god's attributes. They may narrate some myth about the god, or describe the particular power for which the god should be petitioned, rather as a Catholic Book of Saints informs the faithful which saint should be prayed to and for what purpose. Unless we are someday able to translate the glyphs, we may never know the answer.

What we do know is *why* the central pillars in Göbekli Tepe are humanoid, why the different tribes that gathered here would have used the human form to represent their nascent idea of what the gods looked like. They had little choice in the matter.

We are, as we have seen, evolutionarily adapted to implant our own beliefs and desires, our own mental and psychological states, our own *souls,* in other beings, whether they are human or not. Our Hypersensitive Agency Detection Device makes us susceptible to perceiving agency in natural phenomena. Our Theory of Mind makes us inherently biased toward "humanizing" whatever phenomena we encounter. So then, how else would we picture the gods except in human form? We are the lens through which we understand the universe and everything in it. We apply our personal experience to all that we encounter, whether human or not. In doing so, we not only humanize the world; we humanize the gods we think created it.

In the centuries that follow the building of Göbekli Tepe, this unconscious urge to humanize the divine will carry with it certain consequences—both positive and negative. The more we think of the gods in human terms, the more we will project our human attributes upon them. Our values will become the gods' values, our traits will become the gods' traits. Eventually, we will make the heavenly realm a mirror reflecting the earth, so that the gods who take on our personalities will also take on our politics, even our bureaucracies. To get to know the gods better, we will construct entire spiritual systems based on the only thing we can truly know: *ourselves.* The gods need food, because we need food; and so we will offer them sacrifices. The gods need shelter, because we need shelter; and so we will build them temples. The gods need names, so we will name them. They need personalities, so we will give them ours. They need mythic histories to ground them in our reality, formalized rituals so they can be experienced in our world, servants and attendants who can fulfill their wishes (which are nothing more than *our* wishes), rules and regulations to keep them happy, prayers and petitions to ward off their anger. What they need, in short, are religions. And so we will invent them.

But arguably one of the most significant consequences of our compulsion to humanize the divine is what seems to have occurred as a direct result of the building of Göbekli Tepe: the birth of agriculture. For it is the conceptualization of personal gods in human form, and the institutionalized myths and rituals that accompany such a process, that will push us out of the Paleolithic era, that will compel us to stop wandering and to settle down, that will give us the impetus to alter the earth to our advantage by inventing agriculture. Simply put, in transforming the gods of heaven into humans, we will transform humans into the gods of the earth.[1]

FOR NEARLY TWO and a half million years of our evolution—more than 90 percent of our existence as hominids—we foraged the earth for our food. We were predators, stalking through forests and plains, competing for prey with beasts far more adept than we were—though not nearly as clever. This experience as hunter-gatherers shaped and defined us. It enlarged our brains and constructed our cognitive capacities, gradually transforming us from impulsive brutes to discriminating beings.

Our gods, such as they were, were the gods of the hunt. Our rites and rituals, our myths and legends, our subterranean sanctuaries, our very conception of the cosmos were powered by the mystical solidarity that existed between hunter and hunted. That solidarity extended from the animals we killed to the tools we used to kill them: our bone harpoons and wooden spears, our fishhooks and woven nets, became charged with sacred power.

Our reliance on these weapons for our very survival transformed them from mere objects into simulacra of the spirit world.

Hunting gave us mastery over our landscape, obliging us to form a mental map of the world we inhabited—its ridges and slopes, its valleys and rivers. It not only inspired our creative imagination, it entrenched in our consciousness certain societal values that we still strive for today: Our need for mobility as hunters prohibited the accumulation of material possessions, the hoarding of property, and, as a result, the stratification of society into haves and have-nots.

Then, sometime around 12,000 to 10,000 years ago, we inexplicably swapped our spears for plows and transformed ourselves from foragers to farmers. We ceased scavenging for food and started producing it. Rather than hunting for animals, we began to breed them.

Hunting may have made us human, but farming forever altered what being human meant. If hunting gave us mastery over space, farming forced us to master time, to synchronize the movements of the stars and the sun with the agricultural cycle. The mystical solidarity we enjoyed with the animals with whom we shared the earth was transferred to the earth itself. We stopped praying for help with the hunt and prayed instead for help with the harvest. Our spiritual focus shifted from the sky—traditionally associated with fatherly, male deities—to the earth as Mother Goddess, thus elevating the position of women in society. The fertility of the earth became bound up with the fecundity of women, who hold the mystery of life within their wombs, so that, as the legendary historian of religions Mircea Eliade argued, the physical work of plowing the fields became akin to a sexual act.[2]

The process of transforming the earth to our advantage brought with it a whole new set of values and behavioral norms, as well as a new collection of myths to help us make sense of the

changed world we inhabited. It was around this time that the concept of the "immolated deity" first arose—the god who dies and
is dismembered and from whose body creation springs. Think
Phan Ku, the creator god of China, whose skull became the dome
of the sky, whose blood became the rivers and seas, and whose
bones became the mountains and rocks; or the god Osiris, who
taught the ancient Egyptians how to cultivate the earth before
being killed and cut to pieces by his fiendish brother, Seth, who
scattered the pieces of his body along the fertile Nile valley.

Not only did such mythologies better coincide with the birth,
death, and rebirth of our crops, they fostered a more intimate relationship with the divine. After all, if the crops we plant in the
earth are believed to arise from a god's dismembered body, then
when we partake of those plants, we are in fact consuming the
body of the god—a concept that will have a long life in the religious practices of the Ancient Near East, including the Christian
ritual of the Eucharist.

Once we started farming, it is generally assumed, we stopped
moving. We settled down and built villages and temples. Villages
require rules, and so we privileged some among us to make laws
and enforce them (thus the birth of organized society). Temples
require priests, and so we designated others to regulate worship
and speak to the gods on our behalf (thus the birth of organized
religion). The division of labor led to the partitioning of society,
and the novelty of wealth and personal property. We went from
exchanging gifts to bartering and eventually to buying and sell-
ing, hoarding and forfeiting, having and not having.

As food became more readily available, populations soared.
The congregation of large communities into public spaces allowed ideas to be more rapidly exchanged and technologies to be
more seamlessly adopted. Art flourished, technology was shared,

civilization was born, all because of the fateful decision to stop hunting and gathering and start farming and domesticating.

This dramatic shift in human development effectively ended the Paleolithic era and launched what is known as the Neolithic Revolution. The term was coined by the archaeologist Vere Gordon Childe, who considered the birth of agriculture to be the most significant development in human history (after the mastery of fire). Most people would likely agree with Childe that the domestication of animals was obviously beneficial to human beings, and that farming was clearly preferable to foraging. Agriculture must have created more reliable food sources, since there was no longer any need to pursue animals across far-flung hunting grounds or to scour the forests and fields for edible foodstuffs. Rather than randomly decapitating stocks of wheat and barley and stuffing them into our mouths, we could instead plant and harvest acreages of grain. Rather than spend our days combing the wilderness for game, we could capture and pen animals, slaughtering them for food whenever we liked.

Yet the more we learn about the rise of agriculture, the more we realize that it may have cost our ancestors more trouble than it was worth. To begin with, the backbreaking process of spending almost every waking hour—from sunrise to sunset—clearing the land, plowing the earth, collecting and sowing seeds, irrigating the fields by hand, and then guarding the crops day and night against locusts and thieves, was far more time-consuming and labor-intensive than simply going out into the wild and hunting for animals that were still everywhere in abundance.

Farming meant that the skins of freshwater that had to be carried from distant sources to keep the community alive now had to be shared with crops whose thirst was insatiable. It meant that the forests that sheltered us from the elements and protected us from predators had to be burned down to make room for fields and pastures. It meant sharing our food with animals who had to be fed and protected, taken out to pasture, kept clean and free of disease. And what was the reward for all of this drudgery and self-denial? Surprisingly, it was *less* food, not more.[3]

Studies have shown that the agricultural revolution led to the consumption of fewer vitamins and minerals and substantially less protein. Only a few types of grain were suitable for early farming and an even smaller number of animal species were suited to domestication. The hunter survived on dozens of different species of plants and animals. If any species fell in short supply, he could simply focus on another.

The farmer, however, relied on a small variety of domesticated plants and animals. If there was a drought, or if any one of his wheat or barley crops failed, he and his kin would starve and die. If any one of his sheep, goats, or chickens caught a disease, it could wipe out the entire herd, and he and his kin would starve and die. Faced with an exigent crisis, the hunter could simply pack up and follow his meal wherever it led him. The farmer had little choice but to stay put and perish along with his efforts.

It is no wonder that in most ancient agricultural societies, at least one out of every three children died before the age of twenty. As the Israeli historian Yuval Harari observes, the bodies of *Homo sapiens* were adapted to running after game, not to clearing land and plowing fields. Surveys of ancient human skeletons show just how brutal the transition to agriculture was. Farmers were more susceptible than hunters to anemia and vitamin deficiency. They caught more infectious diseases and died younger. They had worse teeth and more broken bones, and they suffered from a host of what were fairly novel ailments, such as slipped discs, arthritis, and hernias. In fact, skeletons unearthed in and around the Ancient Near East indicate that in the first few thousand years of the Neolithic Revolution, humans lost an average of six inches in height, largely as a result of their inadequate diet. In light of all this, the transition from hunting to farming seems not only to have been a bad bet on humanity's part; it was, in Harari's words, "history's biggest fraud."[4]

Given the enormous time, energy, and resources it took to farm, what accounts for the abandonment of hunting for the harsh reality of agricultural life? Childe believed that the abrupt changes in climate that took place at the end of the last Ice Age, around 11,700 years ago, spurred human beings to develop alternative food sources. As the earth warmed and the glaciers retreated, climatic pressures forced populations to squeeze into a few favorable geographical zones, where they experimented with collecting and planting certain varieties of cereals and legumes.

However, subsequent studies of ancient weather patterns have demonstrated that the changes in climate ushered in at the end of the last Ice Age occurred far too slowly to cause the kind of sudden mass migration that Childe imagined. Childe is right that climate change may have allowed for the rise of agriculture and animal domestication. But it caused neither.[5]

Others have argued that the advent of agriculture was the result of population pressures in infertile regions, or that overhunting led to a sharp rise in animal extinction, forcing early humans to devise alternative food sources. The archaeological record supports neither hypothesis. There appears to be no evidence to support the extinction theory, and the first examples of agricultural activity occurred in resource-rich regions like the Fertile Crescent—that arc of moist, bountiful land that rises from the lower Nile valley in Egypt, bends around the Levant and southern Turkey, and dips into Iraq and the western ridge of Iran.[6]

The trouble with most of these theories is that they are based on the widely held assumption that agriculture came first, and permanent settlement followed as a result. We suppose that our ancient ancestors ceased their nomadic ways *because* they started planting seeds and therefore had no choice but to settle down in order to care for their crops. However, the discovery of Göbekli Tepe and other ancient sites built by hunter-gatherers across the Levant has turned this idea on its head. We now know that permanent settlements came first, and then, many years later, farming arose. We were living in villages with booming populations, building giant temples, creating great works of art, sharing our technology for centuries before it occurred to us to grow our food.

So then, if the domestication of plants and animals was not the result of sudden environmental changes or mass extinction or sudden population increase, what was it that spurred the transition from hunting to farming? The discovery of Göbekli Tepe and similar devotional sites across the Ancient Near East suggests that it was the birth of organized religion.

Constructing a temple the size and scope of Göbekli Tepe would have taken many years and required a huge workforce of excavators and quarrymen, masons and artisans, to complete. These workers would have needed a steady supply of food over the course of the project. Hunting the aurochs and gazelles, boars and red deer, that stalked the surrounding area would not have provided enough meat to feed them. So they gradually began to cultivate the indigenous grasses that grew all around the region in order to bolster the workers' food supply. That would have led to the planting of seeds and the harvesting of crops. Eventually, they might have decided to capture animals in large numbers and pen them for easy slaughter. That in turn might have led to the breeding of sheep, pigs, goats, and cattle—all of which, the archaeological records show, were first domesticated in and around eastern Turkey, in the vicinity of Göbekli Tepe, and around the same time as its construction.[7]

The physical act of building the temple may have necessitated the planting of crops and the domestication of animals to feed the workers and worshippers gathered there. But to permanently settle, form, and modify the earth, to exert our will upon animals and utterly disrupt the way they are born, bred, and raised, to create artificial environments that mimic the natural world—all of this would have required a giant psychological leap in the way we think about the relationship between humans and animals, between people and the earth. More than a technological revolution, it would have required a revolution in the way we think about the human condition—a "revolution of symbols," to borrow a phrase coined by the French archaeologist Jacques Cauvin. For our Paleolithic ancestors, that revolution came in the form of an institutionalized religious system dominated by belief in humanized gods.[8]

After all, to conceive of the gods in human form, to claim that we share the same physical and psychic qualities as the gods themselves, is to view humanity as somehow distinct from the rest of the natural world. For the first time in our evolution we began to imagine ourselves not as a part of the universe, but as its center. Gone is the animistic worldview that had bound us in soul and spirit to the natural world. And if we're no longer bound in essence to the animals and the earth, then why not exploit them? Why not intervene in nature to dominate and domesticate it, to transform it to our advantage?

The construction of Göbekli Tepe may not only have inaugurated the Neolithic Era. It likely initiated a whole new conception of humanity. It placed human beings at the center of the spiritual plane, exalted above all living things: rulers of nature, gods over the earth. What followed this tectonic shift from primitive animism to organized religion—in Mesopotamia and Egypt, in Europe and Greece, in Iran and India, China, and beyond—was the formation of entire pantheons of personalized, humanized gods, each embodying a particular human attribute, until there was a unique god for every good and bad quality we possess.

Thus what began as an unconscious cognitive impulse to fashion the divine in our image—to give it our soul—gradually became, over the next ten thousand years of spiritual development, a conscious effort to make the gods more and more humanlike—until, at last, God became literally human.

Chapter Five

Lofty Persons

WHEN THE GODS, *instead of humans, did the work and bore the loads, dug the canals and cleared the channels, dredged the marshes and plowed the fields, they groaned amongst themselves and grumbled over the masses of excavated soil. The labor was heavy, the misery too much. So they set fire to their tools, set fire to their spades. And off they went, one and all, to the gate of the great god Enlil, the counselor of the gods.*

"We have to put a stop to the digging," they cried. "The load is excessive. It is killing us! The labor is heavy, the misery too much!"

Enlil consulted Mami, midwife of the gods. "You are the womb-goddess," he said. "Create a mortal, that he may bear the yoke. Let humans bear the load of the gods."

So Mami, with the help of the wise god Enki, mixed clay with blood and created seven males and seven females. She gave them picks and spades, and led them, two by two, down to earth to relieve the gods of their labor.

Six hundred and six hundred years passed, and the earth be-

came too wide and the people too numerous. The land was as noisy as a bellowing bull. And the gods grew restless at the racket.

"The noise of mankind has become too much," Enlil snapped. "I am losing sleep."

A divine assembly of the gods was convened, and there it was decided by all to make a great flood that would wipe humanity from the face of the earth so that the gods could finally be free of the clamor.

Now, down on the earth, there was a pious man named Atrahasis, whose ear was open to his own god, Enki. He would speak with Enki, and Enki would speak with him.

In a dream, Enki came to Atrahasis and made his voice heard. "Dismantle your house and build a boat," the wise god Enki warned. "Leave all your possessions and put aboard the seed of all living things. Draw out the boat that you will make on a circular plan. Let her length and breadth be equal. Make upper decks and lower decks."

So Atrahasis built a boat and loaded it with the seed of all living things. He put on board his kith and kin. He put on board the birds flying in the heavens. He put on board cattle from the open country, wild beasts from the open country, wild animals from the steppes. Two by two they entered the boat. Then Atrahasis, too, entered the boat and shut the door.

When the first light of dawn appeared, a black cloud rose from the base of the sky. Everything light turned into darkness. The tempest arose like a battle force. Anzu, the storm god—the lion-headed eagle—tore at the sky with his talons.

Then the flood came. Like a wild ass screaming, the winds howled. The darkness was total; there was no sun. No man could see his fellow, no people could be distinguished from the sky. Even the gods were afraid of the deluge. They withdrew to heaven, where they cowered like dogs crouched by a wall.

For seven days and seven nights the torrent, the storm, the flood came on. The tempest overwhelmed the land. Bodies clogged the river like dragonflies. When the seventh day arrived, the storm, which had struggled like a woman in labor, blew itself out. The sea became calm and the flood-plain flat as a roof.

The boat came to rest atop Mount Nimush and Atrahasis exited. He released a dove. The dove came back, for no perching place was visible to it. He released a swallow. The swallow came back, for no perching place was visible to it. He released a raven. The raven did not come back. So Atrahasis and his kith and kin, and the birds of the heavens, and the cattle from the open country, and the wild beasts from the open country, and the wild animals from the steppes came out of the boat. And there he made a sacrifice of thanks to Enki his god.

But when Enlil smelled the sacrifice and saw the boat, he was furious. Once again, he called the divine assembly to order. "We, all of us, agreed together on an oath. No form of life should have escaped. How did any man survive the catastrophe?"

Enki, the wise, spoke. "I did it, in defiance of you! It was I who made sure life was preserved."

The gods were humbled by Enki's words. They wept and were filled with regret. Mami, the midwife of the gods, cried. "How could I have spoken such evil in the gods' assembly? I myself gave birth to them; they are my own people."

So Enlil and Enki came to a compromise. "Instead of imposing a flood, let a lion come up and diminish the people. Instead of imposing a flood, let a wolf come up and diminish the people. Instead of imposing a flood, let famine lessen the land. Let war and plague savage the population."

The divine compromise reached, Enki came down to the boat and took Atrahasis by the hand. He took his wife by the hand. He touched their foreheads and made a declaration.

"Henceforth, this man and this woman shall be as we gods are."[1]

IF THE ANCIENT Sumerian epic of Atrahasis and the flood, composed more than four thousand years ago, sounds familiar, it should. Tales of a world-ending deluge that destroys all of humanity save for a fortunate few are among the oldest and most widely spread in human history. The myth is, in some ways, the quintessential "folk memory," as most scholars believe it is based on an actual catastrophic flood that took place some time in the distant past. Indigenous versions of a flood epic can be found in Egypt, Babylon, Greece, India, Europe, East Asia, North and South America, and Australia. The reasons for the flood differ depending on who is telling the story. There are different settings, different gods, different endings—each reworked to reflect the particular culture and religion of the storyteller.

The hero Atrahasis is known by many names. In the twelfth-century B.C.E. Babylonian *Epic of Gilgamesh,* he is called Utnap-ishtim. In the Greek *Babyloniaka* of Berossus, composed in the third century B.C.E., his name is Xisuthros, and the Sumerian god Enki is replaced with the Greek god Kronos. In the Bible, Atraha-sis is called Noah, while Enki becomes the Hebrew god Yahweh. In the Quran it is Nuh and Allah.

Yet no matter the setting or the reason, the hero or the god, most of these flood narratives can be traced to a single source composed in the first written language, by the first great civilization: Sumer.

The agricultural revolution that took hold around 10,000 B.C.E. spread rapidly through the Fertile Crescent, reaching its zenith in the lush alluvial plains of ancient Mesopotamia. Wedged between the legendary rivers of creation, the Tigris and the Euphrates, in what is today known as Iraq and Syria, Mesopotamia (meaning "between two rivers" in Greek) benefited from a temperate climate and periodic flooding, which created a mineral-rich environment ripe for agricultural growth.

By 9000 B.C.E. there were large, dry farming zones throughout the region, particularly in the south, where small fishing villages clustered against the two great rivers as they met and discharged into the Persian Gulf. By 7000 B.C.E., most common species of plants and animals, with the exception of horses and camels, had been domesticated in Mesopotamia. The next two thousand years saw widespread agricultural expansion stretching west into Egypt and east to the Iranian plateau. The small blocks of fishing and farming villages began merging to form the first proto-cities. At Çatalhöyük in southern Anatolia, between the years 7000 and 6500 B.C.E., nearly a thousand households lived together in a large agricultural settlement boasting elaborately painted shrines dedicated to a fertility goddess. Around 6000 B.C.E., northern Mesopotamia saw the emergence of the Halaf, an advanced culture known for their mastery of pottery. After about a thousand years, the Halaf ceded their cultural domain of the region to the Ubaid, whose reach extended deep into southern Mesopotamia, all the way to modern Bahrain and Oman.

It was the Ubaid, and not the gods, who sometime around 5000 B.C.E. drained the marshes and drew canals from the Tigris and Euphrates, establishing the world's first irrigation system. No one knows exactly when these inhabitants of southern Mesopotamia came to be known as *Sumerians,* or whether the Sumerians and Ubaidis were even related. The word *Sumer* is actually Akkadian—a Semitic language that was the most widely spoken in Mesopotamia. It means "land of the civilized kings." The Sumerians referred to themselves as "the black-headed people." Yet wherever they came from and however they arose, by 4500 B.C.E., the Sumerians had cemented their dominance over Mesopotamia by founding what is regarded as the first major city in the world, *Uruk*.

From their seat at Uruk, the Sumerians created the most advanced civilization the world had ever known. They invented the wheel and the sailboat. They expanded irrigation channels to allow for year-round farming on an immense scale. Mass farming relieved the Sumerians of many of the more burdensome requirements of agricultural life, leading to the flowering of Sumerian culture and religion, the achievement of great works of art and architecture, the creation of complex mythologies such as the Atrahasis epic, and, most earth-shattering of all, the invention of writing.

Writing changes everything. Its development marks the dividing line between prehistory and history. The entire reason why Mesopotamia is known as the Cradle of Civilization is because some time in the fourth millennium B.C.E., the Sumerians began to press blunt reed styluses onto wet clay to make the distinctive wedge-shaped lines we call *cuneiform*, allowing human beings, for the first time in history, to record their most abstract thoughts.[2]

It did not take long for Sumerian cuneiform to be adopted by the other local languages of Mesopotamia, including Akkadian and its two principal dialects: Babylonian in the south, which became the language of literary works and inscriptions, and Assyrian in the north, which was used mostly for economic and political documents until it faded away with the collapse of the Assyrian empire in the seventh century B.C.E. The Akkadian language survived in spoken form throughout the Middle East for three thousand years, until it was fully displaced by Aramaic in the first century B.C.E.[3]

Thanks to cuneiform, we have at our disposal a treasure trove of archives and documents, of kings lists and chronicles of major cities and dynasties, of personal letters that cast light on societal life and government documents that outline the workings of the ancient state. We have temple records detailing the various cults of Mesopotamia. Most spectacularly, we have a veritable library of sprawling, unforgettable myths and legends that offers nearly unfettered access to what is arguably the earliest and most influential advanced religious system ever devised.

The Sumerians were not the only Neolithic civilization to create a sophisticated religion; they were probably not even the first to do so. But they were the first to write about it, and that made all the difference, not only because it allowed their religious ideas to spread across the region, but because, with the invention of writing, the compulsion to humanize the divine—a compulsion rooted in our cognitive processes and crudely expressed at Göbekli Tepe—became *actualized*. The act of writing about the gods, of being forced to describe in words what the gods are like, not only transformed how we envision the gods; it made conscious and explicit our unconscious and implicit desire to make the gods in our own image. That's because when we write about the gods, when we place them in a mythical narrative at the beginning of creation or in the midst of debating an apocalyptic flood, we cannot help but imagine the gods thinking and acting as we ourselves would think and act. We implant in them our attributes and emotions; we ascribe to them our will and our motivations.

The very words we choose to describe the gods affect how we understand their nature, their personality, even their physical form. For example, the word for "god" in Sumerian is *ilu*, which means something like "lofty person," and so that became precisely how the gods were envisioned in Sumerian writings: as elevated beings who had human bodies and wore human clothes, who expressed human emotions and exhibited human personalities. The gods of Sumer were born to mothers who suckled them when they were young. They had fathers with whom they clashed as they grew older. They fell in love and got married. They had sex and birthed children. They lived in houses with their families, and had relatives with whom they formed giant celestial clans. They ate and drank and complained about work. They argued and fought with one another. Occasionally they were wounded and died. They were, in the most meaningful sense, *human*.

As the widespread adoption of the Atrahasis story demonstrates, the myths that germinated in the land between two rivers quickly grew shoots in Europe and North Africa. They blossomed across the Caucasus mountains and over the Aegean Sea. They flowered in the religious systems of the Egyptians and the Greeks, the Indians and the Persians. They fully bloomed in the pages of the Bible and the Quran, where the Sumerian word *ilu* became transliterated as *Elohim* in Hebrew and *Allah* in Arabic. And, not surprisingly, everywhere the myths of Mesopotamia spread, so, too, did the Mesopotamian perception of the gods as "lofty persons."[4]

THE MESOPOTAMIANS WERE *polytheists,* meaning they worshiped multiple gods simultaneously. Indeed, the Mesopotamian pantheon contained more than three thousand deities. There was Aya, the goddess of light, who was wife to Shamash, the god of the sun; Damu, the healer, and Girra, the god of fire and refiner of metals; Sin, the powerful moon god; Enki the wise, who together with Enlil, "the decreer of fates," and An (or Anu), the sky god, made up the three most important deities in the early Mesopotamian pantheon. There were, in fact, so many gods in Mesopotamia that ancient scribes had to compile complex "god lists" to keep track of them all.[5]

Where the Mesopotamians came up with all of these gods is a

difficult question to answer. The nine-thousand-year spiritual journey that took humanity from the faceless, humanoid pillars at Göbekli Tepe to the vibrant, personalized deities of Mesopotamia is obscured by a dearth of material evidence. However, a remarkable series of finds in Jericho, one of the most ancient cities on earth and the prelude to the great city-states of Mesopotamia, has shed some light on this intermediate stage of human spirituality.

In 1953, the famed British archaeologist Dame Kathleen Kenyon was overseeing an excavation in Tell es-Sultan, near the ancient city of Jericho, when she noticed the smooth dome of what appeared to be an intact human skull protruding from a pit she had dug. When she exhumed the skull she was amazed to discover that it was covered in plaster. Its facial features had been perfectly reconstructed with clay so that it looked alive. Inside its hollow eye sockets were two pale, pearly shells. The skull had been removed from a buried corpse and then reburied underneath a private home. Further excavations revealed six more skulls just like it, all buried beneath the same house, and dating to between 8000 and 6000 B.C.E.

Since Kenyon's find at Jericho, similar caches of human skulls have been discovered buried under floors and hearths, beneath beds and platforms, in private homes as far afield as 'Ain Ghazal in Jordan, Tell Ramad and Byblos in Syria, and Çatalhöyük in Turkey. The skulls are often surrounded with jewels and weapons and carefully arranged, either packed in a tight circle and looking inward, or facing outward in the same direction.[6]

We know that Neolithic peoples considered the head (or, rather, the brain) to be the seat of the soul, which is why they so often collected and preserved human skulls. But the presence of these large caches buried under homes in what, for all intents and purposes, look like private household shrines may indicate the

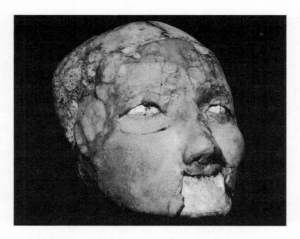

Plastered human skull found in Jericho
Jononmac46 / CC-BY-SA-3.0 / Wikimedia Commons

emergence early in the Neolithic Era of *manism*—a belief popularly referred to as "ancestor worship."

As we have seen, the veneration of ancestors can be traced all the way back to the Paleolithic era. It is the result of the animistic belief that the souls of the dead continue to exist as spirits in the world. Yet with the birth of agriculture, ancestor worship became more complex and pronounced. The earth in which the dead were buried was now the soil from which our sustenance grew. It therefore made sense to focus our spiritual efforts on the recently dead in the hope that they would intercede with the forces of nature on behalf of the living, whether to help preserve the crops or maintain the health and viability of the herd. With the passage of time, some of these deceased ancestors evolved into deities—the better to intercede with the natural forces—until the middleman, as it were, was removed and the forces of nature themselves became deified.

This theory is supported by the fact that many of Mesopotamia's gods began their existence as little more than the deification of the natural elements. An was both the sky god *and the sky itself*. Shamash was both the sun god *and the sun*. It may have been partly the need to better manage these natural forces, to maintain power and influence over them, that spurred the Mesopotamians to personalize these gods, to gradually transform them into a pantheon of individual deities, each with a specific sphere of influence—whether earthly, cultural, or cosmic—and each with a specific function in the lives of their worshippers. From there, it was simply a matter of giving each god a personality, a set of human traits, and a distinct form, and the "lofty persons" were born.

Most of the major gods in Mesopotamia were connected to a particular city-state: Enlil in the city of Nippur, Sin in the city of Ur, Inanna in Uruk, and so on. And while each city-state had its own temple, these were not primarily places of worship; they were, rather, the earthly residences of the gods. Each was thought to be literally a god's second home—a kind of vacation house complete with gardens, walls, doors, and fences, where the gods could take time away from their celestial abodes to dwell with humans on earth. The temples were often built in the form of stepped structures called *ziggurats*—the rectangular pyramidal towers made of baked mud brick that are the hallmark of Mesopotamian architecture. Yet unlike the later Egyptian pyramids, Mesopotamian temples were solid structures, completely filled in, layered in successively receding stories, like staircases that the gods could use to move back and forth between heaven and earth, and capped with a small chamber at the top where the gods could dwell in repose.[7]

The appearance of a god inside one of these chambers was signified by the presence of an idol carved in the god's image. The use of idols was not a Mesopotamian innovation. Like the veneration of ancestors, the carving of idols to represent spirits or gods can be traced to the Paleolithic era. Dozens of idols—the vast majority of them female and pregnant, with round, distended bellies bulging out beneath their plump breasts—have been unearthed in Paleolithic sites across Europe and Asia.[8]

In Mesopotamia, however, efficiencies in sculpting and molding made the use of idols in public devotion far more common and widespread. Each day a priest or priestess—depending on the gender of the god—would enter a temple's chamber, wash, dress, and feed the idol, anoint it with perfumes and incense, embellish it with cosmetics, and, on special occasions, take it out for a stroll so it could visit its fellow gods in neighboring temples. It was only then that the masses would set eyes upon their gods; the laity was not allowed into the temples and thus had no direct access to the deities residing within.

Nevertheless, no Mesopotamian would have thought that the small idol hoisted up in the air by a priest was *actually* a god. This is a complete misunderstanding of the term "idol worship." Ancient peoples did not worship slabs of stone; they worshiped the spirits that resided within them. The idol was not itself a god; it was *imbued* with the god. The god was thought to take form within the idol.

However, the consequence of such a belief is that when the spirit of one of these "lofty persons" entered an idol, the idol became the spirit's body. It reflected the god's physical appearance on earth. Put another way, while no one in Mesopotamia would have considered the idol to actually be the god, most would have readily accepted the idea that the idol *looked like the god*.[9]

This is a complex yet exceedingly important point. In the same way that when we write about a god we instinctively attribute to that god human emotions and motivations, when we visualize a god—when we expertly carve an idol in the god's image or paint the god on a stained-glass window—we instinctively conjure the human form. We may provide that form with wings, as Enlil has, or flames rising from its shoulders, like Shamash. We may exaggerate the god's size or give the god multiple arms and legs. But such embellishments merely provide the *minimally counterintuitive* element necessary to assure that the god will be remembered and successfully transmitted (recall Eve's talking tree). Attenuate these supernatural flourishes slightly, and what remains is not an ethereal force of nature, but a human being with superhuman powers.

The example of Egypt, Mesopotamia's civilizational successor, is highly instructive in this regard. Early in Egyptian history, during what is known as the Pre-Dynastic Period (c. 5000–3000 B.C.E.), the Egyptians were pure animists; they believed that all beings were animated by a single, divine force that permeated the universe. This force manifested itself to some degree in gods and spirits but was itself amorphous—without shape, substance, or will. However, with the invention of Egyptian hieroglyphic writing sometime around 3300 B.C.E.—not long after and probably

Mesopotamian deities on the Adda seal, including Ishtar (with wings), Shamash (rising with sword in hand), and Enki

under the influence of Sumerian cuneiform—there arose a need to make this abstract force more concrete. It had to be visualized so that it could be etched onto the walls of temples or inked onto strips of papyrus. It had to be made real and recognizable in relation to the world so that it could be understood and harnessed. And so, as happened in Mesopotamia, this abstract divine force eventually became realized in human form. By the start of the Old Kingdom (c. 2686–2181 B.C.E.), the Egyptian pantheon of humanized gods had been fully formed and the religion of ancient Egypt firmly established.[10]

Unlike in Mesopotamia, however, the gods of Egypt were often depicted in multifarious ways—rendered as human or animal or, more often than not, a combination of the two. Thus Hathor, the Egyptian goddess of music, dance, and fertility, could be a cow wearing a woman's necklace, a cow/woman hybrid, or a woman with the furry ears of a cow protruding from the sides of her head. Likewise, Anubis, the god of mummification and protector of the dead, could be a jackal, or a man with a jackal's head.

These flourishes not only provided the minimally counterintuitive properties necessary to make the gods more memorable; they allowed Egyptians to manage and, more important, manipulate the god's symbolic function. Anubis was depicted as a jackal-headed man because the jackal is a scavenging animal known for occasionally digging up and devouring corpses buried in the desert. By depicting the protector of graves as a jackal in human form, the Egyptians sought to control what was a widely feared force of nature with the power to disrupt the funerary practices that were so vital to ancient Egyptian spirituality.[11]

Still, no matter what form the gods of Egypt took, they were, like the gods of Mesopotamia, always described in human terms, with human impulses, human desires, and human instincts. Even when the gods were portrayed as animals in Egyptian art and literature, they were still given human traits and behavior; they were still depicted as taking part in human activities. They ate, drank, and slept like humans. They argued with each other and fought over petty jealousies. They had family problems. They displayed good and bad moods. They could be all-knowing or just plain stupid.

Almost the exact same process occurred a thousand years later, this time among the loosely affiliated collective of tribes that scholars refer to as the Indo-Europeans—a designation meant to acknowledge their influence in shaping the languages of Europe and the Near East. Perhaps as long ago as 5000 B.C.E., the Indo-Europeans embarked on a series of migrations from their homeland (likely near the Caucasus, though this is disputed) eastward to the Caspian Sea and the Iranian plateau, southward to the Black Sea and Anatolia and Greece, and westward to the Baltic Sea and Europe. As they settled into their new lands and either merged with or conquered the indigenous populations, the Indo-Europeans left a deep imprint on the religious traditions of this vast region: the hierarchical pantheon of the Canaanite cults; the nature spiritism of the Celts; the religiously inspired caste systems of India; the exceedingly ritualistic practices of ancient Iran; the Hellenic myths of Homer and Hesiod; the philosophical ideals of Plato and Aristotle—in other words, the spiritual landscape from which Judaism, Christianity, and Islam arose.[12]

The Indo-European pantheon of gods was constructed in the same way as that of Mesopotamia and Egypt, by deifying the forces of nature: Dyeus, the sky god; Agni, the god of fire; Indra, the sun god; Varuna, the god of the primordial waters; and so on. But, as happened in Mesopotamia and Egypt, when these gods were written about for the very first time in the Rig Veda—the oldest sacred text of India, composed in Sanskrit around 1500 B.C.E.—they shed their airy natures and took on specific human qualities and appearances. And when in the following centuries these Vedic portrayals became actualized into the vibrant idols of Hindu religiosity, the transformation of these Indo-European deities from deified nature to humanized gods was complete: Indra with his golden skin, hair, and beard, clad in perfumed garments; the two-faced Agni with his many arms and legs; Varuna, resplendent and riding atop a crocodile.[13]

In each of these civilizations, the more accustomed people became to seeing images of their gods displayed in public temples and shrines—the more they heard their stories and legends during public festivals and ceremonies—the more easily they could personalize the abstract forces of nature their ancestors once worshiped. Much as the invention of the printing press made ideas more available to the multitudes, the mass production of personified idols, and the increased technological skill in crafting them, made the gods seem more recognizably human—until, in ancient Greece, they became too human to be taken seriously as gods.

GREEK HISTORY DOES not begin with the grand epics of Homer and Hesiod, which together have given us perhaps the most complete picture possible of the piety and personality of an ancient civilization. It begins, rather, in the Middle Bronze Age, around 1600 B.C.E., with the enigmatic seafaring civilization known as the Mycenaeans. As the first great colonizers of the Aegean, the Mycenaean civilization bestowed upon the Greek Isles many of the gifts for which we now thank ancient Greece, including possibly the classical Greek script.[14]

The Mycenaeans also gave the Greeks many of their gods, in particular Poseidon, the god of the sea, who may have been the supreme god of the Mycenaean pantheon (Zeus, a martial deity, was derived from the Indo-European sky god, Dyeus, and seems to have ascended to the top of the Greek pantheon at a much later date). As the deification of the primordial waters, Poseidon was naturally linked to the Earth Goddess, or Gaia, another major Mycenaean deity (Poseidon's name means "Earth's husband"). Not surprisingly, the Mycenaeans also deified the winds, an element of nature as integral to the spiritual lives of seafarers as water and earth. Other Greek gods familiar to us, including Athena and Hera, were known to the Mycenaeans, and these, too, seem to have begun their existence as deifications of the natural world: Athena likely began as a solar deity, and Hera may have represented the air.

Yet in the Greek epics, these gods became less the personification of the forces of nature and more the divinization of various human attributes: Athena, the goddess of wisdom; Hera, the goddess of maternal love. And while the Greek pantheon originally included dozens of different deities, each with a specific origin and function, by the time they were written about in Homer and Hesiod, they had more or less been condensed into twelve principal gods—known as the *Olympians*—depicted by the Greeks as members of one big family.

In the Greek imagination, Mount Olympus was not just the abode of the gods who ruled over humanity; it was the home of a highly dysfunctional divine family engaged with one another in the same cosmic drama, like characters in a long-running soap opera who are constantly interacting in each other's storylines. There was Zeus, the patriarch, father of gods and men; Hera, whom the Greeks transformed into Zeus's sister and wife; and their firstborn son, Ares, the god of war. There were also Zeus's two brothers: Poseidon, demoted from his perch at the height of the Mycenaean pantheon, and Hades, god of the underworld, as well as his second sister, Demeter, goddess of agriculture. Add to these Zeus's other son, Hermes, whom he bore with the goddess

Maia; his twin children Apollo and Artemis, both born from his tryst with the goddess Leto; Dionysus, the god of wine and ecstasy, whom he sired with a mortal woman; Athena, who in her evolution from Mycenaean to Greek goddess became Zeus's daughter, born directly out of his head after he had swallowed his pregnant wife, Metis; and Zeus's favorite child, Aphrodite, goddess of love and sex.

The ancient Egyptians also organized their gods as a family, modeled after the relationships among Egypt's most beloved trio of deities: Osiris, his sister and wife Isis, and their valiant son, the falcon-headed Horus. But the Greeks perfected the concept of the divine family. And why not? What better way to relate to the gods? This way, when we pray to them for help with our own struggles, we can be certain that they understand us. They understand our trials and tribulations and can address them as if they were their own. As Barbara Graziosi writes in her indispensable book *The Gods of Olympus,* "The Greek gods are familiar to us because they are, quite simply, a family."[15]

Council of the Gods by Raphael and his school, Loggia di Psiche in the Villa Farnesina, Rome (c. 1517–18 C.E.)　*Wikimedia Commons*

For some Greeks, however, that was precisely the problem. The gods written about by the poets of ancient Greece were too morally reproachable, their exploits too maudlin, their concerns *too human,* for them to continue to command respect as gods. How can one have respect for a god like Zeus, who is forever having to settle petty disputes between his wives and children, and who is constantly sneaking away from Mount Olympus to conduct affairs with various goddesses, human women, and young boys?

Pushed to its logical extreme, the impulse to depict the gods in increasingly human terms can quickly seem foolish. It is one thing to ascribe human traits to a deity. It is something else altogether to endow the gods with the full range of human emotions through which they come so vibrantly alive in Greek literature. Are we really to imagine these supreme beings behaving the way they do in the Homeric myths: as adulterous, thieving, jealous, lustful, easily tricked, and utterly corruptible beings who just happen to be immortal?

Even as the Greeks were grappling with the dilemma of so effectively humanizing the gods in their literature, they were making similar objections to the progressively humanlike idols crowding their temples. The earliest expressions of the Greek gods were not the heroic statues we are used to seeing in museums, but rather abstract representations made of unshaped blocks of wood or stone meant to express the god's spirit, not its physical form. Hera, for instance, was represented as a pillar in the port city of Argos and as a plank of wood on the island of Samos. Athena was originally worshiped as a flat piece of olive wood that was washed and bejeweled, wrapped in garments, and carefully tended by a cadre of her priestesses.[16]

But by the time the master Greek artisan Phidias sculpted the magnificent statue of Athena in ivory and gold for the Parthenon— the most famous and widely known cult statue in all the Greek

Isles—the likeness of the goddess with shield in hand and a helmet bearing the image of the sphinx on her head had become the primary form through which she was recognized and worshiped. The same process occurred with images of Hera, of Poseidon, and indeed of all the great gods of Greece.[17]

As with the elaborate depiction of the gods in Greek literature, it was precisely the advanced artistry of Greek sculptors, and the skill they had mastered in rendering the gods so realistically in human form, that created the wedge of doubt about the nature— and indeed the very existence—of the entire Greek pantheon. Could the gods really look exactly like human beings? And not just any humans, but ethnically Greek humans, with their lush beards, curled locks, and sharp, aquiline noses? How could it be that immortal, universal gods responsible for all of creation and everyone in it would look just like a stately fishmonger from Crete?

For many Greeks, the process of so successfully humanizing the gods in writing and in marble exposed the logical fallacy embedded in our innate desire to make the gods in our image. Xenophanes of Colophon, one of the earliest known critics of the ancient Greek religion, put the problem succinctly: "If horses or oxen or lions had hands," he wrote, "horses would draw the figures of the gods as similar to horses, and the oxen as similar to oxen."[18]

Xenophanes was not alone in questioning the premise upon which tens of thousands of years of human spirituality had been built—going back to the pillars at Göbekli Tepe, back to the image of the Sorcerer etched on the wall of the Volp caves, back to the very origins of the religious impulse. Numerous other Greek thinkers—Thales of Miletus, Heraclitus of Ephesus, Plato, and Pythagoras, to name just a few—also began to reconsider the fundamental nature of the gods. These Greeks wanted something from their gods other than mere familiarity. They strove for a religion framed not by the mawkish abuses of Zeus and his family, but by the idea of god as utterly *nonhuman,* either in appearance or in nature—god as the unified principle steering all creation: unchanging and unchangeable, bodiless, and, above all, *singular.*

"One god," Xenophanes wrote. "Like mortals neither in form nor in thought."[19]

For Xenophanes and like-minded Greeks, belief in "one god" was based less on a theological argument than on their conception of the natural world as singular and immutable. After all, if nature is one, then god—"the Mind which shaped and created all things," as Thales called it—must also be one. It was driven by their need for mathematical simplicity: If one is the origin of all numbers and the essence of mathematical unity—the *monad,* as the Pythagoreans termed it—then god must also be one. Finally, it was driven by their understanding of truth: If Plato was right that Truth, in its ideal, eternal form, is one, then god must also be one.

In striving for "one god," these Greek thinkers were trying to redefine god as pure substance, as the underlying reality that permeates all creation. They were seeking to actively suppress the desire to humanize the divine in favor of a more primal, more animistic conception of god: a *dehumanized* god, without form or body, personality or will; a god that, as we shall see, few people, either in Greece or anywhere else in the world, had any interest in worshiping.

Chapter Six

The High God

THE "HERETIC PHARAOH" whom history knows as Akhenaten was born Amenhotep. He was the fourth of his family to bear that name, the tenth pharaoh of the Eighteenth Dynasty, the line that inaugurated the New Kingdom (c. 1570–1070 B.C.E.), a period of peace and prosperity that propelled ancient Egypt to its cultural and political peak.

Akhenaten, whose reign began sometime around the year 1353 B.C.E., was, by all accounts, an odd-looking pharaoh. Tall and long-limbed, with a narrow face, pointed jaw, and droopy eyes, he presents such a curious physical appearance in the statues and reliefs that have survived the ages that scholars do not know what to make of it. In some statues, he is sculpted as sinuous, almost androgynous; in others he has plump breasts and feminine hips—features that would have been as strange and scandalous to the ancient Egyptians as they may be to the modern viewer. In those reliefs in which the pharaoh is portrayed with his famous wife, Queen Nefertiti, it is sometimes difficult to tell the two apart.[1]

Akhenaten's peculiarities did not end with his physical appearance. Even as a young man, he seems to have expressed what can only be described as an unconventional devotion to the sun. Solar worship had always been an integral part of Egyptian spirituality. Like the Mesopotamians before them, and the Indo-Europeans after, the ancient Egyptians deified the sun, giving it an exalted place among the *Ennead,* the nine original gods of creation. There, the sun god was known as *Shu.* But Egyptians worshiped the sun in many other incarnations, the most popular of which was as the god *Re* (pronounced "ray"), the local deity of the southern city named Heliopolis, or Sun City, by the Greeks. (*Re* is also the standard Egyptian word for "sun.")[2]

At the start of the Eighteenth Dynasty, as Egypt was rapidly expanding its borders into new territories, a more universal deity was required to keep pace with its imperial ambitions. It was around this time that the god Re, which dominated the southern region of the empire, merged with a god known as Amun, the local deity of the capital city of Thebes, in the north of Egypt. Together, these two gods became one new and all-powerful national deity called *Amun-Re* ("Amun, who is Re").[3]

By the time Akhenaten became pharaoh nearly two hundred years later, Amun-Re had been elevated to the head of the Egyptian pantheon. He was now known as the king of the gods, not just in Egypt but in all of its vassal states and colonized territories. His temple complex at Karnak in Thebes was the most lavishly adorned in all the land, his priesthood the wealthiest and most powerful in Egypt.[4]

Akhenaten, however, never expressed much devotion to Amun-Re, despite the god's solar origins. The young pharaoh worshiped the sun in an altogether different form, as the ancient yet relatively obscure deity known as the *Aten,* or Sun Disc, the dazzling orb in the sky whose rays were thought to shine upon all people in every corner of the world. The Aten was already an important deity in Akhenaten's family; his father, Amenhotep III, was associated with the god both before and after his death. But Akhenaten's relationship with his god was unique; it was *intimate*. Akhenaten claimed to have "found the Aten." His hymns to his god describe what can only be called a conversion experience—a *theophany*, or visible manifestation of god, in which the Aten spoke to him and revealed its nature. This experience left an indelible mark. For not long after his ascendance to the throne of Egypt, and at his god's behest, Akhenaten single-handedly transformed the Aten from a minor deity of whom most Egyptians would have been only nominally aware to the chief god in the Egyptian pantheon, and then, a few years later, to the sole god in the universe. "Living Aten, there is no other except him!" the young pharaoh decreed.[5]

It was not unusual for a pharaoh to favor one god over the others by, for instance, diverting resources to that god's temple or employing more priests to tend to the god's needs. But the exclusive worship of one god was unprecedented in Egypt, and the denial of the other gods' existence was unfathomable. Yet that is precisely what Akhenaten proposed with his worship of the Aten. As a result, the young pharaoh from the Eighteenth Dynasty of the New Kingdom in ancient Egypt became the first *monotheist* in all of recorded history.

Akhenaten's monotheistic revolution did not happen all at once. First, he changed his name from Amenhotep IV to Akhenaten I: from "Amun is pleased" to "beneficial to Aten." Next, he abandoned his dynasty's traditional seat of power in Thebes, where Amun-Re's temple at Karnak stood, and moved the imperial capital to an undeveloped and barely inhabited region of Egypt revealed to him by the Aten. He christened the new city Akhet-Aten (Aten's Horizon), known today as Amarna. From there, he began a massive temple building project for the Aten across the whole of Egypt. Although he allowed the temples of the other gods, especially Amun-Re's temple at Karnak, to wither and decline for lack of resources, at this stage in his movement, he did not actively persecute the worship of other gods.

But then, in the fifth year of his reign, Akhenaten's monotheistic revolution morphed into full-scale religious repression, an unparalleled effort to impose his monotheistic vision upon an entire empire. The worship of any god but the Aten was declared illegal in Egypt. All temples, save those of the Sun Disc, were shut down and their priesthoods disbanded. A massive military force marched from temple to temple, city to city—from Nubia in the south to Sinai in the east—smashing the idols of the other gods, chiseling their images from public monuments, erasing their names from documents (because ancient Egyptians believed that a name reflected the essence of a thing, erasing a god's name meant wiping out the god's existence). This was nothing short of a pogrom against the gods of Egypt. It was violent, destructive, unforgiving, and ultimately unsuccessful.

Almost immediately after Akhenaten's death, his religion died with him. The zeal with which the pharaoh had destroyed the idols of other gods was directed back at the pharaoh's own god. Monotheism was labeled a heresy, a sacrilege forced upon an unwilling people. The Aten's temples were demolished and thousands of new statues depicting Amun-Re commissioned across the empire. Most of Akhenaten's statues were either destroyed or buried facedown in the desert—a deliberate act of defilement. His tomb was desecrated, and the sarcophagus housing his mummified remains was hacked to pieces. His image was chiseled off public monuments, his name erased from the official list of Eighteenth Dynasty pharaohs. In fact, it is a miracle we know anything about Akhenaten. His son and eventual successor, Tutankhaten, meaning "the living image of Aten," changed his name to Tutankhamun, "the living image of Amun"—the King Tut of legend—in an ostentatious attempt to wipe away any last memory of his father and the heresy of the Atenist years. Thus history's first attempt at monotheism was buried in the sands of Egypt and forgotten.

Stele of Akhenaten and Nefertiti adoring the Aten from Tell el Amarna (c. 1340 B.C.E.)   *Wikimedia Commons*

A LITTLE MORE than two hundred years later, around 1100 B.C.E., monotheism arose once again, this time through the teachings of the Iranian prophet Zarathustra Spitama.[6]

The man the Greeks knew as *Zoroaster* was born in the fertile plains of northeastern Iran to one of a number of Indo-Iranian, or *Aryan*, tribes that had branched off the Indo-European tree to settle across the Central Asian steppes. Aryan society at the time of Zarathustra was strictly stratified into three distinct classes. There were the warriors who protected the tribe from attack, the farmers and herders who fed the population, and the priests—generally known as the *Magi*—who presided over its highly ritualistic religious system.

The religion of ancient Iran was populated by a pantheon of gods, many of them Iranian versions of Vedic deities (Indra, Varuna, Soma, Mithra). However, in contrast to other ancient civilizations, Iran's gods had their origins not in the deification of natural elements, but in the personification of abstract notions such as Truth, Virtue, or Justice. The preeminent scholar of Iranian religions, Mary Boyce, describes the process whereby these abstractions became divinized, acquiring a personality and distinct physical traits, as resembling the making of a pearl, "with layer upon layer of belief and observance being added around the grit of the original concept."[7]

By most accounts, Zarathustra belonged to Iran's priestly class, a hereditary position into which he would have been initiated at the age of seven. His youth was spent diligently memorizing every syllable and caesura in the sacred hymns and mantras (known as *yashts*) meant to please the gods and encourage them to shower their favors upon the people. At age fifteen he completed his training and was fully initiated into the Iranian priesthood.

Priests in ancient Iran were usually attached to individual families who would pay them to perform the time-consuming and rigidly defined rituals and sacrifices on their behalf. Yet Zarathustra unexpectedly abandoned these priestly obligations and, at the age of twenty, began a life of wandering through the steppes and valleys of Iran, searching for a deeper knowledge of the gods than he had discovered in the memorized mantras and routine rituals of the priesthood.

One day, while attending a sacred spring festival near the Saba-lan mountains in northwest Iran, Zarathustra waded into a river to fetch some water for a dawn ceremony. When he turned to head back to shore he was struck by a blinding white light. In a vision, he was brought into the presence of an unfamiliar god, one that was not a part of any known pantheon of the time.

According to Zarathustra's account of this experience written in the *Gathas*—the oldest of the ancient scriptures of *Zoroastrianism,* the religion he would ultimately found—this obscure deity revealed itself to be the sole god in the universe: "the very First and the Last." This was the god who had made the heavens and the earth, the night and the day, the god who had separated the light from the darkness, who determined the paths of the sun and the stars and who caused the moon to wax and wane.[8]

This god was unique in that it was not a tribal deity who had climbed to the top of a pantheon of other gods; *there were no other gods.* It was not connected to a particular tribe or city-state. It did not live inside a temple; it existed everywhere, in all creation, and beyond time and space. Although Zarathustra would come to call this god *Ahura Mazda,* meaning "the Wise Lord," that was merely an epithet; this god had no name. It could be known only through six divine "evocations" that it brought forth into the world from its own being: wisdom, truth, power, love, unity, and immortality. These are not so much Ahura Mazda's attributes as they are the six substances that make up its essence. They are, to put it another way, the reflections of Ahura Mazda in the world.[9]

The encounter between Zarathustra and Ahura Mazda marked

a pivotal moment in religious history, not just because this was only the second recorded attempt to introduce a monotheistic system but because it augured a new kind of relationship between god and human beings. That's because Zarathustra did not merely encounter Mazda; he brought forth a *revelation* from this god. Mazda spoke to Zarathustra, and then Zarathustra wrote down those words for others to read. In doing so, Zarathustra Spitama became the very first human being in history to be characterized as what we now term a *prophet*.

As with most prophets who would follow in his footsteps, Zarathustra was rebuffed by his own community for his monotheistic message. During the first ten years of his preaching, he converted exactly one person to his new religion—his own cousin. Zarathustra's countrymen were generally unwilling to disavow their tribal gods, but they seemed particularly reluctant to accept this one god as the source of all the abstract notions upon which they had formulated the Iranian pantheon: darkness and light, virtue and vice, truth and falsehood. How could one god be the source of both good and evil?

Recognizing this dilemma (and indeed sharing it himself), Zarathustra proposed an ingenious solution. He argued that evil is not an extraneous, created force, but merely the byproduct of good. Mazda did not create evil; Mazda created good. But good cannot exist without non-good (evil), just as light cannot exist without non-light (darkness). Good and evil were therefore opposing spiritual forces that were born from Ahura Mazda's positive creation and its negative opposite.

Zarathustra termed the "good" or "positive" spirit Spenta Mainyu, and the "bad" or "negative" spirit Angra Mainyu. Although he called these the "twin children" of Mazda, they were not separate from Ahura Mazda; they were the spiritual embodiment of Truth and Falsehood. In this way, Zarathustra preserved his *monotheistic* system by supplementing it with a *dualistic* cosmology.

Despite this clever innovation, however, Zarathustra's religion failed to spread among his people. Although he had some success later in life, Zoroastrianism, like Atenism before it, fell into obscurity after its founder's death.

Unlike Atenism, however, Zoroastrianism was unexpectedly revived centuries later, when it became the imperial religion of the Achaemenid Empire—the world-conquering dynasty founded by Cyrus the Great in the sixth century B.C.E. Yet the Magi of Cyrus's royal court who revived Zarathustra's theology completely reimagined it, first by transforming Ahura Mazda's six divine evocations into six divine *beings* who, along with Mazda, became known as the *Amesha Spentas,* or "Holy Immortals," and second, and most dramatically, by transforming Zarathustra's two primordial *spirits*—Spenta Mainyu and Angra Mainyu—into two

Zoroaster/Zarathustra depicted in relief on the door of an Iranian shrine (fifth century C.E.)   *Kuni Takahashi / Contributor / Getty Images*

primordial *deities:* a good god named Ohrmazd (a contraction of
Ahura Mazda), and an evil god named Ahriman. Zarathustran
monotheism became Zoroastrian dualism. Belief in one god that
inhered both good and evil in itself became belief in two gods—
one good, one evil—battling against each other for the souls of
humanity. And once again the experiment with monotheism
failed.[10]

IT IS ASTONISHING that in the hundreds of thousands of
years in which humanity's religious impulse has expressed itself
through belief in the soul, the worship of ancestors, the creation
of spirits, the formation of gods and pantheons, the construction
of temples and shrines, and the establishment of myths and rituals, what we today recognize as *monotheism*—that is, belief in a
sole, singular God—has existed for barely three thousand of
those years. It is not that monotheistic systems didn't sporadically
arise throughout the history of religions; the movements of
Akhenaten and Zarathustra are proof that they did. It's just that
when they did arise, they were routinely rejected and denied,
sometimes violently so. What was it that kept monotheism at bay
for so much of religious history?

Partly it has to do with its exclusivist connotations. Monotheism, it must be understood, is not defined as the sole worship of
one god: that is called *monolatry,* and it is a fairly common phenomenon in the history of religions. Monotheism means the sole
worship of one god *and the negation of all other gods*. It requires
one to believe that all other gods are false. And if all other gods
are false, any truth based on belief in those gods is also false. Indeed, monotheism rejects the very possibility of subjective truth,
which explains why, as we saw with Akhenaten, monotheistic sys-

tems must often be brutally enforced in order to overcome people's natural beliefs and assumptions.

Akhenaten wasn't satisfied with merely forcing his subjects to worship his god and no other. Under his reign, the plural form of the word "god" was excised from the Egyptian vocabulary. That is, the very word "gods," depicted in Egyptian hieroglyphics by three pennants or "staff-flags," ceased to exist *as a word* in Egypt. By eradicating polytheism as a category of thought, Akhenaten was proclaiming that there was now only one true way to conceive of the nature of the universe.[11]

Zarathustra did not have the military might of the pharaoh and so could not physically coerce people into accepting his exclusive claim to truth. But he did present his god as the sole source of human morality—"the veritable Creator of Truth and Right." He vowed that Ahura Mazda would judge every individual on earth by their thoughts, words, and deeds, and then either reward or punish them accordingly after they died. This was an extraordinary idea. The concept of a heaven and hell—for that is what Zarathustra was essentially promoting—was without precedent in human spirituality. Up until this point, most ancients simply accepted the idea that the world of the dead was a continuation of the world of the living: a warrior in this life would continue to fight battles in the next; a farmer on earth would continue plowing fields in the heavens. Morality played no part in how one experienced the afterlife. Zarathustra overturned that notion by suggesting that one's ethical actions on earth—*as judged exclusively by his god alone*—would carry consequences in the next life in the form of eternal reward or eternal punishment.[12]

But while the exclusive nature of monotheism may explain people's reluctance to accept it, the primary reason monotheism failed to take root in our religious imagination for millennia has to do with the ways in which the concept of one god conflicts with our universal compulsion to humanize the divine.

In sophisticated polytheistic systems, such as those we have discussed in Mesopotamia, Egypt, Iran, and Greece, our innate, unconscious desire to project our human attributes onto the gods can be distributed among a host of divine beings, until there is a god for each virtue and vice. Thus we have gods who reflect our various views of love and lust (Ishtar in Mesopotamia, Kama among the Indo-Europeans, Eros and Aphrodite in Greece); gods who reflect our penchant for war and violence (Innana, Anhur, Indra, Ares); gods who represent our maternalistic (Hathor and Hera) and paternalistic (Osiris and Zeus) qualities; and so on.

However, the notion of a single god who encompasses within itself all of our virtues and vices, all of our qualities and attributes at once, simply made no sense to the ancient mind. How could one god be both mother and father? How could one god create both darkness and light? The ancients were perfectly willing to acknowledge the presence of such conflicting qualities in human beings. But they seemed to have preferred their gods to be neatly compartmentalized according to their distinctive attributes; all the better to beseech them for particular favors or needs.

Akhenaten's response to this sentiment was to argue that all the other "gods," and the attributes attached to them, were nothing more than reflections of the Aten and his attributes. "Though alone," the pharaoh sang to his god, "you overflow in your forms . . . you rise and you shine, you depart and approach; *of yourself you make millions of forms*." But that explanation did not seem to satisfy his subjects.

Zarathustra constructed a more creative solution to this problem by transforming the ancient gods of polytheistic Iran into religious history's first expression of "angels" and "demons." Those gods who reflected humanity's virtuous attributes became angels, while those who reflected our negative attributes became demons. But this, too, left the Aryans unsatisfied, which is why, hundreds of years after Zarathustra's death, the Magi were able to successfully reintroduce nearly all the gods of ancient Iran into their revived form of Zoroastrianism.

What the ancient mind seemed willing to accept was the existence of one all-powerful, all-encompassing "High God" who acted as the chief deity over a pantheon of lower gods who were equally worthy of worship. This belief is called *henotheism,* and it quickly became the dominant form of spiritual expression, not only in the Ancient Near East but in nearly every civilization in the world.[13]

The reasons for henotheism's success can be traced to one of the inevitable consequences of our unconscious impulse to humanize the divine: Conceiving the divine in human terms compels us to imagine the world of the gods as an exalted reflection of our own. The heavenly realm becomes a mirror of the earth and its social and political institutions. And as our earthly institutions change, so, too, do those in heaven.

When we organized ourselves in small, wandering packs of hunter-gatherers united by blood and kinship, we envisioned the world beyond ours to be a dreamlike version of our own, bursting with hordes of tame animals, shepherded by the Lord of Beasts for our spirit ancestors to stalk with ease. When we settled down in small villages and began growing our food instead of hunting for it, the Lord of Beasts surrendered to Mother Earth, and the celestial realm was reimagined as a place ruled by a host of fertility gods who maintained an eternal harvest. When those small villages expanded into independent city-states, each with its own tribal deity, in perpetual conflict with each other, the heavens made room for a pantheon of distinct martial deities, each a divine protector of its respective city back on earth. And when those city-states merged into massive empires ruled by all-powerful kings, the gods were rearranged into hierarchies reflecting the new political order on earth.

There is a term for this phenomenon—*politicomorphism,* or "the divinization of earthly politics"—and it is, to this day, one of the central features of nearly every religious system in the world.

A brief look at Mesopotamian history will illustrate precisely how politicomorphism works, and why it so often leads to henotheism. In the fourth millennium B.C.E., during the early development of Mesopotamian civilization, earthly authority was not wholly vested in the king. It resided instead in a "general assembly" that included all free male members of the city-state: "the colony young and old," it was called. This assembly acted like a court of law, settling both civil and criminal cases. It had the power to negotiate disputes with other city-states, and if negotiations failed, it could declare war on its neighbors. It even had the authority to choose and depose the king.[14]

The remarkably democratic nature of early Mesopotamian civilization was, as we saw in the previous chapter, perfectly reflected in early Mesopotamian renderings of the celestial order. Take the Atrahasis epic. There, the gods are quite clearly organized along "democratic" lines. They, too, have an assembly— a "divine assembly"—in which they gather in Enlil's sheltered courtyard to consider both earthly and celestial matters. Being "lofty persons," first, they spend some time catching up with their fellow gods. They chat and embrace each other. They grab a bite to eat, fill their cups with wine, and then, when the small talk is over, they settle down to discuss the matters of the universe. No single god has authority against the will of this divine assembly, though the gods do occasionally foil the assembly's decisions, as when Enki secretly saved Atrahasis from the flood.

Then, in the middle of the third millennium B.C.E., in what is often referred to as the Early Dynastic Period (III), large despotic powers emerged across Mesopotamia. The major city-states of Lagash and Umma launched a century-long border conflict. The legendary king Sargon of Akkad conquered most of the Sumerian city-states in the south to construct Mesopotamia's first empire. The collapse of Sargon's Akkadian Empire ushered in the rise of the Babylonian Empire in the south and the Assyrian Empire in the north. At the same time, marauding bands of nomads from the deserts in the south and the mountains to the north began raiding the settled city-states. Across the region, overpopulation and lack of resources led to a near-permanent state of war.

The paranoid state of affairs in Mesopotamia was expertly exploited by a handful of autocrats who sought absolute authority to protect their people and crush their enemies. Political power became centralized, and a new, despotic conception of kingship arose, as all trace of the general assembly—"the colony young and old"—vanished into history.

The new political reality would be reflected in the Mesopotamian myths written after this period. So we read in the *Enuma Elish*, the great Babylonian epic of creation, composed some time in the middle of the second millennium B.C.E., of a completely different celestial order, one dominated by a Babylonian god who, in Sumerian times, was barely known and utterly unimportant: *Marduk*.

According to the epic, the gods of heaven have come under attack by the primordial sea monster *Tiamat*. They call a meeting in the divine assembly in which they establish a kind of state of emergency. There, the young god Marduk volunteers to fight Tiamat on behalf of the gods, but only if they name him king of the gods and give him absolute authority over the heavens and the earth. "If I should become your avenger, if I should bind Tiamat and preserve you, convene an assembly and proclaim for me an exalted destiny," Marduk demands. "Whatever I instigate must not be changed. Nor may my command be nullified or altered."[15]

Frightened and desperate to reestablish peace and order in the heavens, the gods comply. "Marduk is king!" they shout as they enthusiastically dissolve the divine assembly. "Whatever you command, we will do!" The gods then bestow upon Marduk a scepter and throne to denote his new status atop the Mesopotamian pantheon, and off he goes to defeat Tiamat.

The exact same mythology was developed by the Assyrian Empire, which was facing a similar threat in the north as the Babylonians were facing in the south—only in the Assyrian version it was their local god Ashur, not Marduk, who is crowned king of the gods. At the very same time, in the Isin kingdom, situated twenty miles south of the city of Nippur, the god An was transformed from his original role as the supreme sky god into the undisputed king of heaven.[16]

In each case, in every empire, and throughout all of Mesopotamia, as the politics on earth changed, the politics of heaven changed to match. Just as in the face of fear and terror, the free citizens of Mesopotamia's independent city-states abandoned their primitive democracy and voluntarily handed absolute power to their kings, so, too, did the citizens of heaven make one or another of the gods the unchallenged ruler over the rest. Theology shifted to conform to reality, and the heavens became an amplified projection of the earth.

In such a world order, henotheism—the belief in a High God who rules over all the other gods—makes perfect sense. As more authority is vested in a single individual on earth, more authority is given to a single god in heaven, be it Marduk in Babylon, Ashur in Assyria, An in Isin, Amun-Re in Egypt, Khumban in Elam,

Khaldi in Urartu, Zeus in Greece, Jupiter in Rome, Odin among the Norse, Tian in the Zhou Dynasty of China, and so on.

The problem is that the higher a deity climbs within its pantheon, displacing other, lower gods, the more it has to take upon itself the attributes traditionally ascribed to those other gods, until eventually the contradictions and inconsistencies in the High God's character reach a tipping point. Take the Hindu god Shiva, the High God of *Shaivism,* who, along with Brahma and Vishnu, also forms the triumvirate of supreme gods that make up the so-called Hindu Trinity, or *Trimurti.* Shiva began its existence as a relatively minor deity who is not even mentioned by name in the Rig Veda. But in the post-Vedic literature, especially the Upanishads and the great Indian epic of the Mahabharata, as Shiva climbs higher and higher in the Hindu pantheon, it begins to absorb the attributes and qualities of the gods it displaces, so that today, Shiva is known as creator and destroyer, healer and afflicter, ascetic and hedonist, the god of storms and lord of the dance.[17]

This tipping point is precisely why henotheism rarely evolves into monotheism. It is one thing for a High God to steadily take on the qualities and attributes of lower gods, regardless of whether or not those qualities are at odds, or even in full-blown opposition. It is something else to conceive of a singular god who takes upon itself *all* of those attributes and qualities at once.

There is, of course, a simple and fairly straightforward way of dealing with this dilemma: *Dehumanize* god—strip the divine of any human attributes and redefine god as Xenophanes, Plato, and their fellow Greek philosophers did, as the creative substance underlying the universe. That is in fact what both Akhenaten and Zarathustra attempted to do. Zarathustra presented Ahura Mazda as pure animating spirit—without shape or form—utterly transcendent and apersonal. The Gathas use poetic language to describe Mazda's rewarding hands and all-seeing eyes, but these are nothing more than metaphors. Indeed, human traits ascribed to the divine are rarer in the Gathas than in nearly every other holy scripture.

Akhenaten not only destroyed the idols of the other gods; he forbade his artisans to carve the Aten into a statue or cast it as an idol. Officially, the Aten could be depicted only as a featureless disc with rays of light descending upon the earth like divine hands blessing all creation (the hands being the sole humanistic feature Akhenaten would abide). Although the great hymns written in Akhenaten's time use the masculine singular pronoun "he" to speak of the Aten, the god displays no human qualities, exhibits no human attributes, and has no human emotions or motivations in these poems. And that, as much as anything else, explains why Akhenaten's monotheistic movement, like that of Zarathustra, ultimately failed.

The difficulty Akhenaten and Zarathustra faced is that people generally have a hard time relating to a god who, having no human features or attributes, also has no human needs. If a god has no human form, attributes, or qualities, then how are human beings supposed to connect and commune with it? The very notion of a dehumanized god contradicts the cognitive process whereby the conception of god arose in the first place. It would be like trying to imagine the unimaginable, like conjuring up an image of a being that has no image. It is too slippery and unreal to work.

To accept the proposition of a sole, singular god without human form, attributes, or qualities would require either an enormous cognitive effort on the part of the worshipper or a profound disruption in a religious community's spiritual evolution—a spiritual crisis so great that it would force people to overlook all the contradictory traits inherent in the idea of a singular god and override their natural inclination to fashion that god in their own image.

As it happens, it was precisely such a crisis that—eight hundred years after Akhenaten and six hundred years after Zarathustra—led a small Semitic tribe from the land of Canaan that called itself *Israel* to fashion what would become history's first successful experiment with monotheism.

Part Three

What Is God?

Chapter Seven

God Is One

IN 586 B.C.E., King Nebuchadnezzar II, ruler of the mighty Babylonian Empire and earthly agent of the High God Marduk—king of the gods—broke through the walls of Jerusalem, sacked the capital of the kingdom of Israel, and burned the Jewish temple to the ground. Thousands of Jews were put to the sword; the few who survived—especially the educated elite, the priests, the military, and the royals—were sent into exile in a transparent attempt to put an end to Israel as a nation. And if Israel no longer existed, then neither did its god, Yahweh.[1]

In the Ancient Near East, a tribe and its god were considered a single entity, bound together by a covenant in which the tribe cared for the god by offering it worship and sacrifices, and the god returned the favor by protecting the tribe from harm—be it from flood or famine or, more often than not, from foreign tribes and their gods. In fact, warfare in the Ancient Near East was considered less a battle of armies than a contest between gods. The Babylonians conquered Israel not in the name of Nebuchadnezzar, their king, but in the name of Marduk, their god. Marduk was believed to fight on the battlefield on behalf of the Babylonians and in accordance with the covenant Marduk had made with Nebuchadnezzar.

The Israelites had the same agreement with their god. It was Yahweh who ruled Israel, and thus Yahweh whose task it was to defend it. The bloody battles between the Israelites and their enemies, which take up so much of the early books of the Bible, were explicitly framed as a fight between Yahweh and foreign gods. Indeed, Yahweh was often charged with planning, commanding, and executing those battles on Israel's behalf.

"David inquired of Yahweh, 'Shall I go up against the Philistines? Will you give them into my hand?' Yahweh said to David . . . 'You shall not go up; go around to their rear, and come upon them opposite the balsam trees'" (2 Samuel 5:19–23).[2]

This explicit identification of a tribe with its national god had profound theological implications for ancient peoples. When Yahweh helped the Israelites crush the Philistines, it proved that the Israelite god was more powerful than the Philistine god, Dagon. But when the Babylonians destroyed the Israelites, the theological conclusion was that Marduk, the god of Babylon, was more powerful than Yahweh.

For a great many Israelites, the destruction of their temple—the House of Yahweh—signaled more than the end of their national ambitions. It meant the end of their religion. Cut off from the rites and rituals that had been central to their religious devotion and thus their very identity as a people, they had no choice but to surrender to the new reality. They adopted Babylonian names, studied Babylonian scriptures, and began worshiping Babylonian gods.

But among these exiles was a small band of religious reformers who, faced with the unacceptable prospect of accepting Yahweh's obliteration at the hands of Marduk, offered an alternative explanation: Perhaps Israel's destruction and exile was part of Yahweh's divine plan all along. Perhaps Yahweh was punishing the Israelites for believing in Marduk in the first place. *Perhaps there was no Marduk.*

It was precisely at this moment of spiritual distress, when the kingdom of Israel had been laid waste and the temple of Yahweh torn down and defiled, that a new identity was forged, and with it a wholly new way of thinking about the divine.

THE GOD WHO would come to be known as Yahweh made his first appearance in the form of a burning bush, somewhere perhaps in the rocky deserts of northeastern Sinai. "This is my name forever," Yahweh tells the prophet Moses, "and this is how I will be remembered from generation to generation" (Exodus 3:15).[3]

Moses is in this desert wasteland, the Bible says, because he is fleeing the wrath of the pharaoh. According to the book of Exodus, the Israelites who, a few generations earlier, had followed the descendants of the patriarch Abraham into the land of Egypt, had grown so numerous and powerful that they were stripped of their wealth and freedom and forced into slavery. So feared were they in Egypt that the pharaoh himself commanded that every newborn Israelite son be drowned in the Nile.

Yet somehow this one child was spared. His parents, descendants of Levite priests, placed him in a papyrus basket when he was only three months old and sent it floating among the reeds on the riverbank. The pharaoh's daughter found him there. She took pity on the boy, brought him into her house, and raised him as Egyptian royalty.[4]

One day, after he was grown, Moses went out among the people and witnessed for himself the crushing labor enforced upon the Israelites. He saw an Egyptian master beating an Israelite slave and, in a fit of rage, he killed the Egyptian. Fearing for his life, Moses fled Egypt for what the Bible calls "the land of Midian." There he met a "priest of Midian," who welcomed him into his home and tribe, giving him his own daughter, Zipporah, in marriage.[5]

Many years passed as Moses built a life with his Midianite family in the household of his priestly father-in-law. Late one afternoon, as he was tending his father-in-law's flock, Moses herded them beyond the wilderness, to the foot of a sacred Midianite place known as "the mountain of god." It was there that he came across the mysterious deity who introduced himself as Yahweh.

Where exactly *there* was may be impossible to discern. In the book of Exodus it seems clear that the location of "the mountain of god" is in northeastern Sinai. But in Deuteronomy and elsewhere in the Bible, the mountain where Moses meets Yahweh is located near Seir, in southern Transjordan. It is difficult to know what the Bible even means by "the land of Midian." As far as we know, the Midianites were a loose federation of non-Semitic, desert-dwelling people whose homeland was in northwestern Arabia—not in the Sinai Peninsula, nor near Transjordan. In fact, there is so much confusion and contradiction in the Moses story— Moses's father-in-law is named Reuel in Exodus 2:18, and Jethro just a few verses later (Exodus 3:1)—that historians have had a tough time making much sense of it.[6]

The problem is that no archaeological evidence has ever been unearthed to indicate the presence of Israelites in ancient Egypt. That is a remarkable statement considering the sophisticated bureaucracy of the Egyptian state in the New Kingdom (the period in which the Moses story is supposed to have taken place) and its legendary penchant for recordkeeping. What's more, although the Egyptians regularly employed slave labor, the role and social

Moses and the Burning Bush
Saint Catherine's Monastery, Sinai (Egypt) /
K. Weitzmann: "Die Ikone"/ Wikimedia Commons

status of a slave fell into one of three categories: slaves who had been captured in war, slaves who had sold themselves into slavery in order to pay a debt, and slaves who were, like indentured servants, duty bound to the state for a set period of time.

The Israelites fit into none of these categories, making the notion of Egypt's having enslaved their entire population difficult to swallow. Even more unbelievable is the reason the Bible gives for their wholesale enslavement: that this tribe of Semitic nomads had somehow grown "more numerous and more powerful" than the Egyptians who were, at the time, the largest, wealthiest, most militarily potent empire the world had ever known (Exodus 1:9–10).[7]

But perhaps the most confusing element of the Moses story

has to do with the deity he encounters in the desert. Yahweh's origins are an enigma. The name does not appear in any of the god lists of the Ancient Near East, an extraordinary omission considering the thousands of deities included in these lists. There are, however, two hieroglyphic references to Yahweh in Nubia dating to the New Kingdom period—one at the temple built by Akhenaten's father, Amenhotep III, in the fourteenth century B.C.E., the other at a temple built by Rameses II in the thirteenth century B.C.E.—that mention something called "the land of the nomads of Yahweh." Although there is some debate as to where exactly this land is, the consensus is that it is a reference to the broad desert region lying just south of Canaan—that is, "the land of Midian."

So then, Moses, who had married into a Midianite tribe, came across a Midianite deity (Yahweh) while under the employ of a Midianite priest (his father-in-law) in the land of Midian.[8]

If the story ended there—and if we ignored the historical problems cited above—it would make a certain amount of sense. But the story doesn't end there. Because the first task that this Midianite god gives to Moses is to return to Egypt, free the Israelite slaves from bondage, and shepherd them back to their home in the Land of Canaan: "Thus will you say to the children of Israel, 'Yahweh, the god of your fathers, the god of Abraham, the god of Isaac, and the god of Jacob, has sent me to you'" (Exodus 3:15).

This claim would have come as something of a surprise to Abraham, Isaac, and Jacob. Because the fact of the matter is that these biblical patriarchs did not worship a Midianite desert deity called Yahweh. They worshiped an altogether different god— a Canaanite deity they knew as *El*.

Scholars have known for centuries that there were two distinct deities worshiped by the Israelites in the Bible, each with a different name, different origins, and different traits. The Pentateuch—

the first five books of the Bible (Genesis, Exodus, Leviticus, Numbers, and Deuteronomy)—is actually a composite work stitched together from various sources spanning a period of hundreds of years. Look closely and you can occasionally see the seams where two or more different traditions were sewn together. There are, for instance, two separate creation stories written by two different hands: Genesis chapter 1, in which man and woman are created together and simultaneously, and Genesis chapter 2, the much more popular Adam and Eve story, in which Eve is made from Adam's rib. There are also two different flood narratives, though, unlike the two creation stories, these are woven together to create a single, conflicting account in which the flood lasts either forty days (Genesis 7:17) or one hundred fifty days (Genesis 7:24); the animals are brought aboard the Ark in either seven pairs of male and female (Genesis 7:2) or just one pair of every kind (Genesis 6:19); and the flood begins either seven days after Noah enters the Ark (Genesis 7:10) or immediately after he boards with his kin (Genesis 7:11–13).

By meticulously tracing each of these separate narrative threads, biblical scholars have managed to identify at least four different written sources that make up the bulk of the early books in the Bible. These are named the *Yahwist,* or J, source (*j* is pronounced as *y* in German), which dates to the tenth or ninth century B.C.E. and runs through large parts of Genesis, Exodus, and Numbers; the *Elohist,* or E, source, which dates to the eighth or seventh century B.C.E. and is mostly confined to Genesis and parts of Exodus; the *Priestly,* or P, source, which was written either during or immediately after the Babylonian Exile in 586 B.C.E. and is primarily a reworking of the J and E material; and finally, the *Deuteronomist,* or D, source, which runs from the book of Deuteronomy through First and Second Kings and can be dated to somewhere between the seventh and fifth centuries B.C.E.

There are numerous differences between these sources. For example, the Elohist material, which was probably written by a priest from northern Israel, refers to Mount Sinai as Mount Horeb (Exodus 3:1) and calls the Canaanites "Amorites." In these passages, God tends to reveal himself mostly in visions and dreams, as opposed to the more southern-centered Yahwist material, which often portrays God in uncannily anthropomorphic ways: He creates the world through trial and error, forgetting to craft a mate for Adam (Genesis 2:18); he strolls through the Garden of Eden, enjoying the evening breeze (Genesis 3:8); and at one point, he loses track of his creation, Adam and Eve, unable to find them when they hide among the trees. "Where are you?" Yahweh shouts into the night air (Genesis 3:9).

However, the primary difference between the Yahwist and Elohist sources in the Pentateuch is that God is called by a different name in each. The god of the Elohist is *El* or *Elohim* (the plural form of El), which is rendered in most English translations of the Bible as *God*, with a capital *G*: "After these things, God [Elohim] tested Abraham" (Genesis 22:1). In contrast, the god of the Yahwist tradition is known as *Yahweh*, usually rendered in English Bibles as the *Lord*, spelled with all capital letters: "The LORD [Yahweh] said, 'Surely I have seen the misery of my people who are in Egypt'" (Exodus 3:7). The much later Priestly source tends to go back and forth between using the names Yahweh and Elohim in an obvious attempt to merge these two different gods into one.

Although the Yahwist material is about a hundred years older than the Elohist, the Elohist tradition represents the older deity. In fact, while we know next to nothing about the origins of Yahweh save that he was likely a Midianite god, El is one of the best-known and most well-documented deities in the Ancient Near East.

A mild, distant, fatherly deity traditionally depicted either as a bearded king or in the form of a bull or calf, El was the High God of Canaan. Known as the Creator of Created Things and the Ancient of Days, El also functioned as one of Canaan's chief fertility gods. But El's primary role was as the celestial king who served as father and preserver of the earthly kings of Canaan. Seated on his heavenly throne, El presided over a divine council of Canaanite gods that included Asherah, the Mother Goddess and El's consort; Baal, the young storm god known as the Rider of the Clouds; Anat, the warrior deity; Astarte, also called Ishtar; and a host of other, lower deities.[9]

El was also unquestionably the original god of Israel. Indeed, the very word *Israel* means "El perseveres."

The early Israelites worshiped El by many names—El Shaddai, or El of the Mountains (Genesis 17:1); El Olam, or El Everlasting (Genesis 21:33); El Roy, or El Who Sees (Genesis 16:13); and El Elyon, or El Most High (Genesis 14:18–24), to name a few. And while it may seem incongruous that the Israelites living in Canaan would have so eagerly adopted a Canaanite god as their own, the influence of Canaanite theology runs deep in the Bible—so deep, in fact, that it isn't always so easy to draw a clear distinction ethnically, culturally, or even religiously between the Canaanites and the Israelites, certainly not in the early history of Israel (c. 1200–1000 B.C.E.).[10]

The traditional view of the Israelite people is that they were strict monotheists, dedicated to the one and only God of the universe, surrounded on all sides by the polytheistic Canaanites and their false gods. This view does not stand up to historical and archaeological scrutiny. To begin with, there was no single group called the Canaanites; the term is a general designation for all of the various tribes who inhabited the highlands, valleys, and coastal regions of the land of Canaan (the southern Levant, com-

Seated statue of El   *Courtesy of the Oriental Institute*
of the University of Chicago

prising parts of modern-day Syria, Lebanon, Jordan, and Israel-
Palestine). That has made it next to impossible to cleanly single
out Israelite culture, however that is defined, from the larger umbrella of Canaanite culture. Many scholars now believe that the
Israelites were of Canaanite stock, part of a hill-dwelling clan
that had settled the highlands and then gradually broke free from
the larger Canaanite group of tribes, expressing a distinct identity
that nevertheless remained rooted in Canaanite culture and religion. Both groups were comprised of West Semitic peoples who
spoke a similar language, shared a similar script, and held in common similar rites and rituals. They even employed the same reli-

gious terminology for their ceremonies and sacrifices, leading to
dozens of Canaanite loan words in the Hebrew language, most of
them pertaining to religious matters.[11]

And of course they shared the same god: El.

Actually, it may be more accurate to say that the Israelites and
Canaanites shared the same *gods,* because by no stretch of the
imagination could the early Israelites be considered monotheistic.
At best, they practiced *monolatry,* meaning they worshiped one
god, El, without necessarily denying the existence of the other
gods in the Canaanite pantheon. In fact, the Israelites occasionally worshiped those other gods, too, especially Baal and Asherah
and, to a lesser degree, Anat. And while the Bible is replete with
passages, mostly composed by the later Priestly writer, condemn-
ing the worship of all these other gods, those condemnations only
prove that these gods were indeed worshiped by the Israelites,
both regularly and, as their presence inside the Temple of Jerusalem indicates, officially. King Saul, the first king of Israel, even
named two of his sons after the god Baal—Eshbaal and
Meribbaal—alongside the son he named after Yahweh: *Yeho-
natan,* or Jonathan.[12]

All of this is to say that the early Israelites likely viewed their
god El pretty much the same way the Canaanites viewed El: as the
chief deity presiding over a divine assembly of lower deities, just
as Enlil, or Amun-Re, or Marduk, or Zeus, or any other High
God would. They acknowledged, and occasionally even worshiped, the other deities in the Canaanite pantheon. But their al-
legiance was to the god after whom they were named: El.

It was this same El with whom the patriarch Abraham, who
lived most of his life in the land of Canaan and who was steeped
in Canaanite culture and religion (if not a Canaanite himself),
made a covenant in exchange for a promise of fertility—which
was, after all, one of El's primary functions: "I am *El Shaddai;*

walk before me, and be blameless. . . . I will make you exceedingly fruitful; and I will make nations of you and kings shall come from you" (Genesis 17:1, 6).

It was El who asked Abraham to sacrifice his son, Isaac, as a test of his loyalty and faith; El who renewed the covenant with Isaac's son, Jacob: "You will no longer be called Jacob, rather your name will be Israel" (Genesis 35:10). And it was in the name of this same El—the "El of your father" (Genesis 49:25)—that Jacob passed the covenant on to his own son, Joseph, who, the Bible tells us, was the first of the Israelites to leave Canaan and settle in Egypt, where generations later his descendants would come into contact with a hitherto unknown Midianite god who called himself Yahweh. Indeed, the story of how monotheism—after centuries of failure and rejection—finally and permanently took root in human spirituality begins with the story of how the god of Abraham, El, and the god of Moses, Yahweh, gradually merged to become the sole, singular deity that we now know as God.[13]

AFTER THAT FIRST encounter with Yahweh in the desert, Moses returned to Egypt with a message for the Israelites: The god of their forefathers—of Abraham, Isaac, Jacob, and Joseph—had heard their cry and would soon liberate them from bondage. But the Israelites were unfamiliar with Moses's deity. Even after Moses demonstrated his god's power and persuaded them to follow him back to "the land of Midian"—that is, "the land of the nomads of Yahweh," where the Israelites supposedly encamped after fleeing Egypt—they continued to exhibit little loyalty to this unknown god. As Moses stood atop "the mountain of god" to receive a new covenant from Yahweh (the Ten Commandments), meant to supplant Abraham's covenant with El, the Israelites down below had already reverted to the worship of Abraham's god, fashioning for themselves an idol in the shape of a golden calf—the primary symbol of El.[14]

Writing hundreds of years after the event, the Priestly writer tries to reconcile the conflict between these two separate strands in early Israelite belief by having Moses's god explicitly state, "I am Yahweh. I appeared to Abraham, Isaac, and Jacob as *El Shaddai,* but by my name Yahweh I did not make myself known to them" (Exodus 6:2–3). Yet this claim only highlights the fact that the patriarchs of Israel, in whose memory Yahweh speaks, did not know who Yahweh was.

Reconciliation between Yahweh and El would eventually emerge in Israel, though the history of that reconciliation is a bit rockier than the Priestly source suggests. It seems that Yahweh devotion entered the land of Canaan from the south and was centered there for much of its existence. In the northern regions of Canaan, the Israelites who had been living in the land for generations worshiped El as their High God while also acknowledging, and on occasion worshiping, the other gods of Canaan. It wasn't too difficult, therefore, for them to simply add Yahweh into the mix, though, as the Bible indicates, this occurred slowly and in stages. We can catch a glimpse of this gradual process in the so-called Song of Moses in the book of Deuteronomy:

When Elyon gave the nations their inheritance,
when he separated the sons of man,
he fixed the borders of the people in accordance with the
    number of the gods;
Yahweh's own portion was his people.
DEUTERONOMY 32:8–9

This extraordinary passage not only affirms Israel's recognition of other gods under El's rule, it clearly casts Yahweh as one of those gods. It states that each deity received as a gift or "portion" from El its own nation, and that Yahweh's gift was the nation of Israel.[15]

When the nation of Israel became the kingdom of Israel around 1050 B.C.E., the merging of Yahweh and El was reinforced. Even their names were occasionally fused together as *Yahweh-El* or *Yahweh-Elohim,* presented in most English translations of the Bible as the *Lord God:* "My son, give glory to the *Lord God* [Yahweh-Elohim] of Israel; give thanks to him and tell me what you have done" (Joshua 7:19).[16]

The consolidation of Israel into a kingdom was a response to increased threats from neighboring tribes. To preserve its independence and maintain its viability, Israel centralized its power, transforming itself from a theocratic tribe ruled by prophets and judges into a monarchy ruled by kings. And as happened in Babylon, Assyria, Egypt, and elsewhere, as the nature of the rule of men on earth changed, so, too, did the rule of the gods in heaven to match; in other words, politicomorphism.[17]

Israel's burgeoning monarchy required a national deity: a divine king to reflect the authority of the earthly king. Considering that the capital of this kingdom, Jerusalem, was located in Judah, in the south, it was only natural that Yahweh—by this time already viewed as Yahweh-El—would eventually fill that role. Thus the desert deity worshiped by nomads in the Sinai was elevated to the top of the Israelite pantheon as king of heaven and ruler of all other gods. "Yahweh has established his throne in the heavens and his kingdom rules over all" (Psalms 103:19).

Yahweh essentially became the patron god of the Israelite kings. A temple was built in Jerusalem, and the new national god was placed there in the form of the Ark of the Covenant—Moses's covenant, that is. Under the royal sponsorship of Israel's monarchy, the cult of Yahweh evolved into a structured regiment of ritual sacrifices, mythic narratives, and melodious prayers, according to the common pattern of tribal worship that existed throughout the Ancient Near East.

As with Marduk, Ashur, Amun-Re, and all the other High Gods, the higher Yahweh ascended in Israel's pantheon, the more he absorbed the qualities and attributes of the other gods. So we see Yahweh in the Psalms—the chief form of kingly propaganda in the Bible—subsuming El's role as the celestial king, enthroned and surrounded by a heavenly host in a divine council, just as El had been.

> *Let the heavens praise your wonders, O Yahweh,*
> *and your faithfulness in the assembly of the holy ones.*
> *Who in the sky can be compared to Yahweh?*
> *Who among the sons of god is like Yahweh,*
> *a god feared in the council of the holy ones,*
> *greater and more fearful than any of those who surround him?*
> PSALMS 89:5–7; SEE ALSO PSALMS 82, 97, AND 99

Yahweh began to embody the imagery of the storm god Baal, the Rider of the Clouds, becoming "the one who makes the clouds his chariot, the one who rides upon the wings of the wind" (Psalms 104:3). "You rule over the raging sea," the Psalmist sings; "when its waves rise, you still them" (Psalms 89:9).

Yahweh even took on the female traits of the goddess Asherah, particularly her maternal, nurturing characteristics, as when Yahweh cries out "like a woman giving birth" (Isaiah 42:14). "Listen to me house of Jacob and all of the remnants of the house of Israel," Yahweh says, "those who have been born from my belly, those who were carried in my womb" (Isaiah 46:3).

Yet even at this point of convergence in Israel's history, with Yahweh ascendant, the Israelites did not deny the existence of other deities. While there's some evidence for the presence of a "Yahweh-only" sect in Jerusalem, the monarchy itself neither discouraged nor encouraged the worship of other gods; they merely focused their worship on their own national god. As the renowned biblical scholar Morton Smith wrote, "the attribute of the god of Israel [Yahweh] was merely that of the major god of any ancient near-eastern people . . . to be greater than the gods of their neighbors."

"Who is like you, Yahweh, among the gods? Who is like you, glorious in holiness, awesome doer of deeds, worker of wonders?" (Exodus 15:11).

Again, this is not monotheism. At best it is monolatry, though even that label falls short when one considers how seamlessly other deities were included in Israelite worship. As with most ancients, the Israelites had a difficult time envisioning Yahweh as the sole god in the universe. They thought Yahweh was merely the *best* god in the universe. "For you, Yahweh, are most high over all the earth; you are greatly exalted over all the gods" (Psalms 97:9). They viewed Yahweh as king and ruler over the other gods: the *highest* god, the *strongest* god—the *god of gods*.

And then one day a stronger god, Marduk, appeared and defeated Yahweh, throwing the god of Israel down from the throne of heaven and in the process setting the stage for a new way of thinking, not just about Yahweh but about the very nature of the universe. For it is only at this point in the history of Israel—when the Israelites had been cast out of the land their god had promised them and scattered across the Near East—that we begin to see the first expressions of unambiguous monotheism in the entire Bible: "Thus says Yahweh, the King of Israel and its redeemer . . . 'I am the first and the last; *besides me there are no gods*'" (Isaiah 44:6).[18]

The introduction of monotheism among the Jews was, in other words, a means of rationalizing Israel's catastrophic defeat at the hands of the Babylonians. The crisis of identity posed by the Babylonian Exile forced the Israelites to reexamine their sacred history and reinterpret their religious ideology. The cognitive dissonance created by the Exile required a dramatic, hitherto unworkable religious framework to make sense of the experience. Previous theological ideas that had been difficult to accept—Can one god be responsible for both good and evil? Can one god take upon itself all of our human attributes at once?—suddenly became more palatable. If a tribe and its god were indeed one entity, meaning that the defeat of one signaled the demise of the other, then for these monotheistic reformers suffering exile in Babylon, it was better to devise a single vengeful god full of contradictions than to give up that god and thus their very identity as a people. And so all the historical arguments against belief in a single god were suddenly swept away by the overwhelming desire for this tiny, insignificant Semitic tribe to survive. "I am Yahweh, and there is no other. I form light and create darkness, I make peace and create evil. I, Yahweh, am the maker of all these things" (Isaiah 45:6–7).

This is the birth of Judaism as we know it: not in the covenant with Abraham, nor in the Exodus from Egypt, but in the smoldering ashes of a razed temple and the refusal of a defeated people to accept the possibility of a defeated god. The very testament of faith in Judaism, known as the Shema ("Hear O Israel, Yahweh is our god, Yahweh is *one*"), was composed after this transformational moment in Israelite history, as was most of what we know today as the Hebrew Bible, or Old Testament. Even the biblical material composed before the Exile—that is, the Yahwist and Elohist sources—was reworked and rewritten by the Priestly and Deuteronomistic writers *after* the Exile to reflect this newly found vision of One God.

The God that ultimately arises from the Babylonian Exile is

not the abstract deity that Akhenaten had worshiped. It is not the pure animating spirit that Zarathustra imagined. It is not the formless substance of the universe written about by Greek philosophers. This was a new kind of God, both singular and personal. A solitary God with no human form who nevertheless made humans in his image. An eternal, indivisible God who exhibits the full range of human emotions and qualities, good and bad.

It is an extraordinary development in the history of religions—one that took hundreds of thousands of years to evolve; one that would be overturned a mere five hundred years later by an upstart sect of apocalyptic Jews calling themselves *Christians*.[19]

Chapter Eight

God Is Three

"IN THE BEGINNING was the Logos, and the Logos was with God, and the Logos was God" (John 1:1).

These are the first words of the Gospel of John. And from the moment they were written nearly two thousand years ago, they have formed the principal dividing line between Christianity and the Jewish religion from which it arose.

The Gospel of John is unlike the three other gospels in the New Testament. Matthew, Mark, and Luke are called Synoptic Gospels because they derive mostly from the same source material and thus tell more or less the same story about an itinerant Jewish preacher and peasant from Nazareth named Yeshua (Jesus in Greek) who performed miracles and healed the sick, who preached about the Kingdom of God, who was declared to be the Messiah and savior of the world, and who, as a result of that declaration, was arrested and executed by the Roman authorities before rising from the dead three days later.

John's gospel relies on a separate set of traditions; it relates its own unique stories and offers a completely different timeline of Jesus's activities, including the day of his death and resurrection. The Synoptics begin the story of Jesus either with the launch of his ministry or with his miraculous birth. The Gospel of John begins Jesus's story at the beginning of time.

However, the most significant difference between John and the Synoptics is that while Matthew, Mark, and Luke offer a host of ideas about who Jesus was—a Jewish rabbi (Mark 9:5)? A king in the line of David (Luke 19:38)? A prophet and lawgiver like Moses (Matthew 2:16–18)?—only in the Gospel of John is Jesus unambiguously recognized as the incarnate God.[1]

The claim is there in the first words of the Gospel: "In the beginning was the Logos . . ." The word *logos* is often translated in English Bibles as "word," but that is not what "Logos" means here. *Logos* is a technical term in Greek philosophy meaning "reason" or "logic," though even those definitions fall short of its true sense. For the Greeks, Logos was the underlying rational force of the universe. It is, in other words, *divine reason*—the mind behind creation. The Logos is what Xenophanes, Pythagoras, and Plato meant when they talked about the "one god" as the singular, unified principle steering all creation.[2]

Whoever wrote the Gospel of John (it was not the disciple John; he was long dead by the time the Gospel was written some time around 100 C.E.) was himself a Greek-speaking Roman citizen steeped in Hellenistic philosophy. His readers were also Greek-speaking Roman citizens living in a Hellenistic world. And so, when John uses the word Logos to launch his gospel, he very likely means it the way the Greeks did: as the primal force of creation through which all things came to be.

But then John does something completely unexpected. He argues that this primal force is actually a man. Indeed, the entire purpose of John's gospel is to demonstrate how the abstract, eter-

nal, divine essence of creation, which is both separate from God
and one with God, was made manifest on earth in the form of
Jesus Christ: "And the Logos became flesh and lived among us"
(John 1:14).

To be clear, John is claiming that the maker of heaven and
earth spent thirty years in the backwoods of Galilee, living as a
Jewish peasant; that the one and only God entered the womb of a
woman and was born from her; that the omniscient Lord of the
universe suckled at his mother's breast, ate and slept and shat as a
helpless infant while the universe simply proceeded without him;
that the creator of men was reared by men and then, at the end of
his life on earth, was murdered by men.

"I and the Father are one," Jesus declares in John. "Whoever
has seen me has seen the Father" (John 10:30; 14:9).

The concept of a "god-man" was not new in the Ancient Near
East. The Romans routinely deified their emperors after death,
and sometimes, as in the case of Julius Caesar, during their reigns.
Of the sixty emperors who ruled the Roman Empire between the
first and fourth centuries C.E., thirty-six of them were deified, as
were another twenty-seven of their family members. Altars and
temples were constructed to house their images, priesthoods established to offer them sacrifices, and religious ceremonies devised for people to worship them as gods.[3]

The Romans were likely influenced by the Greeks, who had a
long history of deifying human beings. Greek theology never
made a firm distinction between human and divine; the great
myths of Greece teem with demigods and heroes who achieve divine status as a reward for their service to the gods. Alexander the
Great was considered a god during his reign (336–323 B.C.E.), as
was his father, Philip of Macedon (359–336 B.C.E.), who went so
far as to erect a statue of himself standing alongside the twelve
Olympian gods of the Greek pantheon.[4]

Coin of Augustus Caesar reading CAESAR DIVI F, or "Caesar,
Son of God"   *Classical Numismatic Group, Inc., www.cngcoins.com*

The Greeks themselves probably picked up the practice from
the Egyptians, who viewed their pharaohs as divine. Although the
pharaoh could be the living embodiment of any deity in the Egyptian pantheon, he was most closely associated with the falcon-
headed god Horus. More specifically, Horus inhabited the
pharaoh's body while he sat upon the throne. By taking part in
the activities of what was considered his divine office, especially
the religious rituals and public ceremonies, the pharaoh's human
nature became suffused with divinity. Then, upon his death, he
would shed his humanity and take his place among the stars as a
god worthy of worship.[5]

And it is very likely that the Egyptians were influenced by
Mesopotamian rulers. Indeed, the concept of a divine king originated in Mesopotamia and is often credited to Sargon the Great,
the Akkadian ruler who briefly united nearly all of Mesopotamia
under his control between 2340 and 2284 B.C.E. The fourth king
of Sargon's Akkadian Dynasty, Naram-Sin, created a wholly new
ideology of kingship when he declared himself divine by prefix-

ing his name (Naram) to that of the powerful moon goddess (Sin).[6]

As previously mentioned, the god-man is arguably the single most successful minimally counterintuitive concept in religious history. In fact, practically the only religion in the Near East without a firm tradition of deifying human beings was the religion of Jesus himself: Judaism.

We have seen how the impulse to humanize the divine is embedded in our cognitive processes. But what would compel a society to divinize a human: to worship a man as a god, to imbue him with divine speech, divine knowledge, and divine energy, to pray to him, to seek his aid in this life and the next?

It should not be surprising to learn that the humanization of the divine and the divinization of the human are two sides of the same coin. Over the first few thousand years of organized religion's history, from Göbekli Tepe to Greece, as the gods steadily took on each of our attributes, it was only natural that they would take on our most distinctly human impulse: the desire for power, the need to dominate and control others. The more this motivation was attributed to the gods, the more their relationship with humanity changed, so that the divine was no longer seen as the vital essence of the natural world: nature deified. Now the divine was *king*. No longer did the gods merely dispense light or rain or any of the other forces of nature that sustain us. Now the gods dispensed *justice*. With their mouths they made their will known. With their eyes they saw all of our actions. With their hands they smote those who challenged them.

Of course, the gods have no mouths with which to speak, no eyes with which to see, no hands with which to smite. These are human, not divine, features. So it was left to the gods' representatives on earth to speak for them, to dispense justice on their behalf, to smite their enemies, to bear in their human hands the power that the gods demand for themselves.

The role of human mediator to the gods naturally fell to the gods' counterparts on earth—primarily kings, pharaohs, and emperors, but also priests and prophets, mystics and messiahs. We saw how this process took shape in ancient Mesopotamia, with the consolidation of power into the hands of an autocratic few who wielded the power of the divine. And, as in Mesopotamia, once the need for a human mediator is accepted, it is a short step to deifying the mediator. After all, it makes a certain amount of sense to expect the person acting as the bridge between humans and the divine to also be divine (or at least semidivine).

Nevertheless, there was something uniquely disruptive about the deification of Jesus. It wasn't that Jesus came from a religion with no history of deifying humans. Nor was it the fact that Jesus was a peasant while most other god-men of the Ancient Near East were kings and emperors.[7]

What made Jesus's deification different had less to do with him than it did with the divinity he was said to embody. For while all the other god-men of the Ancient Near East were thought to be one of many human manifestations of one of many gods, Jesus was considered the *sole* human manifestation of the *only* God in the universe.

For a great many Christians in the first few centuries of Christianity, this was a difficult idea to accept. Within the early Church, a dividing line on John's perception of Jesus as the Logos quickly formed: Either John was mistaken and Jesus was just a man and not God, or John was right and Jesus was indeed a god—just not the one and only God of the universe. No less a figure than the preeminent Christian apologist and theologian Justin Martyr (100–165 C.E.) was forced to admit that if Jesus was the divine Logos, as John claimed, then he must have been a different god, one who was "other than the God who made all." Paul of Samosata (200–275 C.E.), the bishop of Antioch, a Christian community that was second only to Rome in its power and influence, argued that John must have meant the Logos dwelt *within* Jesus, not that it *was* Jesus; the Logos was given to him by the one and only God as a reward for his "life of virtue." The influential Church father Arius of Antioch (256–336 C.E.) went one step further: There is only one God, Arius claimed. This God must be, by definition, indivisible, uncreated, and existing from all time. So it is simply impossible to think of Jesus as the Logos. Otherwise, it would mean there are *two* Gods in the universe, and that, for Arius, was simply unthinkable.[8]

Yet not everyone agreed that the concept of two gods was so absurd. In fact, in the polarized debate over whether Jesus was a man or a second god, and in the absence of a compromise between these two positions, which would not be reached until the middle of the fourth century C.E., a great many in the early Church accepted the view that not only were there two gods in the universe—one god named Yahweh and another god named Jesus—but these two gods were enemies.

THE MOST FAMOUS proponent of the two-gods theory of Christianity—known as *ditheism*—was a learned young scholar from Asia Minor named Marcion. Born just around the time that the Gospel of John was being written, Marcion was among the first generation of non-Jews to be raised in the newly formed Christian faith. His father was the bishop of Sinope, a city on the coast of the Black Sea, where the family owned a lucrative ship-building business.

Marcion's wealth accorded him the freedom to pursue a life of leisure and learning. He immersed himself in Greek philosophy and Christian thought, and he seems to have had a deep familiarity with the Hebrew scriptures. Yet it was precisely this depth of knowledge in both the ancient Jewish religion and the brand-new and not yet unified Christian sect that had so recently arisen from it that caused Marcion such consternation. For no matter how he tried, Marcion could not reconcile the God he encountered in the Hebrew Bible, *Yahweh,* with the God that Jesus called *Father.*

The Yahweh of the Bible is a blood-soaked "Man of War" (Exodus 15:3; Isaiah 63:3)—a jealous deity who gleefully calls for the slaughter of anyone who fails to worship him (Exodus 22:20). This is a God who once had forty-two children mauled to death by bears simply because they had teased one of his prophets for being bald (2 Kings 2:23–24). How could the one and only God of the universe be so petty and parochial, so possessive and rapacious? And, more to the point, what could this God have to do with the God revealed by Jesus: a God of love and forgiveness, peace and mercy?

Marcion accepted Jesus's divinity; he fully agreed with John's position that the Logos was God. When he spoke of "the God revealed by Jesus," he meant the God revealed *in the form of Jesus.* At the same time, Marcion recognized Yahweh, the God of the Hebrew Bible, as the creator of the world. In fact, he seems to have read the book of Genesis literally. But his reading only made Jesus and Yahweh seem more dissimilar. What kind of God, he wondered, would make such a wretched world—a world of want and destruction, of enmity and hate? Did not Jesus say that "you shall know them by their fruits?" (Matthew 7:16). If that was true, then the fruits of this God appeared to be rotten to the core.[9]

The only answer that made sense to Marcion was that there must be two gods: the cruel creator God of the Hebrew Bible known as Yahweh, the God of Israel, and the loving, merciful

God, who had always existed as the Logos but who was revealed to the world for the first time in the form of Jesus the Christ.

Marcion was by no means alone among early Christians in coming to this conclusion. A large number of Greek-speaking Christians, whom we today refer to loosely as *Gnostics* (from the Greek word *gnosis,* or "knowledge"), also differentiated between the God of the Hebrew Bible and the God of Jesus, though, unlike Marcion, most Gnostics refused to acknowledge Yahweh as the creator of the world. They believed creation was the work of a lesser god called the *Demiurge,* or "fashioner," a deformed and imperfect deity who foolishly believed himself to be the only god in the universe.

"And he is impious in his arrogance," writes the Gnostic author of *The Secret Gospel of John.* "For he said, 'I am God and there is no other God beside me,' for he is ignorant of his strength, the place from which he had come."[10]

It was the Demiurge who had laid waste to the cities of Sodom and Gomorrah, the Demiurge who had murdered most of humankind in a catastrophic flood, the Demiurge who had expelled Adam and Eve from the Garden of Eden.

"But of what sort is this God?" complained the Gnostic author of *The Testimony of Truth.* "First [he] maliciously refused Adam from eating of the tree of knowledge. And secondly he said, 'Adam, where are you? . . . Surely he has shown himself to be a malicious grudger."[11]

By placing the creation of the universe into the hands of a lesser deity—whether that be Yahweh or the Demiurge—both Marcion and the Gnostics were not only endeavoring to explain a flawed and sinful world at odds with the notion of a flawless and sinless Creator; they were seeking to absolve Jesus of the heinous acts with which Yahweh is credited in the Hebrew Bible.

But there was something else, too. In arguing for the existence of two gods, these Christians were trying to pull Christianity free of its Jewish roots, to declare it a wholly new religion, with a new revelation, and a new God.[12]

In 139 C.E., Marcion left his family home on the Baltic Sea and traveled to Rome to share his ideas with what was the largest and most influential Christian community of the time. He began by ingratiating himself with the Roman Church, offering it a massive donation of 200,000 Roman *sesterces,* an amount that would be equivalent to millions of U.S. dollars in today's currency. The donation allowed Marcion to stay in the city as a revered guest of the Church.

It was in Rome that Marcion began collecting his teachings into two manuscripts, one of which outlined his theology (it is lost to history but we know at least some of what it said through the Church elders who repudiated it), and the other which became the very first attempt at putting together a *New Testament*. Marcion's canon consisted of an edited version of the Gospel of Luke and ten letters from the Apostle Paul, whose writings on the Christ as a cosmic being that existed before time fit perfectly with Marcion's own views.

After five years of meticulously sketching out his argument, Marcion gathered the leaders of the Church in Rome and presented them with his theology of two gods. He began by arguing that Jesus was God incarnate, a position held by many—though not all—of the Church leaders in the room. But then Marcion went on to claim that Jesus was not the God they all knew as Yahweh. Rather, he was a completely different, and hitherto unknown, God who had only just been revealed to humanity. The very purpose of Christ's descent to earth, he told them, was to set humanity free from the evil creator God of the Bible. This meant the religion formed in Jesus's name, Christianity, could no longer

John the Apostle and Marcion of Sinope (the latter's face has
been intentionally disfigured) from an image in an Italian Gospel
codex written in Greek (MS M.748, fol. 150v, eleventh century)
The Morgan Library & Museum / Janny Chiu / Art Resource, NY

be linked to the Judaism out of which it emerged. The Hebrew
scriptures were obsolete; what was needed was a new Bible. And,
as luck would have it, he happened to have brought one with
him.[13]

The Church leaders were not pleased. They returned what was
left of Marcion's substantial contribution and promptly threw
him out of Rome. Marcion, however, was undaunted. He returned
home and began successfully preaching across Asia Minor, where

he found an audience receptive to his doctrine of two gods. In fact, the ditheistic church that Marcion founded became one of the largest in all of Christianity. It thrived in large parts of Turkey and Syria right up until the fifth century C.E.

It's fair to ask why the elders of the Church in Rome were so adamant about maintaining Jewish monotheism. Even at this early stage of its history, Christianity didn't bear much resemblance to Judaism. It had declared a wholly new faith, demonized the Jews as the killers of Christ, begun composing its sacred texts in Greek rather than Hebrew, and imposed upon Jesus a divinity that contradicted Judaism's very definition of God as singular and indivisible.

The truth is that the early Church's desire to maintain fealty to the Jewish belief in one God may have been as much for political reasons as it was for theological ones. For when Marcion and the Gnostics feuded with these Christian leaders over the nature of God, they were also arguing about the nature of authority in the nascent Church. As the acclaimed scholar of religions Elaine Pagels notes, by insisting upon belief in one God, the early church was validating the system of its governance under one bishop—that is, the bishop of Rome. "As God reigns in heaven as master, lord, commander, judge, and king," Pagels writes, "so on earth he delegates his will to members of the church hierarchy, who serve as generals who command an army of subordinates; kings who rule over 'the people'; judges who preside in God's place."[14]

This was politicomorphism, plain and simple: "the divinization of earthly politics." The influential Church elder Ignatius of Antioch (c. 35–108 C.E.) framed this position into a succinct slogan: "One God, One Bishop." Any violation of the former would necessarily diminish the authority of the latter. The Christian's duty, in the words of Ignatius, was to obey the bishop "as if he were God." As Clement I (d. 101 C.E.), the first bishop of Rome and thus the first pope, warned, anyone who failed to "bow the neck" to his authority as bishop was guilty of rebelling against God and should be put to death.

The Church hierarchy's insistence on maintaining One God, One Bishop made little impact either on the followers of Marcion or on the many Gnostic sects that flourished in the early years of Christianity. What it did do, however, was lodge a contradiction in the heart of the burgeoning faith. Because if the Church was going to insist upon accepting the Jewish definition of God that arose out of the Babylonian Exile—God as singular and indivisible—then they needed to come up with a way to explain how a Jewish peasant from the low hills of Galilee could also be God. It was an issue that threatened to tear the Church apart and put an end to Christianity just as it was about to achieve its greatest success.

BY THE END of the second century C.E., Christianity had spread so far and wide throughout the Roman Empire that it was no longer possible for the authorities to ignore it. Some high-ranking members of the imperial court had even converted to the new religion. In 202 C.E., Rome issued an edict forbidding all further conversions, and by the middle of that century, the Empire's Christian subjects were being persecuted on a massive scale. Many Romans blamed the political and economic instability that plagued the Empire during this era on the people's turning their backs on the old gods, and naturally much of this anger was directed toward Christians, who, if nothing else, were conspicuous in their refusal to offer sacrifices to Roman deities.

After a lowborn Roman citizen named Diocletian, who had risen rapidly through the ranks of the military, was named emperor in 284 C.E., he made it his personal mission to rid the Empire of Christianity in all its forms. Churches were burned down, sacred texts were confiscated, and both the Christian laity and the leadership were slaughtered for sport in what became known as the Great Persecution.

When, a few years later, Diocletian abruptly retired as emperor, he made the fateful decision to divide the Empire into a tetrarchy ruled by two sets of junior and senior emperors, one in the east and one in the west. It was an untenable situation that quickly devolved into civil war between rival claimants to the throne. In 312 C.E., one of these claimants rode with his army to the River Tiber in an attempt to reinstitute the rule of a single emperor. His name was Constantine, and he would alter the course of both Rome and Christianity forever.

According to legend, on the eve of the battle at the Tiber, Constantine had a dream in which he saw a cross of light in the heavens and the words CONQUER BY THIS. The next day he had his troops emblazon an unknown symbol upon their shields: the Chi Rho—a cross made from the first two Greek letters of the name *Christ*. His victory in that battle paved the way for Constantine to declare himself the sole, undisputed emperor of Rome.

Attributing his success to the Christian God, Constantine put an end to the persecution of Christians in Rome and legalized Christianity upon his ascension to the throne. However, the new emperor had very little understanding of his adopted faith; he seems to have thought the religion was a kind of sun cult. What mattered most was that, as far as he understood, Christians believed in one God. The man who had fought so many battles to reinstate the rule of a single emperor over Rome seems to have instinctively recognized the political advantage of adopting a monotheistic religion system, though Constantine's slogan was a bit different from the one favored by Ignatius and the Church leadership. He preferred "One God, One Emperor."[15]

One can only imagine Constantine's surprise when he discovered that not only did many of his fellow Christians *not* believe in the existence of only one God, but there was no consensus in the Church over the relationship between this God and Jesus Christ. The Gnostics and the Church in Alexandria stressed Jesus's divinity, with some Gnostics going so far as to deny any humanity in Jesus (Docetism). The Ebionites and the Church in Antioch stressed Jesus's humanity, with the Ebionites (Jewish Christians who represent the earliest form of Christianity) viewing Jesus as a prophet and miracle worker who spoke with the power of the divine but was not himself divine.

Some Christian sects split the difference, arguing that Jesus was born a human being but became divine only after his resurrection (this view is called Dynamism). Others claimed that Jesus was a man who was "adopted" by God as his Son and given divine status when he was baptized by the Holy Spirit in the River Jordan (this view is called Adoptionism).

Constantine was a soldier, not a theologian, and so had little patience for these disagreements. He demanded a firm answer to the question of Jesus's nature and the relationship of the Son to the Father. If he were to present himself to a divided population as the one true leader of the Empire, he needed agreement about the essence of the one true leader of heaven.[16]

In 325 C.E., the emperor summoned the elders of the Church to a council in the city of Nicea to settle the issue once and for all. To emphasize the gravity of the occasion, Constantine decided to preside over the council himself, bedecked in royal garb and flanked by Imperial guards. The one thing that the assembled old men knew for certain was that the emperor had no tolerance for any outcome that would violate the oneness of God. That immediately excluded the position of the Gnostics, the followers of Marcion, and any other Christian sect that accepted ditheism. At the same time, the elders of the Church were unwilling to accept any position that denied the divinity of Christ, which ruled out the positions held by the Ebionites, the followers of Arius, and much of the Church in Antioch.

But how to reconcile these two demands? What kind of doctrinal gymnastics could possibly overcome the unalterable fact that a singular, indivisible God who exists in multiple forms is, *by definition,* not a singular, indivisible God?

The compromise that came out of Nicea was to declare that Jesus Christ, the Son, was "of one substance" with God, the Father. The idea was based on the writings of one of the most prominent of all early Christian theologians, Tertullian of Carthage (c. 160–220 C.E.). Tertullian channeled the Greek philosophers of the past by arguing that God was a "substance." However, unlike those Greeks, Tertullian believed this substance had taken form as three separate beings: the Father (Yahweh), the Son (Jesus Christ), and the Holy Ghost (the divine spirit of God in the world). To help explain his theory, Tertullian relied on analogy. "When a ray is shot forth from the sun," he wrote, "a part is taken from the whole; but there will be sun in the ray because it is a sun ray; its nature is not separated, but extended. . . . Thus, too, what proceeds from God is God and the Son of God, and both are one." Tertullian coined a new word to describe this innovative theology: He called it *trinitas,* or Trinity.[17]

The Nicean compromise satisfied the emperor, but it left nearly everyone else in the Church with even more questions. Do the Father, Son, and Holy Spirit share the divine substance in equal amounts? After all, while a ray of light from the sun contains the substance of the sun, it does not contain *the same amount* of substance as the sun. And who among the three beings had the divine substance first? The sun and the ray may be made of the same substance, but the sun is the *sole source* of that substance; the ray is utterly dependent upon the sun. Is the same true for the Father and the Son? Is the Father the originator of the substance and the Son dependent upon the Father? If that is the case, then how could an indivisible God create Jesus out of himself? Wouldn't that violate God's Oneness? Wouldn't it make Jesus part of the created order, hence contradicting the Gospel of John's claim that Jesus was with God "from the beginning"? Alternatively, if the Father and Son contained the divine substance simultaneously, then does that not mean there were two separate yet equal divine beings at the beginning of creation?[18]

Some Church elders, following the teachings of the theologian Athanasius of Alexandria (298–373 C.E.), tried to address the confusion by suggesting the Father and Son were not made of "the same substance" but rather of a "similar substance." But that only further confused matters.

In the end, it was Augustine of Hippo (354–430 C.E.), the man who, more than any other figure, would shape Christian theology in the Western world, who had the final word. God is One, Augustine declared in his masterwork, *On the Trinity*. God is eternal and unchanging. But while that may be true, God nevertheless exists in three forms: Father, Son, and Holy Spirit. No one of these forms is subordinate to another. All three share the same measure of divinity. All three existed at the beginning of time. And if this idea causes confusion, if it defies logic and reason, if it seems to contradict the very definition of God, then it is simply the task of the believer to accept it as a mystery and move on.[19]

When, a few years after Augustine's death, the Church at the Council of Chalcedon (451 C.E.) affirmed its position that Jesus Christ, while *truly* God, was also *truly* human—"the same essence with the father as to his Godhead, and the same essence with us as to his manhood"—Christianity not only effectively annulled the postexilic Jewish conception of God as singular and indivisible, it surrendered itself completely to humanity's oldest and most deeply embedded impulse. It made the God of heaven and earth *fully* human. In doing so, it set the religion on a collision course with a new monotheistic faith that, a little more than a century after Chalcedon, would arise out of the deserts of Arabia to confront Christianity's conception of the humanized God.[20]

Chapter Nine

God Is All

TWO ARMIES FACED each other from opposite sides of the battered walls of Jerusalem. The year was 614 C.E. Inside the besieged city, a few thousand fighting men loyal to the Byzantine emperor, Flavius Heraclius the Younger—the handsome young warrior who had seized the throne after personally drawing and quartering its previous occupant—anxiously awaited the onslaught they knew was coming at the hands of the royal army of King Khosrow II, king of kings and ruler of the Persian (Sassanian) Empire.

For three hundred years, these two superpowers—one Christian, the other Zoroastrian—had warred with each other for control over the Near East, the balance of power swinging back and forth with each destructive battle. This was not just a struggle over land; it was a clash between the divergent religious views of two theocratic kingdoms, each founded upon an officially sanctioned and legally enforced conception of the divine as existing in

either two forms (Zoroastrian Dualism) or three (Christian Trinitarianism).

By the start of the seventh century C.E., the incessant conflict
had drained both empires of their wealth and strength. And yet so
great was their animus that neither could shake the instinct to
inflict just one more measure of violence upon the other. The recent ascension of Heraclius had left the Byzantine Empire in dis-
array, and Khosrow thought to take advantage of his adversary's
situation by sending his nearly bankrupted army on a rampage
across Christian lands. His forces had already captured Antioch
and Damascus. Now they stood at the walls of Jerusalem, poised
to conquer the holy city and in the process to strike a symbolic
blow to Christianity.

Circling the city walls were Khosrow's ten thousand heavily
armed Persian troops, along with an auxiliary force of about two
thousand Jewish fighters hoping to avenge three centuries of op-
pression, mass slaughter, and forced conversion under Christian
rule. The Jews would get their wish. When the walls were breached
and the Persian army victorious, King Khosrow handed Jerusalem back to the Jews, who promptly unleashed a wave of death
and destruction upon the city's Christian inhabitants.

The Byzantines rebounded. Heraclius reconstituted his army
and forced the Sassanian troops out of the cities they had so recently conquered. In 630 C.E., he recaptured Jerusalem, sending
the Persians back to their capital city, Ctesiphon, in defeat, but
massacring the Jews who remained. Weak and weary from war,
the two superpowers sued for peace and prepared for what each
assumed would be another brief respite in this unending battle
between withering empires. But then something happened that
neither could have imagined.

A few months after Heraclius and Khosrow had hammered
out their peace deal in the city of Cappadocia, each was visited by

an emissary from the forgotten desert wastelands of the Arabian Peninsula. The emissaries carried letters addressed to both emperors from an Arab prophet who claimed to speak on behalf of a god that neither the Trinitarians nor the Dualists had ever heard of, but whom the prophet claimed was the sole God in the universe.

In the name of Allah, the Beneficent, the Merciful, the letters began. *Peace be upon him who follows the right path. I invite you to Islam, and if you become a Muslim you will be safe, and Allah will double your reward, and if you reject this invitation of Islam you will be committing a sin by misguiding your subjects.*

The letters were signed Muhammad Rasulullah: Muhammad the Messenger of Allah.[1]

King Khosrow, in defiance of all kingly codes of conduct, killed the emissary and commanded his viceroy to find this desert prophet and cut off his head. Heraclius, however, was so amused by the audacity of the letter that he reportedly fell into a fit of laughter. He dismissed the emissary, tore up the missive, and apparently thought nothing more of it.

Before the decade was out, the followers of this same desert prophet had swallowed up nearly the whole of the Sassanian Empire, putting an end to Zoroastrianism as a global religion. They had pushed the Byzantine Empire out of the Near East, leaving it a hollow shell barely a fifth of its former size. They had even allowed the Jews to once again return to Jerusalem and practice their religion there. Having sprung out of the Arabian wilderness to confront a world dominated by two prevailing perceptions of the divine—God as Three and God in Two—the armies of this new religion, called *Islam,* sought to root out both beliefs from the known world, and replace them with the Jewish view of God as it had been wholeheartedly embraced by their prophet, Muhammad: God as One.[2]

———

MUHAMMAD IBN ABDALLAH ibn Abd al-Muttalib was
born some time around the latter half of the sixth century C.E. in
the city of Mecca, in the Arabian Peninsula. He came into the
world the only son of a widow, in a city where widows were left
without protection. He became an orphan while still a child, in a
society that treated orphans as chattel to be bought and sold.
Through the assistance of a kindly uncle, the young Muhammad
was able to avoid this fate and to earn a meager living making
trade runs north to Syria and south into Yemen. In his twenties
his prospects suddenly improved when he married an older merchant named Khadija and took over the management of her successful caravan business.

Yet despite the relative wealth and comfort of his new life, Muhammad could never shake the feeling that there was something
profoundly wrong with a society that had brought him so close to
a life of slavery and despair—a society in which the unprotected
masses could be so easily exploited by the powerful and affluent
for their own gain. He became restless and dissatisfied. He began
giving away his wealth and seeking solace in the mountains and
glens of the Meccan valley, where he would spend his nights in
prayer and meditation, beseeching the heavens for an answer to
the misery and sorrow that he saw in his world.

Then, one day, the heavens responded.

According to tradition Muhammad was meditating in a cave
on Mount Hira when he was seized by an invisible presence commanding him, "Recite." What followed that initial experience was
twenty-two years of nearly uninterrupted prophetic revelations
from a god he called *Allah*—revelations that would eventually be
collected into what is now known as the *Quran,* or the Recitation.

The ancient Arabs were already familiar with Allah, who was

likely conceived as the Arabian equivalent of the Indo-European deity Dyeus, or its Greek counterpart Zeus: that is, as a sky god who steadily rose through the ranks of the Arab pantheon to become High God. But it's unclear whether the Arabs thought of Allah as a personalized deity or as a kind of abstract spirit, somewhat akin to the divine force that the ancient Egyptians and Mesopotamians believed underpinned the universe. Allah is not a proper name, after all, but a contraction of the Arabic word *al-ilah,* meaning simply, "the god"—an indication that Allah may have been viewed more as divine *spirit* than as divine *personality.* And unlike the hundreds of other deities recognized by the ancient Arabs, Allah seems never to have been represented by an idol, which would make sense if he was perceived as an animating spirit without physical form.

At the same time, the Arabs credited Allah with being the creator of the heavens and the earth, so they clearly ascribed will and intention to the god. They thought of Allah as a material being who, like Zeus, had sired both sons and daughters. Indeed, Allah's three daughters—Allat, who was associated with the Greek goddess Athena; Manat, who was likely connected with the Mesopotamian goddess Ishtar; and al-Uzza, who was the Arab equivalent of Aphrodite—played a central role in ancient Arab spirituality as Allah's intermediaries.

Whatever the case, the ancient Arabs had little use for an abstract deity they could neither see nor interact with in their day-to-day lives. The Arab pantheon was littered with a host of gods and goddesses, angels and demons, and djinn, all of whom served the specific needs of their desert worshippers and nearly all of whom were conceived of in unambiguously human terms. The gods of the Arab world ate and drank, had sex and sired children, wore clothes and carried weapons (the goddess Manat wore two coats of mail and carried two swords). Most of these gods, save

Page from "Journey of the Prophet Muhammad," from the *Majma al-Tararikh* by Hafiz-i Abru (c. 1425 C.E.)   *Metropolitan Museum of Art / CC0 1.0*

Allah, were carved in stone to look like human beings (or occasionally some other living creature) and housed inside Mecca's central sanctuary, the Kaaba, where they could be visited by Arabs across the region bearing gifts and sacrifices in exchange for their favors and blessings.[3]

Yet this was a highly evolved form of polytheism, one that freely absorbed the deities of other religions, including Judaism and Christianity. The Jewish patriarch Abraham had his own idol in the Kaaba, as did Jesus Christ and his mother, Mary. In fact, a great many Arabs considered all these gods to be nothing more than multiple manifestations of a single divine, albeit distant and unapproachable being: Allah.

So when Muhammad came down from Mount Hira with a message from this same Allah claiming to be the sole deity in the universe, he did not arouse a great deal of theological resistance. Mecca was a vibrant, religiously pluralistic, cosmopolitan city—a center of trade and commerce—in which Jews, Christians, Zoroastrians, Hindus, and polytheists intermingled in an environment that encouraged bold religious experimentation. Muhammad's declaration of monotheism would have been neither new nor particularly offensive to most of its residents. Even the vocabulary that Muhammad used to describe Allah as creator and king, as the Subduer of Men and the Bestower of Fates, was nearly identical to the vocabulary the ancient Arabs used to describe Allah.

Muhammad did, however, make two principal innovations to the Arab religious system that set him at odds with the Meccan establishment and made his movement unique. First, he firmly embraced the exclusivist connotations of his monotheistic system. It wasn't enough for the Arabs to believe that Allah was the sole God in the universe; they had to deny the existence of any other god. "Oh my people. Worship Allah. You have no god but Him!" (Surah 7:59).

This was not just a new way of thinking about Allah; it was a direct attack on the established order. For by claiming that no other gods existed, Muhammad was undermining Mecca's economy, which was predicated on its status as a sanctuary city open to worshippers of all the known gods of Arabia. If there were no other gods, then there was no need for the Kaaba and thus no reason for Mecca's elevated position as the religious and the economic center of Arabia.

The second innovation, somewhat related to the first, was that Muhammad explicitly identified Allah with Yahweh, the god of the Jews. The Arabs were, of course, well aware of Yahweh. Jews had been living in the Arabian Peninsula for hundreds of years, perhaps as far back as the Babylonian Exile, and they participated in Arab society at every level. The Arabs even accepted Yahweh's association with Allah, more or less, particularly when it came to Allah's role as creator.

But Muhammad re-envisioned the relationship between these two deities by claiming that it was Allah who had made the covenant with Abraham in exchange for a promise of fertility (Surah 2:124–133); that it was Allah who had appeared to Moses in the form of a burning bush and instructed him to return to Egypt to free the Israelites (Surah 28); that it was Allah who had devastated the world with a catastrophic flood, sparing only Noah and his family from the onslaught (Surah 71); that it was Allah who sent an angel to Mary bearing the good news that she would give birth to the Messiah, Jesus (Surah 3:45–51); that in fact it was Allah who had revealed the Torah and the Gospels (Surah 5:44–46).

To be clear, Muhammad was not *replacing* Yahweh with Allah; he simply viewed Yahweh and Allah as *the same God*. The core of Muhammad's message was that he himself was merely one in a long line of prophets going all the way back to Adam, entrusted with revealing not a new scripture but the "confirmation of previous scriptures" (Surah 12:111). "We believe in Allah, and what has been revealed to us, and what has been revealed to Abraham, Ishmael, Isaac, Jacob, and the [twelve] tribes [of Israel]; we believe in what was revealed to Moses and Jesus and the prophets from their Lord. We make no distinction between any of them" (Surah 3:84).

There can be little doubt that Muhammad had a deep familiarity with Judaism, in light of his recounting of Jewish myths, his reverence for Jewish prophets, his veneration of the sacred Jewish city of Jerusalem, and his nearly wholesale adoption of Jewish dietary and purity laws. So great was Judaism's impact on Muhammad's thinking that a few historians have gone so far as to suggest that Islam, like Christianity, may have originated as a Jewish sect before branching off to become an independent religion. Although most scholars reject that position, what cannot be denied is that Muhammad was greatly influenced by his contacts with the Jews of Arabia. And nowhere is that influence more evident than in Muhammad's unqualified acceptance of the Jewish understanding of God as singular and indivisible. "Allah is *One,*" the Quran states emphatically. "Allah is *Unique.* He has neither begotten anyone, nor is he begotten of anyone. And there is none like Him" (Surah 112:1–3).[4]

What makes this statement so significant is that at this point in time, Jewish monotheism as a religious idea was being strangled in one corner of the Near East by Byzantine Trinitarianism and subsumed in the other by Zoroastrian Dualism. Whether he was conscious of it or not, Muhammad's decision to renounce both Zoroastrianism and Christianity ("Do not say 'Three'!" the Quran warns. "God in truth is One!" Surah 4:171), and to unequivocally support Jewish monotheism instead, not only injected new life into the fledgling Jewish definition of a singular, personal God; it resulted in the creation of a brand-new global religion.[5]

At the center of that new religion was a kind of doubling down on the very concept of monotheism, which in Islam is founded upon a complex theological idea called *tawhid*. Arabic for "making one," tawhid is less an affirmation of God's *singularity* than it is a description of God's *essence*. It does not mean there is only one God. It means that God is, in form and nature, *oneness*.

As an expression of "Divine Unity," tawhid requires that God be not only indivisible, but also utterly unique. Allah is "a thing, not as other things," wrote Abu Hanifa al-Nu'man (699–767 C.E.), one of the first Muslim theologians to tackle the subject. "He resembles none of the created things, nor do any created things resemble Him."[6]

What this means in principle is that there can be no physical similarity between Allah and his creation, which is why, unlike nearly every other creation myth that arose from the Ancient Near East, the Quran expressly rejects the belief that God created human beings in his image. God has no image. He has no body, is of no substance, takes no shape in any form, human or otherwise.

On the surface it appears that Muhammad was consciously attempting to dehumanize Allah. Certainly his disdain for the worship of idols was well known. Among his first acts after conquering Mecca in the name of his new religion was to empty the Kaaba of all its idols and smash them to pieces.

Yet the Quran is replete with anthropomorphic descriptions of God. Allah is described as "holding humanity in his hands" and having "all-seeing eyes" and a face—"wherever you turn there is the face of Allah" (Surah 2:11). The Quran also ascribes to Allah a host of human qualities and attributes—sometimes referred to as Allah's Beautiful Names—which are clearly meant to create a divine personality for a being who, were one to take the doctrine of tawhid seriously, should technically be without personality.

The obvious explanation for this seeming inconsistency between what Allah is supposed to be and how Allah is described in the Quran is to read such descriptions metaphorically, not as literal descriptions of God's body. Otherwise it would violate the principle of tawhid.

The problem is that most Muslims do not read the Quran that way. Abu Hanifa certainly did not. As the founder of one of the four main schools of law in Sunni Islam, he set the precedent for Quranic exegesis by vehemently rejecting the possibility of any figurative reading of the Quran. In fact, nearly every school of law in Islam insists that God's words in the Quran must be taken literally. After all, if God is indivisible, as tawhid demands, then he cannot be separated from his words. He *is* his words. Therefore, his words must be as eternal and divine, as unchanging and unchangeable as God himself is. So if the Quran happens to mention Allah's hands or eyes or face, it means that Allah must literally have hands and eyes and a face. Never mind the theological twists and turns necessary to make sense of such a view (Does Allah have only two hands? Why not three, or a thousand? Would not two hands restrain or limit Allah's all-encompassing power?). As Abu Hanifa's spiritual successor, Abu al-Hasan al-Ashari (874–936 C.E.), founder of the most powerful traditionalist school of thought in Islam, argued, Allah has a face because the Quran says so. And if such a literal reading happens to contradict the core tenet of tawhid and thus everything that Islam as a religion was founded upon, so be it.[7]

The position of these Muslim theologians—and the vast majority of Muslims who, to this day, follow their teachings—not only proves just how durable our innate evolutionary impulse to humanize the divine can be; it also lays bare the paradox at the very heart of the Islamic definition of God. For if God does indeed have qualities and attributes, and if God is in fact indivisible, as the concept of Divine Unity requires, then that means God cannot be divided from any of those qualities and attributes. If God is eternal and has always existed, then God's attributes must also be eternal; they, too, must have always existed with God. Otherwise they would be separate from God, and that would violate tawhid. Even Abu Hanifa was forced to admit as much: "He knows by virtue of his knowledge, knowledge being an eternal quality; he is Almighty by virtue of his power, his power being an eternal quality; he creates by virtue of his creative power, his creative power being an eternal quality."

It is that last attribute mentioned by Abu Hanifa—God's creative power—in which the paradox is most spectacularly revealed. The issue is fairly straightforward: If God is indivisible, and God is Creator, how could there be any division between Creator and creation? Are they not necessarily one and the same?

That question has vexed Islam from the moment the Prophet Muhammad first began preaching in Mecca, though, to be frank, most Islamic scholars have chosen to ignore the issue altogether. In fact, such theological concerns have often been dismissed by the learned class in Islam as mere "babble." The word for theology in Arabic is *kalam,* or "talking," and throughout Islamic history those Muslims who have tried to tackle theological conundra have often been scorned as *ahl al-kalam,* "the people of talking," which is why the overwhelming focus of Islamic thought over the centuries has been on legal and not theological matters.

But from the start, a number of Muslim thinkers publicly wrestled with the fundamental issue of how to reconcile God's unity with God's creative power. In doing so, these Muslims not only revitalized Islamic theology in the face of orthodox rigidity, they created a wholly new branch of Islamic mysticism popularly called *Sufism*.

THERE ARE MANY stories told about the first meeting between the legendary Sufi poet of love, Jalal ad-Din Rumi, and his friend and spiritual mentor, Shams-i Tabrizi, to whom many of Rumi's poems were addressed. The two men would go on to form Sufism's most celebrated friendship: Shams will one day pass into sainthood, and Rumi, of course, will become history's most famous Sufi, recognized around the world simply as Mawlana, "our Master." But on the day of their first meeting in the year 1244 C.E., Rumi was just an obscure scholar and member of the "turbaned class" in the city of Konya, in modern-day Turkey, and Shams was a wild, wandering dervish whom people mocked as "the Bird" for his peripatetic ways.

Accounts of the initial encounter between Rumi and Shams have passed into legend; like most Sufi biographies they should be read as allegories meant to reveal some hidden truth, and not as history. In some versions of the story, Rumi is sitting alone by a pond reading his books when Shams comes upon him.

"What are you doing?" Shams asks.

Glancing up at the filthy traveler dressed in rags and standing before him, Rumi assumes he is a homeless peasant and replies, "It is something you cannot understand."

At that moment, the books in Rumi's hand either burst into flames or jump from his lap and fall into the pond, depending on the version of the story. In either case, the books end up miraculously unharmed.

"What is this?" Rumi exclaims at the miracle.

"It is something you cannot understand," Shams replies.

There is a less well known but more prosaic version of this

Rumi (seated on horse) meeting Shams. Folio from Jâmi al-Siyarby
Mohammad Tahir Suhravardî.

Topkapi Palace Museum / Wikimedia Commons / public domain

story, supposedly recounted by Shams himself, in which he sees Rumi riding a horse through Konya's market and steps in front of him, blocking his path. Yet regardless of how the story of their first encounter begins—whether beside a pond or at the market— it always ends the same way, with Shams asking Rumi his thoughts about another Sufi mystic, long since dead, named Tayfur Abu Yazid al-Bastami—known to all as *Bayazid*.[8]

Born around 804 C.E. in the town of Bastam in northeastern Iran, Bayazid came from a family of Zoroastrian priests who had converted to Islam not long after the Arab invasion of Persia and the fall of the Sassanian Empire in 651 C.E. He began his formal education within the Hanafi school, where he steeped himself in the theology of tawhid, the concept of Divine Unity, and the enigma of God's eternal attributes.

Something about the nature of these inquiries left Bayazid disturbed and deeply unsatisfied. He abandoned his formal education and struck off on his own in search of a more intimate experience of God, one that could not be taught in any school. He eventually fell under the influence of a group of Sufis led by a Persian mystic named Sahl al-Tustari.

As a spiritual movement, Sufism defies categorization. Its chief concern is with seeking direct access to God, which is why Sufis tend to rebuff the traditional concerns of Islamic law and theology in favor of an unmediated experience of the divine. Sufis are unconcerned with the debate over whether the Quran should be read literally or figuratively. Instead they argue that the Quran has two distinct layers of meaning: There is the external layer that all Muslims can access simply by reading the scripture and interpreting it for themselves, and there is a secret, hidden layer that only a select few can comprehend, and then only through the kind of intuitive knowledge that comes from a lifetime of prayer and meditation. The external layer helps the believer to learn about God; the hidden layer allows the believer to *know* God.

It was precisely this desire to know God that led Bayazid to join this Sufi order. Day and night Bayazid meditated, desperately trying to unlock the secret truth he thought was concealed in the concept of tawhid. And then one day it came to him, shaking him to his core. He jumped out of his seat and cried out in ecstasy: "Glory be to Me! How great is My majesty!"

To those who heard these words, Bayazid had uttered the most shocking heresy. He was, in no uncertain terms, calling himself God. Actually, such statements had become fairly routine among a certain group of Sufi mystics sometimes called the Drunken Sufis because of their propensity for making similar ecstatic utterances. Bayazid's master, al-Tustari, himself once famously said, "I am the proof of God," while another of his fellow disciples, Mansur al-Hallaj, was crucified for having run out into the streets of Baghdad shouting, "I am the Truth!"[9]

But while most Muslims assumed these Drunken Sufis were associating themselves with the divine, to Sufis like Shams, such statements concealed an even more startling, and more consequential, proclamation about the very nature of reality. Indeed, it was the recognition of that reality—the ability to understand intuitively what Bayazid, al-Tustari, and al-Hallaj meant by their words—that formed a kind of initiatory rite into Sufism. That is why, when Shams first meets Rumi in Konya, he asks him about Bayazid's statement. What did the Sufi master mean when he cried out, "Glory be to Me"?

As with most mystical queries, the answer to Shams's question is irrelevant. Shams is merely assessing Rumi's worthiness to become one of his disciples. In some versions of the story, Rumi does not even bother to respond. He simply swoons, or falls into a trance, or gazes deep into Shams's eyes, lost in a secret that only the two of them seem to share. What matters is the truth hidden within the question. For by wondering what Bayazid meant, Shams is asking an altogether different question: "What is God?"

That question has been at the center of the human quest to make sense of the divine from the very beginning. Is God the animating force that connects all living beings, as our prehistoric ancestors seemed to believe? Or nature deified, as the early Mesopotamians thought? Or an abstract force that permeates the universe, the way some Greek philosophers described it? Or a personalized deity who looks and acts just like a human being? Or is God literally a human being?

No matter how one answers it, the question of what God is has been the abiding concern of believers and nonbelievers alike for hundreds of thousands of years. The question itself has led to the building of entire civilizations, and it has also torn them down. It has created peace and prosperity, and it has led to war and violence.

Yet here now was a group of mystics who, propelled by their adherence to a strict form of monotheism, were making a radical proposition: The only way to make sense of the unity of the Creator is to accept the unity of all creation. In other words, if God is *one*, then God must be *all*.

The term for this concept is *wahadat al-wujud,* or the Unity of Being, first coined by one of the greatest philosophical minds in history, Muhyiddin ibn al-Arabi (1165–1240 C.E.). Seeking to provide a firm philosophical basis for the Sufi conception of the divine, Ibn al-Arabi began by addressing the fundamental flaw in the doctrine of tawhid: If, in the beginning, there was nothing but God, how could God have created anything, unless God created it from himself? And if God did make creation from himself, wouldn't that violate the oneness and unity of God by dividing God between Creator and creation?

Ibn al-Arabi's solution to this problem was to confirm what Sufis like Shams and Bayazid had been saying all along: If God is indivisible, then nothing can come into existence that isn't also God. At the very least, Creator and creation must share the exact same eternal, indistinguishable, *inseparable* essence, meaning everything that exists in the universe exists only insofar as it shares in the existence of God. Therefore, God must be, in essence, the sum total of all existence.[10]

This, then, is the answer to the question Shams asked Rumi. It is what Bayazid meant when he said, "Glory be to Me." It is why Tustari called himself "the proof of God." These Sufis were not claiming to be divine; they were claiming *unity* with the divine. Indeed, for most Sufis, the mistake of Christianity lies not in violating the indivisible nature of God by transforming God into a human being; rather, it lies in believing that God is only *one* particular human being and no other. According to Sufism, if God is truly indivisible, then God is all beings, and all beings are God.

And so, at last, we arrive at the inevitable end point of the monotheistic experiment—the climax of the fairly recent belief in a single, singular, nonhuman, and indivisible creator God as defined by postexilic Judaism, as renounced by Zoroastrian Dualism and Christian Trinitarianism, and as revived in the Sufi interpretation of tawhid: God is not the creator of everything that exists.

God *is* everything that exists.[11]

Conclusion

The One

IN THE BIBLICAL VERSION of creation—or rather, in one of the two biblical versions of creation (the Yahwist)—God, having made Adam and Eve in his own image, sets them loose in the Garden of Eden with a simple command: "You may eat from any tree in the garden but do not eat of the tree of knowledge of good and evil. If you do, you shall die."

But the serpent, the craftiest of God's creations, tells them otherwise. "You will certainly not die," he says. "For God knows that when you eat of it your eyes will be opened, and *you will be like God,* knowing good and evil."

Man and woman both eat the forbidden fruit, and neither die. The serpent was right. God admits as much to his heavenly court: "The man has now become *like one of us,* knowing good and evil. He must not be allowed to reach out his hand and take also from the tree of life and eat, and live forever."

So God banishes Adam and Eve from the garden and places

angels bearing flaming swords at Eden's gates to ensure that neither man nor woman ever return.

When I read this story as a kid, I regarded it as a warning never to disobey God lest I, too, be punished as Adam and Eve were. Now it seems clear to me that Adam and Eve were punished not for disobeying God, but for trying to become God. Perhaps this ancient folk memory is hiding a deeper truth, one that our prehistoric ancestors seem to have understood intuitively but which we, who have transitioned from the pure animism of the past to the rigid religious doctrines of today, have forgotten: God did not make us in his image; nor did we simply make God in ours. Rather, we *are* the image of God in the world—not in form or likeness, but in *essence*.[1]

I arrived at this epiphany through my own long, and admittedly circuitous, spiritual journey—both as a scholar of religions and as a person of faith. Indeed, the history of human spirituality that I outline in this book closely mirrors my own faith journey from a spiritually inclined child who thought of God as an old man with magical powers, to a devout Christian who imagined God as the perfect human being; from a scholastic Muslim who rejected Christianity in favor of the purer monotheism of Islam, to a Sufi forced to admit that the only way to accept the proposition of a singular, eternal, and indivisible God was to obliterate any distinction between Creator and creation.

There is a modern term for this conception of the divine: *pantheism*, meaning "God is all" or "all is God." In its simplest form, pantheism is the belief that God and the universe are one and the same—that nothing exists outside of God's necessary existence. As the pantheistic philosopher Michael P. Levine puts it: "Nothing can be substantially independent of God because there is nothing else but God." In other words, what we call the world and what we call God are not independent or discrete. Rather, the world is God's self-expression. It is God's essence realized and experienced.[2]

Think of God as a light that passes through a prism, refracting into countless colors. The individual colors seem different from each other but in reality they are the same. They have the same essence. They have the same source. In this way, what seems on the surface to be separate and distinct is in fact a single reality, and that reality is what we call God.[3]

This is essentially what our prehistoric ancestors believed. Their primitive animism was predicated on the belief that all things—living or not—share a single essence: a single *soul,* if you will. The same belief spurred the ancient Mesopotamians to deify the elements of nature, long before they began to transform those elements into individual, personalized gods. It lay at the heart of the early Egyptian belief in the existence of a divine force that manifested itself in both gods and humans. It is what the Greek philosophers meant when they spoke of "one god" as the singular, unified principle steering all of creation. All of these belief systems can be viewed as different expressions of the pantheistic conception of God as the sum of all things.

I arrived at pantheism through Sufism. But one can find the same belief in nearly every religious tradition. Pantheism exists in Hinduism, both in the Vedas and the Upanishads, but particularly in the Vedanta tradition, which holds that the *Brahman* (Absolute Reality) alone is real and everything else is illusion: "Nothing is which is not God, and God is everything which is." It can be found in the Buddhist principle that the world and everything in it are merely aspects of the Buddha—that all phenomena have their being in a single reality. As the great Zen master Dogen Zenji (1200–1253 C.E.) said, "All existents are Buddha nature." It is deeply embedded in Taoism, where the divine principle is presented as the ground of all being. "There is nowhere [the Tao] is not. . . . There is not a single thing without Tao," wrote the fourth-century B.C.E. Chinese philosopher Chuang-Tze.[4]

One can arrive at a form of pantheism through Jewish mysticism and the concept of *tzimtzum*, or "divine withdrawal"—the belief that God had to make room within himself to allow for the universe to come into being. Even in Christianity, the quintessentially humanizing religion, one finds pantheistic trends in the works of mystical thinkers such as Meister Eckhart, who famously wrote, "God is Being and from him all being comes directly."[5]

One need not arrive at pantheism through religion at all, but rather through philosophy. It was in fact the rationalist philosopher Benedict Spinoza (1632–1677 C.E.) who is credited with popularizing pantheism in the west by arguing that since there could be but one "substance" in the universe displaying infinite attributes, then whether that substance is called God or Nature, it must exist as a single, undifferentiated reality.[6]

Or ignore God altogether and simply look to science and its unifying conception of nature, in the conservation of energy and matter and the inseparable nature of the two: the unalterable fact that everything that exists today has always existed and will always exist as long as the universe itself exists.

Either way this fundamental truth remains: All is One, and One is All. It is simply up to the individual to decide what "the One" is: how it should be defined, and how it should be experienced.

For me, and for countless others, "the One" is what I call God. But the God I believe in is not a personalized God. It is a *dehumanized* God: a God with no material form; a God who is pure existence, without name, essence, or personality.

Often when I speak about God like this I am confronted with the same negative reaction that Akhenaten, Zarathustra, Xenophanes, and nearly every other religious reformer who has tried to dehumanize the divine faced. People simply do not know how to commune with a God who has no human features, attributes, or needs. How can one form a meaningful relationship with such a God? After all, we are, as we have seen, evolutionarily adapted to conceptualize God in human terms. It is a function of our brains, which is why those who have managed to cast off this humanizing impulse have done so deliberately and with great effort.

But perhaps we should consider the possibility that the entire reason we have a cognitive impulse to think of God as a divine reflection of ourselves is because we are, *every one of us,* God. Perhaps rather than concerning ourselves with trying to form a relationship with God, we should instead become fully aware of the relationship that already exists.

I have spent most of my spiritual life trying to bridge the chasm that I imagined exists between God and me, either through faith or scholarship or some combination of the two. What I believe now is that there is no chasm because there is no distinction between us. I am, in my essential reality, God made manifest. We all are.

As a believer and a pantheist, I worship God not through fear and trembling but through awe and wonder at the workings of the universe—for the universe is God. I pray to God not to ask for things but to become one with God. I recognize that the knowledge of good and evil that the God of Genesis so feared humans might attain begins with the knowledge that good and evil are not metaphysical things but moral choices. I root my moral choices neither in fear of eternal punishment nor in hope of eternal reward. I recognize the divinity of the world and every being in it and respond to everyone and everything as though they were God—because they are. And I understand that the only way I can truly know God is by relying on the only thing I can truly know:

myself. As Ibn al-Arabi said, "He who knows his soul knows his Lord."

It is no coincidence that this book ends where it began, with the soul. Call it what you want: whether *psyche,* per the Greeks; or *nefesh,* as the Hebrews preferred; or *chi'i,* as in China; or *brahman* in India. Call it Buddha Nature or *purusa.* Consider it comaterial with the mind, or coexistent with the universe. Imagine it reuniting with God after death, or transmigrating from body to body. Experience it as the seat of your personal essence or as an impersonal force underlying all creation. However you define it, belief in the soul as separate from the body is universal. It is our *first* belief, far older than our belief in God. It is the belief that begat our belief in God.

Numerous studies on the cognition of children have shown an instinctual propensity for "substance dualism"—the belief that the body and mind/soul are distinct in form and nature. That means we enter the world with an innate sense—untaught, unforced, unprompted—that we are more than just our physical bodies. There are certain cognitive processes that can lead us to apply this inborn belief in the soul to others—human and nonhuman alike. But when it comes to belief in the soul, we are, to put it simply, born believers.[7]

Whether we *remain* believers is, once again, nothing more or less than a choice. One can choose to view humanity's universal belief in the soul as born of confusion or faulty reasoning: a trick of the mind or an accident of evolution. Indeed, one can believe that everything—the Big Bang, the distribution of space and time, the balance between mass and energy, and so on—is all just an accident of atoms. Creation may very well have originated purely through physical processes that reflect nothing more than the articulation of the most basic properties of matter and energy—without cause, value, or purpose. That is a perfectly plausible explanation for the existence of the universe and everything in it. It is, in fact, just as plausible—and just as impossible to prove—as the existence of an animating spirit that underlies the universe, that binds together the souls of you and me and everyone else— perhaps every*thing* else—that is or was or has ever been.

So then, make your choice.

Believe in God or not. Define God how you will. Either way, take a lesson from our mythological ancestors Adam and Eve and eat the forbidden fruit. You need not fear God.

You *are* God.

Acknowledgments

I owe this book, and pretty much everything else I do, to the undying support of my wife, Jessica Jackley, who is not only the love of my life but also my best friend and partner in life. The book could not have been written without the assistance of my friend and colleague Dr. Ian Werrett, whose meticulous research and late-night debates with me on the nature of the divine were instrumental in creating the finished product. Additional research for the book was done by Safa Sameizade-Yazd and Joseph Lerner. I am, as ever, grateful to my amazing literary agent, Elyse Cheney, as well as my editors, Will Murphy and Hilary Redmon, and my tireless publicist, London King, at Random House.

Bibliography

Abadia, Oscar Moro, and Manuel R. Gonzalez Morales. "Paleolithic Art: A Cultural History." *Journal of Archaeological Research* 21 (2013): 269–306.

Adovasio, J. M., Olga Soffer, and Jake Page. *The Invisible Sex*. New York: HarperCollins, 2007.

Albright, William Foxwell. "Jethro, Hobab, and Reuel in Early Hebrew Tradition." *Catholic Biblical Quarterly* 25/1 (1963): 1–11.

Allam, Schafik. "Slaves." Pages 293–96 in *The Oxford Encyclopedia of Ancient Egypt*. Edited by Donald Redford. Oxford: Oxford University Press, 2001.

Anonymous. *Cultus Arborum: A Descriptive Account of Phallic Tree Worship, with Illustrative Legends, Superstitions, Usages, &c., Exhibiting Its Origin and Development Amongst the Eastern & Western Nations of the World, from the Earliest to Modern Times; with a Bibliography of Works upon and Referring to the Phallic Cultus*. London: privately published, 1890.

Anthes, Rudolf. "Egyptian Theology in the Third Millennium B.C." *Journal of Near Eastern Studies* 18/3 (1959): 169–212.

Arapura, J. G. "Transcendent Brahman or Transcendent Void: Which Is

Ultimately Real? Transcendence and the Sacred." Pages 83–99 in *Transcendence and the Sacred*. Edited by A. M. Olson and L. S. Rouner. Notre Dame, Ind.: University of Notre Dame Press, 1981.

Archer, W. G. "Review: *Four Hundred Centuries of Cave Art* by Abbé H. Breuil." *Burlington Magazine* 95/607 (1953): 343–44.

Armitage, Simon, et al. "The Southern Route 'Out of Africa': Evidence for an Early Expansion of Modern Humans into Arabia." *Science* 331/6016 (2011): 453–56.

Arnold, Bettina, and Derek B. Counts. "Prolegomenon: The Many Masks of the Master of Animals." Pages 9–24 in *The Master of Animals in Old World Iconography*. Edited by Derek B. Counts and Bettina Arnold. Budapest: Archaeolingua Alapitvany, 2010.

Aslan, Reza. "Thus Sprang Zarathustra: A Brief Historiography on the Date of the Prophet of Zoroastrianism." *Jusur* 14 (1998–99): 21–34.

———. *No god but God: The Origins, Evolution, and Future of Islam*. New York: Random House, 2005.

———. *Zealot: The Life and Times of Jesus of Nazareth*. New York: Random House, 2013.

Assman, Jan. *The Mind of Egypt*. New York: Metropolitan, 1996.

———. *The Search for God in Ancient Egypt*. Translated by David Lorton. Ithaca and London: Cornell University Press, 2001.

———. *Of Gods and Gods: Egypt, Israel, and the Rise of Monotheism*. Madison: University of Wisconsin Press, 2008.

———. *From Akhenaten to Moses: Ancient Egypt and Religious Change*. Cairo: American University in Cairo, 2014.

Astour, Michael C. "Yahweh in Egyptian Topographic Lists." Pages 17–19 in *Festschrift Elmar Edel* in *Ägypten und Altes Testament*. Edited by Manfred Görg. Bamberg, Germany: Görg, 1979.

Atlas, S. "The Philosophy of Maimonides and Its Systematic Place in the History of Philosophy." *Philosophy* 11/41 (1936): 60–75.

Atran, Scott. *In Gods We Trust: The Evolutionary Landscape of Religion*. New York: Oxford University Press, 2002.

Atwell, James. "An Egyptian Source for Genesis." *Journal of Theological Studies* 51/2 (2000): 441–77.

Aubert, Maxime, et al. "Pleistocene Cave Art from Sulawesi, Indonesia." *Nature* 514 (2014): 223–27.

Bahn, Paul. *The Cambridge Illustrated History of Prehistoric Art*. Cambridge: Cambridge University Press, 1998.

Bahn, Paul, Natalie Franklin, and Matthias Stecker, eds. *Rock Art Studies: News of the World IV*. Oxford: Oxbow Books, 2012.

Baines, John. "Kingship, Definition of Culture, and Legitimation." Pages 3–48 in *Ancient Egyptian Kingship*. Edited by David O'Connor and David P. Silverman. Leiden: Brill, 1995.

Bandstra, Barry. *Reading the Old Testament: Introduction to the Hebrew Bible*. 4th ed. Belmont, Calif.: Wadsworth, 2009.

Banning, E. B. "The Neolithic Period: Triumphs of Architecture, Agriculture, and Art." *Near Eastern Archaeology* 61/4 (1998): 188–237.

Barkley, Russell A. *Executive Functions: What They Are, How They Work, and Why They Evolved*. New York: Guilford Press, 2012.

Barks, Coleman. *The Essential Rumi*. New York: HarperOne, 2004.

Barrett, Justin L. "Cognitive Constraints on Hindu Concepts of the Divine." *Journal for the Scientific Study of Religion* 37 (1998): 608–19.

———. "Theological Correctness: Cognitive Constraint and the Study of Religion." *Method and Theory in the Study of Religion* 11 (1998): 325–39.

———. "Exploring the Natural Foundations of Religion." *Trends in Cognitive Sciences* 4/1 (2000): 29–34.

———. *Why Would Anyone Believe in God?* Lanham, Md.: Altamira Press, 2004.

———. "Cognitive Science, Religion and Theology." Pages 76–99 in *The Believing Primate: Scientific, Philosophical, and Theological Reflections on the Origin of Religion*. Edited by J. Schloss and M. Murray. Oxford: Oxford University Press, 2009.

———. *Born Believers: The Science of Children's Religious Belief*. New York: Atria Books, 2012.

Barton, C. Michael, G. A. Clark, and Allison E. Cohen. "Art as Information: Explaining Upper Palaeolithic Art in Western Europe." *World Archaeology* 26/2 (1994): 185–207.

Barua, Ankur. "God's Body at Work: Rāmānuja and Panentheism." *International Journal of Hindu Studies* 14/1 (2010): 1–30.

Bar-Yosef, Ofer. "The PPNA in the Levant—An Overview." *Paléorient* 15/1 (1989): 57–63.

Bausani, Alessandro. "Theism and Pantheism in Rumi." *Iranian Studies* 1/1 (1968): 8–24.

Begouën, Robert, and Jean Clottes. "Les Trois-Frères after Breuil." *Antiquity* 61 (1987): 180–87.

Begouën, Robert, Carole Fritz, and Gilles Tosello. "Parietal Art and Ar-
chaeological Context: Activities of the Magdalenians in the Cave of
Tuc d'Audoubert, France." Pages 364–80 in *A Companion to Rock
Art*. Edited by Jo McDonald and Peter Veth. London: Chichester,
U.K.: Wiley-Blackwell, 2012.

Berghaus, Gunter. *New Perspectives on Prehistoric Art*. Westport, Conn.:
Praeger, 2004.

Bering, Jesse M. "Intuitive Conceptions of Dead Agents' Minds: The
Natural Foundations of Afterlife Beliefs as Phenomenological Boundary." *Journal of Cognition and Culture* 2/4 (2002): 263–308.

———. "The Cognitive Psychology of Belief in the Supernatural: Belief
in a Deity or an Afterlife Could Be an Evolutionarily Advantageous
By-product of People's Ability to Reason About the Minds of Others." *American Scientist* 94/2 (2006): 142–49.

———. "The Folk Psychology of Souls." *Behavioral and Brain Sciences*
29/5 (2006): 462–98.

Berlejung, Angelika. "Washing the Mouth: The Consecration of Divine
Images in Mesopotamia." Pages 45–72 in *The Image and the Book:
Iconic Cults, Aniconism, and the Rise of the Book Religion in Israel
and the Ancient Near East*. Edited by K. van der Toorn. Leuven:
Peeters, 1997.

Binford, Lewis R. "Post-Pleistocene Adaptations." Pages 313–42 in *New
Perspectives in Archaeology*. Edited by L. R. Binford and S. R. Binford.
Chicago: Aldine, 1968.

Binns, L. Elliott. "Midianite Elements in Hebrew Religion." *Journal of
Theological Studies* 31/124 (1930): 337–54.

Bird-David, Nurit. "'Animism' Revisited: Personhood, Environment, and
Relational Epistemology." *Current Anthropology* 40/S1 (1999): S67–S91.

Black, Whitney Davis, et al. "Art for Art's Sake in the Paleolithic [and
Comments and Reply]." *Current Anthropology* 28/1 (1987): 63–89.

Blanc, Alberto C. "Some Evidence for the Ideologies of Early Man."
Pages 119–36 in *Social Life of Early Man*. Edited by Sherwood Washburn. London: Routledge, 2004.

Bloch, Maurice. *In and Out of Each Other's Bodies: Theory of Mind, Evolution, Truth, and the Nature of the Social*. New York: Routledge, 2016.

Bloom, Paul. *Descartes' Baby: How the Science of Child Development
Explains What Makes Us Human*. New York: Basic Books, 2004.

———. "Religious Belief as an Evolutionary Accident." Pages 118–27 in

The Believing Primate. Edited by Jeffrey Schloss and Michael J. Murray. Oxford: Oxford University Press, 2009.

———. "Religion, Morality, Evolution." *Annual Review of Psychology* 63 (2012): 179–99.

Boak, Arthur Edward Romilly. "The Theoretical Basis of the Deification of Rulers in Antiquity." *The Classical Journal* 11/5 (1916): 293–97.

Bosch-Gimpera, P. "Review *Four Hundred Centuries of Cave Art* by Abbé H. Breuil." *Boletín Bibliográfico de Antropología Americana* 15/2 16/2 (1952–1953): 80–82.

Bottéro, Jean. *Religion in Ancient Mesopotamia*. Translated by Teresa Lavender Fagan. Chicago: University of Chicago Press, 2004.

Boutwood, Arthur. "A Scientific Monism." *Proceedings of the Aristotelian Society*, New Series 1 (1900–1901): 140–66.

Boyce, Mary. *History of Zoroastrianism*. 3 vols. Leiden: Brill, 1975–1991.

Boyd, Robert, et al. "The Evolution of Altruistic Punishment." *Proceedings of the National Academy of Sciences* 100/3 (2003): 3531–35.

Boyer, Pascal. *The Naturalness of Religious Ideas: A Cognitive Theory of Religion*. Berkeley and Los Angeles: University of California Press, 1994.

———. *Religion Explained: The Evolutionary Origins of Religious Thought*. New York: Basic Books, 2001.

Braidwood, Robert J. "The Agricultural Revolution." *Scientific American* 203 (1960): 130–41.

———. *Prehistoric Men*. 6th ed. Chicago: Chicago Natural History Museum, 1963.

Brandon, S.G.F. "The Ritual Perpetuation of the Past." *Numen* 6/2 (1959): 112–29.

Breasted, James. *Ancient Records of Egypt*. Vol. 2. Chicago: University of Chicago Press, 1906.

Breuil, Abbé Henri. *Four Hundred Centuries of Cave Art*. Translated by Mary E. Boyle. New York: Hacker Art Books, 1979 [1952].

———. *White Lady of Brandberg: Rock Paintings of South Africa*. Vol. 1. London: Faber and Faber, 1955.

Breuil, Abbé Henri, and Raymond Lantier. *The Men of the Old Stone Age*. New York: St. Martin's Press, 1965.

Brisch, Nicole. "The Priestess and the King: The Divine Kingship of Šū-Sîn of Ur." *Journal of the American Oriental Society* 126/2 (2006): 161–76.

Broadie, Sarah. "Theological Sidelights from Plato's 'Timaeus.'" *Proceedings of the Aristotelian Society, Supplementary Volumes* 82 (2008): 1–17.

Brown, Francis, S. R. Driver, and Charles Briggs. *A Hebrew and English Lexicon of the Old Testament*. Oxford: Oxford University Press, 1951.

Burckhardt, Titus. *Introduction to Sufism*. London: Thorsons, 1995.

Burger, Peter. *The Sacred Canopy: Elements of a Sociological Theory of Religion*. New York: Doubleday, 1967.

Burkert, Walter. *Greek Religion*. Translated by John Raffan. Cambridge, Mass.: Harvard University Press, 1985.

———. *Creation of the Sacred: Tracks of Biology in Early Religions*. Cambridge, Mass.: Harvard University Press, 1996.

Burkit, Miles C. "13. Review of *La Signification de l'Art Rupestre Paléolithique*." *Man* 63 (1963): 14.

Call, Josep, and Michael Tomasello. "Does the Chimpanzee Have a Theory of Mind? 30 Years Later." *Trends in Cognitive Sciences* 12/5 (2008): 187–92.

Carneiro, Robert L. "Review of *The Birth of the Gods and the Origins of Agriculture* by Jacques Cauvin." *American Antiquity* 67/3 (2002): 575–76.

Cartailhac, Émile. "Les mains inscrites de rouge ou de noir de Gargas." *L'anthropologie* 17 (1906): 624–25.

Carter, Tim. "Marcion's Christology and Its Possible Influence on Codex Bezae." *The Journal of Theological Studies* 61/2 (2010): 550–82.

Cauvin, Jacques. *The Birth of the Gods and the Origins of Agriculture*. Translated by Trevor Watkins. New Studies in Archaeology; Cambridge: Cambridge University Press, 2007.

Cauvin, Jacques, Ian Hodder, Gary O. Rollefson, Ofer Bar-Yosef, and Trevor Watkins. "Review of *The Birth of the Gods and the Origins of Agriculture* by Jacques Cauvin." *Cambridge Archaeological Journal* 11/01 (2001): 105–21.

Chalupa, Aleš. "How Did Roman Emperors Become Gods? Various Concepts of Imperial Apotheosis." *Anodos—Studies of the Ancient World* 6–7 (2006–2007): 201–207.

Childe, Vere Gordon. "The Urban Revolution." *Town Planning Review* 21/1 (1950): 3–17.

———. *Man Makes Himself: History of the Rise of Civilization*. 3rd ed. London: Watts and Company, 1936.

Chipp, Herschel B. "Review of *Palaeolithic Art*." *Art Journal* 22/1 (1962): 54–56.

Chittenden, Jacqueline. "The Master of Animals." *Hesperia: The Journal of the American School of Classical Studies at Athens* 16/1 (1947): 89–114.

Chittick, William C. *The Sufi Path of Knowledge: Ibn al-Arabi's Metaphysics of Imagination*. Albany: SUNY Press, 1989.

Cicero. *The Nature of the Gods*. Translated by P. G. Walsh. Oxford: Oxford University Press, 2008.

Clark, Geoffrey A. "Grave Markers: Middle and Early Upper Paleolithic Burials and the Use of Chronotypology in Contemporary Paleolithic Research." *Current Anthropology* 42/4 (2001): 449–79.

Clottes, Jean, and David Lewis-Williams. *The Shamans of Prehistory: Trance Magic and the Painted Caves*. New York: Abrams, 1998.

Coats, George W. "Moses in Midian." *Journal of Biblical Literature* 92/1 (1973): 3–10.

Cohen, Martin. "The Role of the Shilonite Priesthood in the United Monarchy of Ancient Israel." *Hebrew Union College Annual* 36 (1965): 59–98.

Conard, Nicholas J. "Palaeolithic Ivory Sculptures from Southwestern Germany and the Origins of Figurative Art." *Nature* 426/18 (2003): 830–32.

Conkey, Margaret W. "A Century of Palaeolithic Cave Art." *Archaeology* 34/4 (1981): 20–28.

Coogan, Michael David. "Canaanite Origins and Lineage: Reflections on the Religion of Ancient Israel." Pages 115–84 in *Ancient Israelite Religion: Essays in Honor of Frank Moore Cross*. Edited by Patrick D. Miller, et al. Philadelphia: Fortress Press, 1987.

Cooper, Rodney A. *Tao Te Ching: Classic of the Way and Virtue; An English Version with Commentary*. Bloomington, Ind.: AuthorHouse, 2013.

Corduan, Winfried. "A Hair's Breadth from Pantheism: Meister Eckhart's God-Centered Spirituality." *Journal of the Evangelical Theological Society* 37/2 (1994): 263–74.

Crone, Patricia, and Michael Cook. *Hagarism: The Making of the Islamic World*. Cambridge: Cambridge University Press, 1977.

Cross, Frank Moore. "Yahweh and the God of the Patriarchs." *Harvard Theological Review* 55/4 (1962): 225–59.

————. *Canaanite Myth and Hebrew Epic: Essays in the History of the Religion of Israel*. Cambridge, Mass.: Harvard University Press, 1997.

Csibra, Gergely, et al. "Goal Attribution Without Agency Cues: The Perception of 'Pure Reason' in Infancy." *Cognition* 72/3 (1999): 237–67.

Dalley, Stephanie. *Myths from Mesopotamia: Creation, the Flood, and Others*. New York: Oxford University Press, 1989.

Davenport, Guy. "Robot." *Hudson Review* 25/3 (1972): 413–46.

Deimel, Antonius. *Pantheon Babylonicum: Nomina Deorum e Textibus Cuneiformibus Excerpta et Ordine Alphabetico Distributa*. Rome: Sumptibus Pontificii Instituti Biblici, 1914.

De La Torre, Miguel A., and Albert Hernández. *The Quest for the Historical Satan*. Minneapolis: Fortress Press, 2011.

De Moor, Johannes C. *The Rise of Yahwism: The Roots of Israelite Monotheism*. 2nd ed. Leuven: Peeters, 1997.

Dever, William G. "Asherah, Consort of Yahweh? New Evidence from Kuntillet 'Ajrûd." *Bulletin of the American Schools of Oriental Research* 255 (1984): 21–37.

————. *Did God Have a Wife? Archaeology and Folk Religion in Ancient Israel*. Grand Rapids: Eerdmans, 2008.

de Wet, Chris. "Mystical Expression and the 'Logos' in the Writings of St. John of the Cross." *Neotestamentica* 42/1 (2008): 35–50.

Dexter, Miriam Robbins. "Proto-Indo-European Sun Maidens and Gods of the Moon." *Mankind Quarterly* 55 (1984): 137–44.

Diaz-Andreu, Margarita. "An All-Embracing Universal Hunter-Gatherer Religion? Discussing Shamanism and Spanish Levantine Rock-Art." Pages 117–33 in *The Concept of Shamanism: Uses and Abuses*. Edited by Henri-Paul Francfort and Roberte N. Hamayon. Budapest: Akademiai Kiado: 2001.

Dion, Paul E. "YHWH as Storm-God and Sun-God: The Double Legacy of Egypt and Canaan as Reflected in Psalm 104." *Zeitschrift für die Alttestamentliche Wissenschaft* 103/1 (1991): 43–71.

Duling, Dennis C. *Jesus Christ Through History*. New York: Harcourt, 1979.

Dumbrell, William J. "Midian: A Land or a League?" *Vetus Testamentum* 25/2 (1975): 323–37.

Durkheim, Émile. *The Elementary Forms of Religious Life*. New York: Free Press, 1995.

Ehrman, Bart D. *Lost Christianities: The Battle for Scripture and the Faiths We Never Knew.* New York: Oxford University Press, 2003.

Eliade, Mircea. *Shamanism: Archaic Techniques of Ecstasy.* Princeton: Princeton/Bollingen, 1974.

———. *From the Stone Age to the Eleusinian Mysteries.* Volume 1 of *History of Religious Ideas.* Translated by Willard Trask. Chicago: University of Chicago Press, 1978.

Eliade, Mircea, et al. *The Encyclopedia of Religion.* 16 vols. New York: Macmillan, 1987.

Eshraghian, Ahad, and Bart Loeys. "Loeys-Dietz Syndrome: A Possible Solution for Akhenaten's and His Family's Mystery Syndrome." *South African Medical Journal* 102/8 (2012): 661–64.

Fagan, Brian M., and Charlotte Beck, eds. *The Oxford Companion to Archaeology.* New York: Oxford University Press, 1996.

Fakhry, Majid. "Philosophy and Theology: From the Eighth Century C.E. to the Present." Pages 269–304 in *The Oxford History of Islam.* Edited by John L. Esposito. New York: Oxford University Press, 1999.

Faulkner, Raymond O. *The Ancient Pyramid Texts.* Oxford: Clarendon Press, 1969.

Feeley-Harnik, Gillian. "Issues in Divine Kingship." *Annual Review of Anthropology* 14 (1985): 273–313.

Feld, Edward. "Spinoza the Jew." *Modern Judaism* 9/1 (1989): 101–19.

Feuerbach, Ludwig. *The Essence of Christianity.* Translated by Marian Evans. New York: Calvin Blanchard, 1855.

———. *Lectures on the Essence of Religion.* Translated by Ralph Manheim. New York: Harper and Row, 1967.

———. *Principles of the Philosophy of the Future.* Translated by Manfred Vogel. Indianapolis: Hackett, 1986.

Finkel, Irving. *The Ark Before Noah: Decoding the Story of the Flood.* New York: Doubleday, 2014.

Fitzmyer, Joseph. "The Aramaic Language and the Study of the New Testament." *Journal of Biblical Literature* 99/1 (1980): 5–21.

Forrest, Peter, and Roman Majeran. "Pantheism." *Roczniki Filozoficzne / Annales de Philosophie / Annals of Philosophy* 64/4 (2016): 67–91.

Foster, Benjamin R. *Before the Muses: An Anthology of Akkadian Literature.* Bethesda: University of Maryland Press, 2005.

Frankfort, Henri. *Kingship and the Gods: A Study of Ancient Near East-*

ern Religion as the Integration of Society and Nature. Chicago: University of Chicago Press, 1948.

Fraser, Douglas. "Review of *Palaeolithic Art: Indian Art in America*." *Art Bulletin* 45/1 (1963): 61–62.

Freed, Rita. "Art in the Service of Religion and the State." Pages 110–29 in *Pharaohs of the Sun: Akhenaten, Nefertiti, Tutankhamun*. Boston: Museum of Fine Arts in association with Bulfinch Press/Little, Brown, 1994.

Freeman, L. G. "The Significance of Mammalian Faunas from Paleolithic Occupations in Cantabrian Spain." *American Antiquity* 38/1 (1973): 3–44.

Freud, Sigmund. *Totem and Taboo: Resemblances Between the Psychic Lives of Savages and Neurotics*. Translated by Abraham Arden Brill. New York: Moffat, Yard and Company, 1918.

———. *The Future of an Illusion*. Translated by W. D. Robson-Scott. London: Hogarth Press, 1928.

Gamble, Clive. "Interaction and Alliance in Palaeolithic Society." *Man* 17/1 (1982): 92–107.

———. *The Palaeolithic Settlement of Europe*. Cambridge: Cambridge University Press, 1986.

Garcia-Diez, M., D. L. Hoffman, J. Zilhao, C. de las Heras, J. A. Lasheras, R. Montes, and A.W.G. Pike. "Uranium Series Dating Reveals a Long Sequence of Rock Art at Altamira Cave (Santillana del Mar, Cantabria)." *Journal of Archaeological Science* 40 (2013): 4098–106.

Garr, W. R. *In His Own Image and Likeness: Humanity, Divinity, and Monotheism*. Leiden: Brill, 2003.

Geertz, Clifford. *The Interpretation of Cultures*. New York: Basic Books, 1973.

Giedion, Sigfried. "Review: *Four Hundred Centuries of Cave Art* by Abbé H. Breuil." *College Art Journal* 12/4 (1953): 381–83.

Girard, René. *Violence and the Sacred*. Baltimore, Md.: Johns Hopkins University Press, 1979.

Giversen, Soren, and Birger A. Pearson. "The Testimony of Truth." Pages 448–59 in *The Nag Hammadi Library in English*. Edited by James M. Robinson. San Francisco: HarperSanFrancisco, 1978.

Goedicke, Hans. "Remarks on the 'Israel-Stela.'" *Wiener Zeitschrift für die Kunde des Morgenlandes* 94 (2004): 53–72.

Gooch, Brad. *Rumi's Secret: The Life of the Sufi Poet of Love*. New York: Harper, 2017.

Goodrich, Norma Lorre. *Ancient Myths*. London: Mentor Books, 1960.

Gottwald, Norman K. *The Tribes of Yahweh: A Sociology of the Religion of Liberated Israel, 1250–1050 B.C.E.* Maryknoll, N.Y.: Orbis Books, 1979.

Gowlett, John, Clive Gamble, and Robin Dunbar. "Human Evolution and the Archaeology of the Social Brain." *Current Anthropology* 53/6 (2012): 693–722.

Graziosi, Barbara. *The Gods of Olympus: A History*. New York: Picador, 2014.

Green, Alberto R. W. *The Storm-God in the Ancient Near East*. Winona Lake, Ind.: Eisenbrauns, 2003.

Green, Richard E., et al., "A Draft Sequence of the Neanderthal Genome." *Science* 328 (2010): 701–22.

Gregory, Curtis. *The Cave Painters: Probing the Mysteries of the World's First Artists*. New York: Alfred A. Knopf, 2006.

Grun, Rainer, et al. "U-series and ESR analyses of bones and teeth relating to the human burials from Skhul." *Journal of Human Evolution* 49/3 (2005): 316–34.

Guenevere, Michael, and Hillard Kaplan. "Longevity of Hunter-Gatherers: A Cross-Cultural Examination." *Population and Development Review* 33/2 (2007): 321–65.

Gunther, Hans F. K. *The Religious Attitudes of the Indo-Europeans*. Translated by Vivian Bird. London: Clare Press, 1967.

Guthrie, R. Dale. *The Nature of Paleolithic Art*. Chicago: University of Chicago Press, 2005.

Guthrie, Stewart. *Faces in the Clouds*. New York: Oxford University Press, 1995.

———. "On Animism." *Current Anthropology* 41/1 (2000): 106–107.

Hahn, Joachim. *Kraft und Aggression: Die Botschaft der Eiszeitkunst im Aurignacien Süddeutschlands?* Tübingen: Verlag Archaeologica Venatoria, 1986.

Hall, Edith. *Introducing the Ancient Greeks: From Bronze Age Seafarers to Navigators of the Western Mind*. New York: W. W. Norton, 2015.

Hallowell, Alfred Irving. "Ojibwa Ontology, Behavior, and World View." Pages 20–52 in *Culture in History: Essays in Honor of Paul Radin*. Edited by Stanley Diamond. New York: Columbia University Press, 1960.

Halverson, John, et al. "Art for Art's Sake in the Paleolithic [and Comments and Reply]." *Current Anthropology* 28/1 (1987): 63–89.

Hammond, Norman. "Palaeolithic Mammalian Faunas and Parietal Art in Cantabria: A Comment on Freeman." *American Antiquity* 39/4 (1974): 618–19.

Harari, Yuval Noah. *Sapiens: A Brief History of Humankind*. New York: HarperCollins, 2015.

Harrison, Paul. *Elements of Pantheism*. Coral Springs, Fla.: Lumina Press, 2004.

Harvey, Paul, ed. *The Oxford Companion to Classical Literature*. Oxford: Clarendon Press, 1951.

Hasel, Michael G. "Israel in the Merneptah Stela." *Bulletin of the American Schools of Oriental Research* 296 (1994): 45–61.

Hawkes, Jacquetta, and Sir Leonard Woolley. *Prehistory and the Beginnings of Civilization*. New York: Harper and Row, 1963.

Hayden, Brian. "Review of *The Birth of the Gods and the Origins of Agriculture* by Jacques Cauvin." *Canadian Journal of Archaeology/ Journal Canadien d'Archéologie* 26/1 (2002): 80–82.

———. *Shamans, Sorcerers and Saints*. Washington, D.C.: Smithsonian, 2003.

Hedley, Douglas. "Pantheism, Trinitarian Theism and the Idea of Unity: Reflections on the Christian Concept of God." *Religious Studies* 32/1 (1966): 61–77.

Herodotus. Translated by A. D. Godley. Loeb Classical Library. Cambridge, Mass.: Harvard University Press, 1960.

Hodder, Ian. "The Role of Religion in the Neolithic of the Middle East and Anatolia with Particular Reference to Catalhöyük." *Paléorient* 37/1 (2001): 111–22.

———. "Symbolism and the Origins of Agriculture in the Near East." *Cambridge Archaeological Journal* 11/1 (2001): 107–14.

Hodin, J. P. "Review: *Four Hundred Centuries of Cave Art* by Abbé H. Breuil; *Art in the Ice Age* by Johannes Maringer, Hans-Georg Bandi." *Journal of Aesthetics and Art Criticism* 13/2 (1954): 272–73.

Hoffmeier, James K. *Akhenaten and the Origins of Monotheism*. Oxford: Oxford University Press, 2015.

Holland, Tom. *In the Shadow of the Sword: The Birth of Islam and the Rise of the Global Arab Empire*. New York: Doubleday, 2012.

Hornung, Erik. "The Rediscovery of Akhenaten and His Place in Religion." *Journal of the American Research Center in Egypt* 29 (1992): 43–49.

————. *Akhenaten and the Religion of Light*. Translated by David Lorton. Ithaca and London: Cornell University Press, 1999.

Hovers, Erella, Shimon Ilani, Ofer Bar-Yosef, and Bernard Vandermeersch. "An Early Case of Color Symbolism: Ochre Use by Modern Humans in Qafzeh Cave." *Current Anthropology* 44/4 (2003): 491–522.

Hublin, Jean-Jacques, and Shannon P. McPherron, eds. *Modern Origins: A North African Perspective*. New York: Springer, 2012.

Huchingson, James E. "The World as God's Body: A Systems View." *Journal of the American Academy of Religion* 48/3 (1980): 335–44.

Hume, David. *Four Dissertations*. London: A. and H. Bradlaugh Bonner, 1757.

Hutton, Ronald. *Witches, Druids, and King Arthur*. New York: Bloomsbury Academic, 2003.

Ingold, Tim, and Gisli Palsson, eds. *Biosocial Becomings: Integrating Social and Biological Anthropology*. Cambridge: Cambridge University Press, 2013.

Irani, Dinshaw J. *Understanding the Gathas: The Hymns of Zarathushtra*. Womelsdorf, Pa.: Ahura Publishers, 1994.

Jacobsen, Thorkild. "Ancient Mesopotamian Religion: The Central Concerns." *Proceedings of the American Philosophical Society* 107/6 (1963): 473–84.

————. "Primitive Democracy in Ancient Mesopotamia." *Journal of Near Eastern Studies* 2/3 (1943): 159–72.

————. *The Treasures of Darkness: A History of Mesopotamian Religion*. Revised edition. New Haven: Yale University Press, 1978.

James, E. O. "The Threshold of Religion. The Marett Lecture, 1958." *Folklore* 69/3 (1958): 160–74.

Jaubert, Jacques, et al. "Early Neanderthal Constructions Deep in Bruniquel Cave in Southwestern France." *Nature* 534 (2016): 111–27.

Jochim, Michael. "Palaeolithic Cave Art in Ecological Perspective." Pages 212–19 in *Hunter Gatherer Economy in Prehistory*. Edited by G. N. Bailey. Cambridge: Cambridge University Press, 1983.

Johnson, Raymond. "Monuments and Monumental Art under Amenhotep III: Evolution and Meaning." Pages 63–94 in *Amenhotep III: Perspectives on His Reign*. Edited by David O'Connor and Eric H. Cline. Ann Arbor: University of Michigan Press, 2001.

Jones, Rufus M. "Jewish Mysticism." *Harvard Theological Review* 36/2 (1943): 155–63.

Karamustafa, Ahmet. *Sufism: The Formative Period*. Berkeley: University of California Press, 2007.

Kelemen, Deborah. "Are Children Intuitive Theists? Reasoning About Purpose and Design in Nature." *Psychological Science* 15/5 (2004): 295–301.

Kelemen, Deborah, and Cara DiYanni. "Intuitions About Origins: Purpose and Intelligent Design in Children's Reasoning About Nature." *Journal of Cognition and Development* 6/1 (2005): 3–31.

Kenyon, Kathleen. *Digging up Jericho*. New York: Praeger, 1957.

Keyser, James D., and David S. Whitley. "Sympathetic Magic in Western North American Rock Art." *American Antiquity* 71/1 (2006): 3–26.

Knight, Nicola, Paulo Sousa, Justin L. Barrett, and Scott Atran. "Children's Attributions of Beliefs to Humans and God: Cross-Cultural Evidence." *Cognitive Science* 28 (2004): 117–26.

Köhler, Ludwig. *Old Testament Theology*. Translated by A. S. Todd. Philadelphia: Westminster Press, 1957.

Kreitzer, Larry. "Apotheosis of the Roman Emperor." *Biblical Archaeologist* 53/4 (1990): 210–17.

Kubler, George. "Eidetic Imagery and Paleolithic Art." *Yale University Art Gallery Bulletin* 40/1 (1987): 78–85.

Kuiper, F.B.J. "Ahura 'Mazda' 'Lord Wisdom'?" *Indo-Iranian Journal* 18/1–2 (1976): 25–42.

Lambert, Wilfred G. "The God Aššur." *Iraq* 45/1 (1983): 82–86.

———. *Babylonian Creation Myths*. Winona Lake, Ind.: Eisenbrauns, 2013.

Larson, Gerald James, ed., *Myth in Indo-European Antiquity*. Berkeley: University of California Press, 1974.

Lasheras, Jose Antonio. "The Cave of Altamira: 22,000 Years of History." *Adoranten* (2009): 5–33.

Leeming, David, and Margaret Leeming, eds. *A Dictionary of Creation Myths*. New York: Oxford, 1994.

Legrain, Georges. "Second rapport sur les travaux exécutés à Karnak du 31 octobre 1901 au 15 mai 1902." *Annales du Service des Antiquités de L'Égypte* 4 (1903): 1–40.

Leroi-Gourhan, André. *The Dawn of European Art: An Introduction to Palaeolithic Cave Painting*. Cambridge: Cambridge University Press, 1982.

————. "The Hands of Gargas: Toward a General Study." *October* 37 (1986): 18–34.

————. *The Hunters of Prehistory*. Translated by Claire Jacobson. New York: Atheneum, 1989.

————. "The Religion of the Caves: Magic or Metaphysics?" *October* 37 (1986): 6–17.

————. *Treasures of Prehistoric Art*. New York: Harry Abrams, 1967.

Lesher, James H. *Xenophanes of Colophon: Fragments: A Text and Translation with Commentary*. Toronto: University of Toronto Press, 1992.

Levine, Michael P. *Pantheism: A Non-Theistic Concept of Deity*. New York: Routledge, 1994.

————. "Pantheism, Substance and Unity." *International Journal for Philosophy of Religion* 32/1 (1992): 1–23.

Levine, Morton H. "Review *Four Hundred Centuries of Cave Art* by Abbé H. Breuil." *American Anthropologist*, New Series, 59/1 (1957): 142–43.

————. "Prehistoric Art and Ideology." *American Anthropologist* 59/6 (1957): 949–64.

Lévi-Strauss, Claude. *Totemism*. Translated by Rodney Needham. London: Merlin Press, 1991.

Lewis, David Levering. *God's Crucible: Islam and the Making of Europe, 570–1215*. New York: W. W. Norton, 2008.

Lewis-Williams, David. *Conceiving God: The Cognitive Origin and Evolution of Religion*. London: Thames and Hudson, 2010.

————. "Debating Rock Art: Myth and Ritual, Theories and Facts." *South African Archaeological Bulletin* 61/183 (2006): 105–14.

————. *Inside the Neolithic Mind*. London: Thames and Hudson, 2009.

————. *The Mind in the Cave: Consciousness and the Origins of Art*. London: Thames and Hudson, 2004.

Lewis-Williams, David, and David Pearce. *Inside the Neolithic Mind: Consciousness, Cosmos, and the Realm of the God*. London: Thames and Hudson, 2005.

Lommel, Herman. *Die Religion Zarathustras. Nach dem Awesta dargestellt*. Hildesheim: Olms, 1971.

Lorblanchet, Michel. "The Origin of Art." *Diogenes* 214 (2007): 98–109.

————. "Claw Marks and Ritual Traces in the Paleolithic Sanctuaries of the Quercy." Pages 165–70 in *An Enquiring Mind: Studies in Honour of Alexander Marshack*. Edited by Paul Bahn. Oxford: Oxbow Books, 2009.

MacCulloch, Diarmaid. *Christian History: An Introduction to the Western Tradition*. London: SCM Press, 2012.

MacIntyre, Alasdair. "Pantheism." Pages 31–35 in vol. 6 of *Encyclopedia of Philosophy*. Edited by Paul Edwards. 10 vols. New York: Macmillan, 1967.

Macquarrie, John. *In Search of Deity*. London: SCM Press, 1984.

Mallory, James Patrick. *In Search of the Indo-Europeans: Language, Archaeology and Myth*. New York: Thames and Hudson, 1989.

———, and D. Q. Adams, eds. *The Encyclopedia of Indo-European Culture*. London and Chicago: Fitzroy Dearborn Publishers, 1997.

Marett, Robert Ranulph. *The Threshold of Religion*. London: Methuen, 1914.

Marinatos, Nanno. *The Goddess and the Warrior: The Naked Goddess and Mistress of the Animals in Early Greek Religion*. London: Routledge, 2000.

Maringer, Johannes. "Priests and Priestesses in Prehistoric Europe." *History of Religions* 17/2 (1977): 101–20.

Marshack, Alexander. "Images of the Ice Age." *Archaeology* 48/4 (1995): 28–36.

McFarland, Thomas. *Coleridge and the Pantheist Tradition*. Oxford: Oxford University Press, 1969.

Mehr, Farhang. *The Zoroastrian Tradition: An Introduction to the Ancient Wisdom of Zarathustra*. Rockport, Mass.: Element, 1991.

Mendenhall, George E. "The Hebrew Conquest of Palestine." *Biblical Archaeologist* 25/3 (1962): 65–87.

Mendenhall, George E., and G. A. Herion. *Ancient Israel's Faith and History: An Introduction to the Bible in Context*. Louisville: Westminster John Knox Press, 2001.

Menocal, Maria Rosa. *Ornament of the World: How Muslims, Jews and Christians Created a Culture of Tolerance in Medieval Spain*. New York: Back Bay Books, 2003.

Metso, Sarianna. *The Serekh Texts*. New York: T&T Clark, 2007.

Mithen, Steven J. "To Hunt or to Paint: Animals and Art in the Upper Palaeolithic." *Man*, New Series, 23/4 (1988): 671–95.

Mohr, Richard D. "Plato's Theology Reconsidered: What the Demiurge Does." *History of Philosophy Quarterly* 2/2 (1985): 131–44.

Momigliano, Arnaldo. "How Roman Emperors Became Gods." *American Scholar* 55/2 (1986): 181–93.

Moore-Colyer, R. J. "Review of *The Birth of the Gods and the Origins of Agriculture* by Jacques Cauvin." *Agricultural History Review* 49/1 (2001): 114–15.

Morenz, Siegfried. *Egyptian Religion*. Translated by Ann E. Keep. Ithaca: Cornell University Press, 1992.

Morkot, James. "Divine of Body: The Remains of Egyptian Kings—Preservation, Reverence, and Memory in a World Without Relics." *Past and Present*, Supplement 5 (2010): 37–55.

Morris-Kay, Gillian. "The Evolution of Human Artistic Creativity." *Journal of Anatomy* 216 (2010): 158–76.

Mowinckel, Sigmund. "The Name of the God of Moses." *Hebrew Union College Annual* 32 (1961): 121–33.

Muesse, Mark. *The Hindu Traditions: A Concise Introduction*. Minneapolis: Fortress Press, 2011.

Müller, Max. *Introduction to the Science of Religion*. London: Longmans, Green, 1873.

———. *Comparative Mythology: An Essay*. London: Routledge and Sons, 1909.

Murray, Gilbert. *Five Stages of Greek Religion*. New York: Anchor Books, 1955.

Murray, Michael. "Scientific Explanations of Religion and the Justification of Religious Belief." Pages 168–78 in *The Believing Primate: Scientific, Philosophical, and Theological Reflections on the Origin of Religion*. Edited by Jeffrey Schloss and Michael Murray. Oxford: Oxford University Press, 2009.

Nadeau, Randall L., ed. *Asian Religions: A Cultural Perspective*. Chichester, U.K.: Wiley-Blackwell, 2013.

Nederhof, Mark-Jan. "Karnak Stela of Ahmose," n.p. [cited 24 April 2014]. https://mjn.host.cs.st-andrews.ac.uk/egyptian/texts/corpus/pdf/urkIV-005.pdf.

Nicholson, Reynold A. *Rumi: Poet and Mystic (1207–1273)*. Oxford: Oneworld, 1995.

O'Connor, David, and David P. Silverman, eds. *Ancient Egyptian Kingship*. Leiden: Brill, 1995.

O'Connor, David, and Eric H. Cline, eds. *Amenhotep III: Perspectives on His Reign*. Ann Arbor: University of Michigan Press, 2001.

Olyan, Saul M. *Asherah and the Cult of Yahweh in Israel*. Atlanta: Society of Biblical Literature, 1988.

Osborne, Catherine. *Presocratic Philosophy: A Very Short Introduction*. Oxford: Oxford University Press, 2004.

Owen, Huw Parri. *Concepts of Deity*. London: Macmillan, 1971.

Pagels, Elaine. "The Demiurge and his Archons: A Gnostic View of the Bishop and Presbyters?" *Harvard Theological Review* 69/3–4 (1976): 301–24.

———. *The Gnostic Gospels*. New York: Random House, 1979.

Pardee, Dennis. *Ritual and Cult at Ugarit*. Atlanta: Society of Biblical Literature, 2002.

———. "A New Aramaic Inscription from Zincirli." *Bulletin of the American Schools of Oriental Research* 356 (2009): 51–71.

Parkinson, George Henry Radcliffe. "Hegel, Pantheism, and Spinoza." *Journal of the History of Ideas* 38/3 (1977): 449–59.

Pausanias. *Description of Greece*. Translated by W.H.S. Jones. 5 vols. Loeb Classical Library. Cambridge, Mass.: Harvard University Press, 1935.

Peregrine, Peter, and Melvin Ember, eds. *Encyclopedia of Prehistory*, vol. 3: *East Asia and Oceania*. New York: Springer, 2001.

Peters, Joris, et al. "Early Animal Husbandry in the Northern Levant." *Paléorient* 25/2 (1999): 27–48.

Pettitt, Paul. *The Palaeolithic Origins of Human Burial*. New York: Routledge, 2010.

Pettitt, Paul, and Alistair Pike. "Dating European Palaeolithic Cave Art: Progress, Prospects, Problems." *Journal of Archaeological Method and Theory* 14/1 (2007): 27–47.

Pettitt, Paul, et al. "New Views on Old Hands: The Context of Stencils in El Castillo and La Garma Caves (Cantabria, Spain)." *Antiquity* 88 (2014): 47–63.

Piaget, Jean. "Children's Philosophies." Pages 534–47 in *A Handbook of Child Psychology*. Edited by C. Murchison. Worcester, Mass.: Clark University Press, 1933.

———. *The Child's Conception of the World*. New Jersey: Littlefield, Adams, 1960.

Picton, J. Allanson. "Pantheism: Some Preliminary Observations." *New England Review*: 24/1 (2003): 224–27.

Pike, Alistair, et al. "U-Series Dating of Paleolithic Art in 11 Caves in Spain." *Science* 336 (2012): 1409–13.

Pitulko, Vladimir V., et al. "Early Human Presence in the Arctic: Evidence from 45,000-Year-Old Mammoth Remains." *Science* 351/6270 (2016): 260–63.

Pollack, Gloria Wiederkehr. "Eliezer Zvi Hacohen Zweifel: Forgotten Father of Modern Scholarship on Hasidism." *Proceedings of the American Academy for Jewish Research* 49 (1982): 87–115.

Pope, Marvin H. *El in the Ugaritic Texts.* Leiden: Brill, 1955.

Potts, Daniel T. "Accounting for Religion: Uruk and the Origins of the Sacred Economy." Pages 17–23 in *Religion: Perspectives from the Engelsberg Seminar 2014.* Stockholm: Axel and Margaret Ax:son Johnson Foundation, 2014.

Preuss, Horst Dietrich. *Old Testament Theology.* Louisville: Westminster John Knox Press, 1995.

Radcliffe-Brown, Alfred Reginald. *Structure and Function in Primitive Society: Essays and Addresses.* New York: Free Press, 1952.

———. "Taboo." Pages 46–56 in *Reader in Comparative Religion: An Anthropological Approach.* Edited by William A. Lessa and Evon Z. Vogt. New York: Harper and Row, 1979.

Radhakrishnan, Sarvepalli. "The Vedanta Philosophy and the Doctrine of Maya." *International Journal of Ethics* 24/4 (1914): 431–51.

Rainey, Anson F. "Israel in Merneptah's Inscription and Reliefs." *Israel Exploration Journal* 51/1 (2001): 57–75.

Rauf, Bulent. "Concerning the Universality of Ibn 'Arabi." *Journal of the Muhyiddin Ibn 'Arabi Society,* vol. 6, 1987.

Redford, Donald B. *Akhenaten the Heretic King.* Princeton: Princeton University Press, 1984.

———. "The Sun-Disc in Akhenaten's Program: Its Worship and Antecedents, I." *Journal of the American Research Center in Egypt* 13 (1976): 47–61.

———. "The Sun-Disc in Akhenaten's Program: Its Worship and Antecedents, II." *Journal of the American Research Center in Egypt* 17 (1980): 21–38.

Reed, Robert C. "An Interpretation of Some Anthropomorphic Representations from the Upper Palaeolithic." *Current Anthropology* 17/1 (1976): 136–38.

Rendu, William, et al. "Evidence Supporting an Intentional Neandertal Burial at La Chapelle-aux-Saints." *Proceedings of the National Academy of Sciences of the United States of America* 111/1 (2014): 81–86.

Reynolds, Gabriel Said. *The Emergence of Islam: Classical Traditions in Contemporary Perspective.* Minneapolis: Fortress Press, 2012.

Rice, Patricia C., and Ann L. Paterson. "Cave Art and Bones: Exploring the Interrelationships." *American Anthropologist,* New Series, 87/1 (1985): 94–100.

———. "Validating the Cave Art–Archeofaunal Relationship in Cantabrian Spain." *American Anthropologist,* New Series, 88/3 (1986): 658–67.

Riel-Salvatore, Julien, and Geoffrey A. Clark. "Grave Markers: Middle and Early Upper Paleolithic Burials and the Use of Chronotypology in Contemporary Paleolithic Research." *Current Anthropology* 42/4 (2001): 449–79.

Riel-Salvatore, Julien, and Claudine Gravel-Miguel. "Upper Palaeolithic Mortuary Practices in Eurasia: A Critical Look at the Burial Record." Pages 303–46 in *The Oxford Handbook of the Archaeology of Death and Burial.* Edited by Sarah Tarlow and Liv Nilsson Stutz. Oxford: Oxford University Press, 2013.

Riesebrodt, Martin. *The Promise of Salvation: A Theory of Religion.* Chicago: University of Chicago Press, 2010.

Robins, Gay. "The Representation of Sexual Characteristics in Amarna Art." *Journal of the Society for the Study of Egyptian Antiquities* 23 (1993): 29–41.

Rollefson, Gary. "2001: An Archaeological Odyssey." *Cambridge Archaeological Journal* 11/01 (2001): 112–14.

Rossano, Matt J. "Supernaturalizing Social Life: Religion and the Evolution of Human Cooperation." *Human Nature* 18/3 (2007): 272–94.

———. "Ritual Behaviour and the Origins of Modern Cognition." *Cambridge Archaeological Journal* 19/2 (2009): 249–50.

Rowe, William. "Does Panentheism Reduce to Pantheism? A Response to Craig." *International Journal for Philosophy of Religion* 61/2 (2007): 65–67.

Safi, Omid. "Did the Two Oceans Meet? Historical Connections and Disconnections Between Ibn 'Arabi and Rumi." *Journal of Muhyiddin Ibn 'Arabi Society* 26 (1999): 55–88.

Sahly, Ali. *Les Mains mutilées dans l'art préhistorique.* Toulouse: privately published, 1966.

Sampson, Geoffrey. *Writing Systems: A Linguistic Introduction.* Palo Alto: Stanford University Press, 1990.

Sandman, Maj. *Texts from the Time of Akhenaten.* Bruxelles: Édition de la Fondation Égyptologique Reine Élisabeth, 1938.

Schimmel, Annemarie. *I Am Wind, You Are Fire: The Life and Works of Rumi.* Boston and London: Shambhala, 1992.

Schjoedt, Uffe. "The Religious Brain: A General Introduction to the Experimental Neuroscience of Religion." *Method and Theory in the Study of Religion* 21/3 (2009): 310–39.

Schloen, J. David, and Amir S. Fink. "New Excavations at Zincirli Höyük in Turkey (Ancient Sam'al) and the Discovery of an Inscribed Mortuary Stele." *Bulletin of the American Schools of Oriental Research* 356 (2009): 1–13.

Schloss, Jeffrey, and Michael J. Murray. *The Believing Primate: Scientific, Philosophical, and Theological Reflections on the Origin of Religion.* Oxford: Oxford University Press, 2009.

Schneider, Laurel. *Beyond Monotheism: A Theology of Multiplicity.* London: Routledge, 2007.

Sellers, Robert Victor. *Council of Chalcedon: A Historical and Doctrinal Survey.* London: SPCK, 1953.

Selz, Gebhard. " 'The Holy Drum, the Spear, and the Harp': Towards an Understanding of the Problems of Deification in Third Millennium Mesopotamia." Pages 167–209 in *Sumerian Gods and Their Representations.* Edited by I. J. Finkel and M. J. Geller. Groningen: Styx, 1997.

Shafer, Byron E., ed. *Religion in Ancient Egypt: Gods, Myths and Personal Practice.* Ithaca and London: Cornell University Press, 1991.

Sharpe, Kevin, and Leslie Van Gelder. "Human Uniqueness and Upper Paleolithic 'Art': An Archaeologist's Reaction to Wentzel van Huyssteen's Gifford Lectures." *American Journal of Theology & Philosophy* 28/3 (2007): 311–45.

Shaviv, Samuel. "The Polytheistic Origins of the Biblical Flood Narrative." *Vetus Testamentum* 54/4 (2004): 527–48.

Shaw, Ian, ed. *The Oxford History of Ancient Egypt.* Oxford: Oxford University Press, 2003.

Shear, Jonathan. "On Mystical Experiences as Support for the Perennial

Philosophy." *Journal of the American Academy of Religion* 62/2 (1994): 319–42.

Shults, LeRon. "Spiritual Entanglement: Transforming religious symbols at Çatalhöyiik." Pages 73–98 *in Religion in the Emergence of Civilization: Çatalhöyiik as a Case Study*. Edited by Ian Hodder. Cambridge: Cambridge University Press, 2010.

Siddiqi, Mazheruddin. "A Historical Study of Iqbal's Views on Sufism." *Islamic Studies* 5/4 (1966): 411–27.

Silverman, David. "The Nature of Egyptian Kingship." Pages 49–94 in *Ancient Egyptian Kingship*. Edited by David O'Connor and David P. Silverman. Leiden: Brill, 1995.

Simmons, Allan. *The Neolithic Revolution in the Near East: Transforming the Human Landscape*. Tucson: University of Arizona Press, 2007.

Smart, Ninian. *Dimensions of the Sacred: An Anatomy of the World's Beliefs*. Berkeley: University of California Press, 1996.

Smith, Huston. *The World's Religions: Our Great Wisdom Traditions*. New York: HarperCollins, 1991.

———. "Is There a Perennial Philosophy?" *Journal of the American Academy of Religion* 55/3 (1987): 553–66.

Smith, Mark S. *The Early History of God: Yahweh and the Other Deities in Ancient Israel*. 2nd ed. Grand Rapids: Eerdmans, 2002.

Smith, Morton. *Studies in the Cult of Yahweh*. 2 vols. Leiden: Brill, 1996.

———. "The Common Theology of the Ancient Near East." *Journal of Biblical Literature* 71/3 (1952): 135–47.

Smith, Noel. *An Analysis of Ice Age Art: Its Psychology and Belief System*. American University Studies: Series XX, "Fine Arts," vol. 15 (book 15). New York: Peter Lang, 1992.

Smith, W. Robertson. *Lectures on the Religion of the Semites: Fundamental Institutions*. New York: Ktav Publishers, 1969.

Snow, Dean R. "Sexual Dimorphism in Upper Palaeolithic Hand Stencils." *Antiquity* 80 (2006): 390–404.

———. "Sexual Dimorphism in European Upper Paleolithic Cave Art." *American Antiquity* 4 (2013): 746–61.

Sobat, Erin. "The Pharaoh's Sun-Disc: The Religious Reforms of Akhenaten and the Cult of the Aten." *Hirundo: McGill Journal of Classical Studies* 12 (2013–2014): 70–75.

Sprigge, Timothy Lauro Squire. "Pantheism." *Monist* 80/2 (1997): 191–217.

Sproul, Barbara C. *Primal Myths*. New York: HarperCollins, 1991.

Srinivasan, Doris. "Vedic Rudra-Śiva." *Journal of the American Oriental Society* 103/3 (1983): 543–56.

Stone, Alby. *Explore Shamanism*. Loughborough, U.K.: Explore Books, 2003.

Stringer, Chris. *Lone Survivors: How We Came to Be the Only Humans on Earth*. New York: Henry Holt and Company, 2012.

Stringer, Martin D. "Rethinking Animism: Thoughts from the Infancy of Our Discipline." *Journal of the Royal Anthropological Institute* 5/4 (1999): 541–55.

Struble, Eudora J., and Virginia Rimmer Herrmann. "An Eternal Feast at Sam'al: The New Iron Age Mortuary Stele from Zincirli in Context." *Bulletin of the American Schools of Oriental Research* 356 (2009): 15–49.

Taraporewala, Irach J. S. *The Divine Songs of Zarathustra: A Philological Study of the Gathas of Zarathustra, Containing the Text and Literal Translation into English, a Free English Rendering and Full Critical and Grammatical Notes, Metrical Index and Glossary*. Bombay: D. B. Taraporevala Sons, 1951.

Tattersall, Ian. *Becoming Human: Evolution and Human Uniqueness*. New York: Harvest, 1999.

Tertullian, *Apologetical Works,* and Minucius Felix, *Octavius*. Translated by Rudolph Arbesmann, Sister Emily Joseph Daly, and Edwin A. Quain. Fathers of the Church, volume 10. Washington, D.C.: The Catholic University of America Press, 1950.

Teske, Roland. "The Aim of Augustine's Proof that God Truly Is." *International Philosophical Quarterly* 26 (1986): 253–68.

Thomassen, Einar. "Orthodoxy and Heresy in Second-Century Rome." *Harvard Theological Review* 97/3 (2004): 241–56.

Tobin, Frank. "Mysticism and Meister Eckhart." *Mystics Quarterly* 10/1 (1984): 17–24.

Treves, Marco. "The Reign of God in the O.T." *Vetus Testamentum* 19/2 (1969): 230–43.

Tylor, Edward Burnett. *Primitive Culture*. London: J. Murray, 1889.

Ucko, Peter. "Subjectivity and the Recording of Palaeolithic Cave Art." Pages 141–80 in *The Limitations of Archaeological Knowledge*. Edited by T. Shay and J. Clottes. Liege: University of Liege Press, 1992.

Urquhart, William Spence. *Pantheism and the Values of Life with Special Reference to Indian Philosophy*. London: Epworth Press, 1919.

———. "The Fascination of Pantheism." *International Journal of Ethics* 21/3 (1911): 313–26.

VanderKam, James. *The Dead Sea Scrolls Today.* 2nd ed. Grand Rapids: Eerdmans, 2010.

van der Toorn, Karel. *Family Religion in Babylonia, Ugarit, and Israel: Continuity and Change in the Forms of Religious Life.* Leiden: Brill, 1996.

van Inwagen, Peter. "Explaining Belief in the Supernatural: Some Thoughts on Paul Bloom's 'Religious Belief as an Evolutionary Accident.'" Pages 128–38 in *The Believing Primate: Scientific, Philosophical, and Theological Reflections on the Origin of Religion.* Edited by Jeffrey Schloss and Michael Murray. Oxford: Oxford University Press, 2009.

VanPool, Christine S., and Elizabeth Newsome. "The Spirit in the Material: A Case Study of Animism in the American Southwest." *American Antiquity* 77/2 (2012): 243–62.

Verhoeven, Marc. "The Birth of a Concept and the Origins of the Neolithic: A History of Prehistoric Farmers in the Near East." *Paléorient* 37/1 (2001): 75–87.

Vinnicombe, Patricia. *People of Eland: Rock Paintings of the Drakensberg Bushmen as a Reflection of Their Life and Thought.* 2nd ed. Johannesburg: Wits University Press, 2009.

von Franz, Marie-Louise. *Creation Myths.* Boston: Shambhala, 1995.

Walker, Williston. *A History of the Christian Church.* New York: Scribner, 1918.

Walton, John H. *Ancient Near Eastern Thought and the Old Testament: Introducing the Conceptual World of the Hebrew Bible.* 3rd ed. Grand Rapids: Baker Academic, 2009.

Watkins, Trevor. "Building Houses, Framing Concepts, Constructing Worlds." *Paléorient* 30/1 (2004): 5–23.

Weinberg, Saul S. "A Review Article: Man's Earliest Art." *Archaeology* 6/3 (1953): 174–80.

Weisdorf, Jacob L. "From Foraging to Farming: Explaining the Neolithic Revolution." *Journal of Economic Surveys* 19/4 (2005): 561–86.

Wengrow, David. "Gods and Monsters: Image and Cognition in Neolithic Societies." *Paléorient* 37/1 (2011): 154–63.

Wensinck, Arent Jan. "The Two Creeds, Fikh Akbar II." Pages 1553–59 in *The Norton Anthology of World Religions: Volume II.* Edited by Jack Miles. New York: W. W. Norton, 2015.

West, Martin. "Towards Monotheism." Pages 21–40 in *Pagan Monothe-ism in Late Antiquity*. Edited by Polymnia Athanassiadi and Michael Frede. Oxford: Oxford University Press, 1999.

White, Randall. *Prehistoric Art: The Symbolic Journey of Humankind*. New York: Harry N. Abrams, 2003.

Williams, David Salter. "Reconsidering Marcion's Gospel." *Journal of Biblical Literature* 108/3 (1989): 477–96.

Williams, Lukyn. *Dialogue with Trypho the Jew*. New York: Macmillan, 1930.

Wilson, David Sloan. *Darwin's Cathedral: Evolution, Religion, and the Nature of Society*. Chicago: University of Chicago Press, 2002.

Wise, Michael. *Language and Literacy in Roman Judaea: A Study of the Bar Kokhba Documents*. New Haven: Yale University Press, 2015.

Wisse, Frederik. "The Apocryphon of John." Pages 104–23 in *The Nag Hammadi Library in English*. Edited by James M. Robinson. San Francisco: HarperSanFrancisco, 1978.

Wobst, H. Martin. "The Archaeo-Ethnology of Hunter-Gatherers or the Tyranny of the Ethnographic Record in Archaeology." *American Antiquity* 43/2 (1978): 303–309.

Wolf, Laibl. *Practical Kabbalah: A Guide to Jewish Wisdom for Everyday Life*. New York: Three Rivers Press, 1999.

Wood, Bryant. "The Rise and Fall of the 13th-Century Exodus-Conquest Theory." *Journal of the Evangelical Theological Society* 48/3 (2005): 475–89.

Wray, Tina J., and Gregory Mobley. *The Birth of Satan: Tracing the Devil's Biblical Roots*. New York: Palgrave Macmillan, 2005.

Wynn, Thomas, and Frederick Coolidge. "Beyond Symbolism and Language: An Introduction to Supplement 1, *Working Memory*." *Current Anthropology* 51 (2010): S5–S16.

Wynn, Thomas, Frederick Coolidge, and Martha Bright. "Hohlenstein-Stadel and the Evolution of Human Conceptual Thought." *Cambridge Archaeological Journal* 19/1 (2009): 73–84.

Yarshater, Ehsan, ed. *Mystical Poems of Rumi*. Chicago: University of Chicago Press, 2008.

Zagorska, Ilga. "The Use of Ochre in Stone Age Burials of the East Baltic." Pages 115–24 in *The Materiality of Death: Bodies, Burials, Beliefs*. Edited by Fredrik Fahlander and Terje Oestigaard. Oxford: Archaeopress, 2008.

Zarrinkoob, Abdol-Hosein. "Persian Sufism in Its Historical Perspective." *Iranian Studies* 3/4 (1970): 139–220.

Zeder, Melinda A. "Religion and the Revolution: The Legacy of Jacques Cauvin." *Paléorient* 37/1 (2011): 39–60.

Zimmerli, Walther. *Old Testament Theology in Outline*. Edinburgh: T&T Clark, 1978.

Notes

INTRODUCTION: IN OUR IMAGE

1. Subsequent studies of children have shown that while it is true that their concepts of God are dependent upon their understanding of people in general and their parents in particular, they do not treat God as being limited by human abilities. For example, when asked to account for the origins of natural objects such as large rocks or mountains, four-year-olds credited God, not people. See Jean Piaget, *The Child's Conception of the World* (Paterson, N.J.: Littlefield, Adams, 1960), and Nicola Knight, Paulo Sousa, Justin L. Barrett, and Scott Atran, "Children's Attributions of Beliefs to Humans and God: Cross-Cultural Evidence," *Cognitive Science* 28 (2004): 117–126.

2. Ludwig Feuerbach, *The Essence of Christianity* (New York: Pantheon, 1957), 58.

3. Much of my theory on the humanization of god is reliant on the anthropologist Stewart Guthrie, one of the foremost theorists on the subject. In *Faces in the Clouds: A New Theory of Religion* (New York: Oxford University Press, 1995), Guthrie posits that all forms of religiosity can be traced down to some form of anthropomorphism. This occurs, according to the theory, because there are innate cogni-

tive structures that psychologically bias humans to find persons in their natural, social, and cosmological environment. Anthropomorphizing the world, according to Guthrie, "is a good bet because the world is uncertain, ambiguous, and in need of interpretation. It is a good bet because the most valuable interpretations usually are those that disclose the presence of whatever is most important to us. That usually is other humans" (3).

Guthrie's argument can be outlined in three aspects. First, he forms a theoretical basis for his argument, suggesting that religion consists of seeing the world as humanlike. He offers ethnographic data as evidence for his claim, citing animistic ideas of souls and spirits to gods, mythical beings, and even natural phenomena like the flight of birds, earthquakes, and other disasters. Second, he examines why viewing religion as essentially anthropomorphizing the world is plausible. He gives four reasons: (1) our world is ambiguous and perpetually inchoate, (2) our first need therefore is to interpret it, (3) interpretation gambles on the most significant possibilities, and (4) the most significant possibilities are humanlike. Third, he offers evidence from the cognitive sciences and developmental psychology to support the claims made above. In general, Guthrie sees religiosity as a sort of wager against perceived instabilities in nature. His main concern is not to establish or document how religion is important in society, but rather to generate a theory that explains the origins of religious behavior.

4. In the larger and more mainstream Mahayana branch of Buddhism (as opposed to the smaller, less theistic Theravada branch), the Buddha's appearance on earth is traditionally viewed as the manifestation of pure dharma, but in human form. On devas as humanized godlike spirits, see Ninian Smart, *Dimensions of the Sacred: An Anatomy of the World's Beliefs* (Berkeley: University of California Press, 1996).

5. According to studies done by the cognitive psychologist Justin Barrett, religiously devout participants, when given questionnaires to reflect on what properties they believed God has, routinely provided "theologically correct" answers about God being omnipresent or omniscient, having infallible perception or unlimited attention. However, in conversation, these same participants were also equally willing to attribute certain properties to God—such as having a lim-

ited focus of attention, or exhibiting fallible perception, or simply not knowing everything—that contradicted each and every one of their written answers. See Justin L. Barrett, "Theological Correctness: Cognitive Constraint and the Study of Religion," *Method and Theory in the Study of Religion* 11 (1998): 325–39, and "Cognitive Constraints on Hindu Concepts of the Divine," *Journal for the Scientific Study of Religion* 37 (1998): 608–19.

1. ADAM AND EVE IN EDEN

1. Humans first evolved from apes (*Australopithecus*) some 2.5 million years ago in East Africa, from which they eventually migrated to settle in North Africa, Europe, and Asia. For much of the next two million years, there were numerous genera of humans (Homo) occupying the earth, including *Homo neanderthalensis, Homo erectus, Homo soloensis, Homo denisova, Homo ergaster,* and so on. European *Homo sapiens* are sometimes referred to as Cro-Magnon, named after the discovery of five *Homo sapiens* skeletons in 1868 in a cave of the same name near the village of Les Eyzies, France. The theory generally known as the "recent single-origin hypothesis" holds that anatomically modern humans evolved in Africa some 200,000 years ago and that around 125,000 years ago, one branch of these early humans, *Homo sapiens,* began to migrate to and settle in Eurasia, where they replaced an earlier human species, Neanderthals. This theory has recently been corroborated by DNA evidence. However, a recent discovery of *Homo sapiens* fossils in Jebel Irhoud, Morocco, dating to at least 300,000 B.P. [Before the Present], suggests that our species may be older than originally thought. See Jean-Jacques Hublin et al., "New Fossils from Jebel Irhoud, Morocco, and the Pan-African Origin of *Homo sapiens,*" *Nature* 546 (June 8, 2017): 289–92.

Some researchers argue convincingly that the origins of *Homo sapiens* can be found not in East or South Africa, as is often presumed, but rather in North Africa, and 50,000 years earlier than the previous estimate of 60,000 to 70,000 years ago. On this point see Jean-Jacques Hublin and Shannon P. McPherron, eds., *Modern Origins: A North African Perspective* (New York: Springer, 2012), and Simon J. Armitage et al., "The Southern Route 'Out of Africa': Evidence for an Early Expansion of Modern Humans into Arabia," *Science* 331/6016 (2011): 453–56.

It is commonly believed that *Homo sapiens* and Neanderthals shared Europe for at least ten thousand years, probably between 40,000 and 30,000 B.C.E., and there is ample evidence of cross-breeding between these two species (all living non-Africans possess approximately 2 percent Neanderthal DNA). A likely explanation for this discovery is that Neanderthals and *Homo sapiens* interbred during the Upper Paleolithic Period. However, a recent discovery of a bone found on the banks of a Siberian river has been traced to a man related to both humans and Neanderthals who lived as long as 45,000 years ago. Because researchers estimate that mating with Neanderthals took place 7,000 to 10,000 years before the Siberian man lived, that could place human/Neanderthal interbreeding as far back as 60,000 years ago. See Richard E. Green et al., "A Draft Sequence of the Neanderthal Genome," *Science* 328 (2010): 701–22, and Jennifer Viegas, "45,000-Year-Old Man Was Human-Neanderthal Mix," abc.net.au/science/articles/2014/10/23/4113107.htm.

2. An excellent primer on the lives of our *Homo sapiens* ancestors is Ian Tattersall, *Becoming Human: Evolution and Human Uniqueness* (New York: Harvest, 1999); the best and most accessible introduction to the role of women in Paleolithic societies is *The Invisible Sex,* by J. M. Adovasio, Olga Soffer, and Jake Page (New York: HarperCollins, 2007).

3. "Body decoration," notes Gillian Morris-Kay, "is likely to have been an important precursor to the creation of art separate from the body. The use of colour to decorate skin, bones and beads suggests enjoyment of form and colour. The practice of piercing teeth, shells and bones, and stringing them, singly or multiply, to make a pendant or necklace is the oldest known form of personal decoration after body painting." Gillian Morris-Kay, "The Evolution of Human Artistic Creativity," *Journal of Anatomy* 216 (2010): 161.

4. The skull of a woman was found at the Le Mas-d'Azil cave in southwestern France whose empty eye sockets were decorated with carved bone to simulate a gaze and whose lower jaw seems to have been replaced with that of a reindeer. The skull is dated to the Magdalenian period, about 12,000 B.C.E.

According to Paul Pettitt, "mortuary activity was fully symbolically structured after 30,000 BP, possibly beforehand; and that a degree of symbolic underpinning is evident in Middle Palaeolithic
burial back to 100,000 BP." Paul Pettitt, *The Palaeolithic Origins of
Human Burial* (New York: Routledge, 2011), 269.

"While Paleolithic burials are clear indications of concepts of afterlife," argues Brian Hayden, "they also raise the possibility of the
existence of very early forms of ancestral cults. Up until about
150,000 years ago, there does not seem to have been any form of
burial. When individuals died, they must have been simply left on the
ground to decay or to be stripped of their flesh, just as Tibetans leave
bodies in the open to be consumed by animals. . . . It is also possible
that early humans could have placed bodies on raised platforms or in
trees so that birds and insects rather than carnivores would consume
the bodies. . . . What is most significant when burials begin to appear
in the archaeological record is that there is not a wholesale change in
this traditional practice. It is not as though a new belief and ritual
system replaced the old practices, and it is not the case that people
had suddenly become more conscious of hygiene . . . nor that they
had suddenly developed awareness of death. Rather, burial is clearly
symbolic. It requires special efforts and is often accompanied by fires
or symbolic offerings or selections of special stones." Brian Hayden,
Shamans, Sorcerers and Saints (Washington, D.C.: Smithsonian,
2003), 115.

I certainly agree with David Wengrow that "if we are searching for
a sustained interest in the cultural realization of composite beings
among early hunter-gatherers, we are more likely to find it in the funerary record of Palaeolithic and Mesolithic societies—extending
back in time to the earliest attested combinations of human and animal parts in deliberate formations, within the burials of Skhul and
Qafzeh caves (ca 100–80,000 B.C.), and forwards to the so-called 'shamanic' grave assemblages of the Natufian period—rather than in their
surviving pictorial art." David Wengrow, "Gods and Monsters: Image
and Cognition in Neolithic Societies," *Paléorient* 37/1 (2011): 154–55.

5. A note about the word "soul." Clearly this is a "Western" word that
carries specific religious connotations and should not be applied to
all religious faiths. As used here, however, it is a byword for "spiritual

essence" and can, if you like, be replaced with "mind." For one of the earliest uses of the word "soul," see the recent discovery of a stele at Zincirli (ancient Sam'al) near modern-day Gaziantep, Turkey, in Dennis Pardee, "A New Aramaic Inscription from Zincirli," *Bulletin of the American Schools of Oriental Research* 356 (2009): 51–71; J. David Schloen and Amir S. Fink, "New Excavations at Zincirli Höyük in Turkey (Ancient Sam'al) and the Discovery of an Inscribed Mortuary Stele," *Bulletin of the American Schools of Oriental Research* 356 (2009): 1–13; and Eudora J. Struble and Virginia Rimmer Herrmann, "An Eternal Feast at Sam'al: The New Iron Age Mortuary Stele from Zincirli in Context," *Bulletin of the American Schools of Oriental Research* 356 (2009): 15–49.

6. Although it is unanimously agreed that Upper Paleolithic Period (UPP) humans buried their dead, there is still a great deal of debate over whether the practice also existed in the Middle and Lower Paleolithic periods. See Julien Riel-Salvatore and Geoffrey A. Clark, "Grave Markers: Middle and Early Upper Paleolithic Burials and the Use of Chronotypology in Contemporary Paleolithic Research," *Current Anthropology* 42/4 (2001): 449–79.

    "For several decades," notes William Rendu, "scholars have questioned the existence of burial in Western Europe prior to the arrival of Anatomically Modern Humans. Therefore, an approach combining a global field recovery and the reexamination of the previously discovered Neandertal remains has been undertaken in the site of La Chapelle-aux-Saints (France), where the hypothesis of a Neandertal burial was raised for the first time. This project has concluded that the Neandertal of La Chapelle-aux-Saints was deposited in a pit dug by other members of its group and protected by a rapid covering from any disturbance. These discoveries attest the existence of West European Neandertal burial and of the Neandertal cognitive capacity to produce it." William Rendu, "Evidence Supporting an Intentional Neandertal Burial at La Chapelle-aux-Saints," *Proceedings of the National Academy of Sciences of the United States of America* 111/1 (2014): 81.

    The earliest and least controversial material evidence for Neanderthal burials comes from interment sites at Skhul and Qafzeh, in Israel, dating to about 100,000 years ago. However, Neanderthal bones have been found buried throughout Europe and Asia, for instance in Teshik Tash, Central Asia, and in Shanidar, Iraq, where a large cave was discovered with several Neanderthals buried in it. Some of these burials indicate cannibalistic activity. See Rainer Grun et al., "U-series and ESR Analyses of Bones and Teeth Relating to the Human Burials from Skhul," *Journal of Human Evolution* 49/3 (2005): 316–34, and André Leroi-Gourhan, *The Hunters of Prehistory,* trans. Claire Jacobson (New York: Atheneum, 1989), 52.

7. Animism is not really a religion, of course; at that point in our evolution, there was simply no such thing. Better to think of animism as a belief system, a lens through which Adam and Eve viewed the world and their place in it.

8. There is no shortage of theories about the meaning and use of Paleolithic cave art. There are those who follow the "art for art's sake" model, wherein no inherent meaning is prescribed to cave art. Although this theory, which is primarily driven by a low estimation of prehistoric man's cognitive abilities, has been more or less abandoned in modern scholarship, it still has some contemporary proponents, for example John Halverson, who writes, "It is proposed that cave art has no 'meaning' in any ordinary sense of the word, no religious, mythic, or metaphysical reference, no magical or practical purpose. It is to be understood, rather, as a reflection of an early stage of cognitive development, the beginnings of abstraction in the form of represented images. The activity would have been autotelic, a kind of play, specifically a free play of signifiers. Thus Paleolithic art may well have been, in a fairly precise and instructive sense, art for art's sake." John Halverson, "Art for Art's Sake in the Paleolithic," *Current Anthropology* 28/1 (1987): 63. Many other scholars view Paleolithic cave art as a means of information exchange. For instance, cave art may be a reflection of "demographic stress" resulting from the "closing of social networks under conditions of increasing population density." According to Barton, Clark, and Cohen, cave art produced during the Paleolithic era might have been involved with claims for property rights. "Claims to these rights could have been expressed symbolically through art. While portable art could conceivably have served this function, parietal art would more effectively have communicated claims of eminent domain by visibly (and 'permanently') modifying the landscape." See C. Michael Barton, G. A. Clark, and Allison E. Cohen, "Art as Information: Explaining Upper Palaeolithic Art in

Western Europe," *World Archaeology* 26/2 (1994): 199–200. See also
Clive Gamble, "Interaction and Alliance in Palaeolithic Society,"
Man 17/1 (1982): 92–107, and *The Palaeolithic Settlement of Europe*
(Cambridge: Cambridge University Press, 1986), and Michael Jo-
chim, "Palaeolithic Cave Art in Ecological Perspective," in *Hunter-
Gatherer Economy in Prehistory,* ed. G. N. Bailey (Cambridge:
Cambridge University Press, 1983), 212–19.

Those who subscribe to the structuralist argument posit that Paleolithic cave art is an expression of a larger worldview, cosmology, or
system of thought that rigidly organized Paleolithic life and culture
into a universal pattern of meaning. The originator and most prominent proponent of this theory was André Leroi-Gourhan, who nevertheless rejected the religious significance of the caves. According to
Leroi-Gourhan and Michelson, "We would, in this case, possess not
the vestiges of practices, as the older prehistorians believed, not even
a religion or a metaphysics, but rather an infrastructural framework
which could serve as a basis for an infinite number of detailed moral
symbols and operational practices . . . the themes which emerge from
Paleolithic art more directly invite psychoanalytical study than that
of the history of religion . . ." André Leroi-Gourhan and Annette
Michelson, "The Religion of the Caves: Magic or Metaphysics?" *October* 37 (1986): 16.

Perhaps the most well-known theory of Paleolithic cave art involves the notion of "sympathetic magic." In brief, this theory holds
that cave art was intended to facilitate success in the hunt in a magi-
cal/spiritual sense. Such art was designed to ensure the safety of the
hunters and yield sustenance by giving the artists/hunters spiritual
and physical power over their prey. One of the chief arguments for
this theory is the belief—mistaken, in my view, as I show in the
book—that much of the Paleolithic cave art depicts images of animals that appear to be struck by spears, bleeding, and/or with cut
marks incised on the image.

The most significant proponent of the "art as sympathetic magic"
theory was Abbé Henri Breuil, who argued that the prehistoric paintings were made in the mysterious depths of the earth in an attempt to
exert control over the natural realm. These early artists were endeavoring to ensure success in the hunt and the continued fertility of their
prey by descending into the earth's bowels (a possible relation to pro-

creation/pregnancy?) and magically capturing the spirit of certain animals in the darkest/most inaccessible recesses of the cave. Henri Breuil, *Four Hundred Centuries of Cave Art,* trans. Mary Boyle (New York: Hacker Art Books, 1979).

Finally, there are those scholars, myself among them, who argue that Paleolithic cave art is the expression of a religious impulse and therefore exudes spiritual significance. David Lewis-Williams believes that the art is the result of trancelike states (possibly drug-induced) achieved by a shaman, and that the cave itself was a kind of veil or a boundary between this world and the spirit world. See Jean Clottes and David Lewis-Williams, *The Shamans of Prehistory: Trance Magic and the Painted Caves* (New York: Abrams, 1998), and David Lewis-Williams and David Pearce, *Inside the Neolithic Mind: Consciousness, Cosmos, and the Realm of the God* (London: Thames and Hudson, 2005).

However, Kevin Sharpe and Leslie Van Gelder have challenged the notion that the paintings and images in the caves are religious "art." According to Sharpe and Van Gelder: "The shamanic hypothesis follows in the grand tradition of interpreting the cave 'art' in southwestern Europe by imputing religious meanings and intentions to the Upper Paleolithic creators of the 'art.' (Note that, along with many others, we use quotation marks around the word 'art' because, while the corpus of such artifacts contains some artistic images, not all of it obviously appears as such and its creators may not have intended it all as art.) The key pioneer of the discovery, recording, and interpretation of prehistoric 'art' in southwestern Europe was Henri Breuil. . . . Breuil, like his prominent successor, André Glory, was a Roman Catholic priest (the Jesuit archaeologist-theologian Pierre Teilhard de Chardin adds to the point), and it therefore seems natural that they, when confronted by the majesty of the 'art' and the awe-inspiring nature of its antiquity, read religious meaning and intention into it. They similarly approached the caves containing the 'art' by naming places 'sanctuaries,' 'cathedrals,' 'chapels,' and the like. They started a tradition that reflects the cultural ethos of late nineteenth and much of twentieth century France and Spain, and strongly continues today; all one needs to do is take a cursory glance at web sites about prehistoric art or much new age literature to see this. Lewis-Williams fits firmly into this tradition. The 'art' feels romantic and mysterious. The religious interpretation now arises automatically. It makes a good story. And it does not require the current speculators to dirty themselves in caves." Kevin Sharpe and Leslie Van Gelder, "Human Uniqueness and Upper Paleolithic 'Art': An Archaeologist's Reaction to Wentzel van Huyssteen's Gifford Lectures," *American Journal of Theology and Philosophy* 28/3 (2007): 313–14.

Obviously, I disagree with this analysis and will simply quote Lewis-Williams in response: "Notwithstanding all the variety [of parietal art in the French caves], we can discern some consistencies. The most obvious is the stunning fact that people made images deep underground, often in places where their creations could be seen by only one person at a time; many may even have been seen by the maker only. It is hard to imagine any reason for making these remote images if those ancient artists did not believe there was a nether realm filled with supernatural animals and possibly spirit beings as well. Like communities all over the world, Upper Palaeolithic people probably believed in a tiered cosmos: an underworld, the level on which human beings lived, and a realm above the sky. Just what be-ings were believed in Upper Palaeolithic times to inhabit the spiritual levels and how they may have influenced human beings is a matter for conjecture." David Lewis-Williams, "Into the Dark: Upper Palaeoli-thic Caves in Western Europe," *Digging Stick* 27/2 (2010): 5. See also Sharpe and Van Gelder, "Human Uniqueness and Upper Paleolithic 'Art,'" 311–45.

9. It is Lewis-Williams who brilliantly formulated the thesis of the "tiered cosmos" mentioned here, noting that "Upper Paleolithic peo-ple probably understood entry into the caves as equivalent to entry into an underworld. . . . The cave passages were the 'entrails' of the underworld, and the walls, floors, and ceilings were thin 'membranes' that could be penetrated for access to what lay beyond them. Activity areas were therefore subdivisions of a nether realm." David Lewis-Williams, *Conceiving God: The Cognitive Origin and Evolution of Religion* (London: Thames and Hudson, 2010), 210.

10. Other wonderfully preserved examples of cave art include Altamira and Tito Bustillo in Spain. The image from El Castillo is a "large red stippled disk" on the "Panel de las Manos." Pike et al., "U-Series Dat-ing of Paleolithic Art in 11 Caves in Spain," *Science* 336 (2012): 1411–12. See also M. Garcia-Diez, D. L. Hoffman, J. Zilhao, C. de las

Heras, J. A. Lasheras, R. Montes, and A.W.G. Pike, "Uranium Series Dating Reveals a Long Sequence of Rock Art at Altamira Cave (Santilana del Mar, Cantabria)," *Journal of Archaeological Science* 40 (2013): 4098–106.

For helpful discussions on the parietal and mobile art of the UPP, as well as its geographical distribution, age, and diversity, see Oscar Moro Abadia and Manuel R. Gonzalez Morales, "Paleolithic Art: A Cultural History," *Journal of Archaeological Research* 21 (2013): 269–306; Paul Bahn, Natalie Franklin, and Matthias Stecker, eds., *Rock Art Studies: News of the World IV* (Oxford: Oxbow Books, 2012); Gillian M. Morris-Kay, "The Evolution of Human Artistic Creativity," *Journal of Anatomy* 216 (2010): 158–76; Michel Lorblanchet, "The Origin of Art," *Diogenes* 214 (2007): 98–109; Paul Pettitt and Alistair Pike, "Dating European Palaeolithic Cave Art: Progress, Prospects, Problems," *Journal of Archaeological Method and Theory* 14/1 (2007): 27–47; Curtis Gregory, *The Cave Painters: Probing the Mysteries of the World's First Artists* (New York: Alfred A. Knopf, 2006); Gunter Berghaus, *New Perspectives on Prehistoric Art* (Westport, Conn.: Praeger, 2004); Randall White, *Prehistoric Art: The Symbolic Journey of Humankind* (New York: Harry N. Abrams, 2003); Paul Bahn, *The Cambridge Illustrated History of Prehistoric Art* (Cambridge: Cambridge University Press, 1998); and Margaret W. Conkey, "A Century of Palaeolithic Cave Art," *Archaeology* 34/4 (1981): 21–22.

11. The Volp caves were first explored by the three sons of Count Henri Bégouën, professor of prehistory at the University of Toulouse (hence the name *Les Trois-Frères*). On a lazy summer day in 1912, the brothers built themselves a homemade boat out of discarded boxes and empty gasoline cans and rowed it along a slender arm of the Volp River into the half-submerged entrance of one of the caves. Even in the semidarkness they could make out the faint etchings on the cave walls, though they could not have known then the significance of what they were seeing. Their exploration of the caves came to a halt with the launch of the First World War, as one after another, the brothers were called to the front. It wasn't until the end of the war in 1918 that the boys returned to their childhood adventures in the caves. By then, however, their father, Count Bégouën, had recognized the importance of the find and contacted his friend, the archaeologist

and French priest Henri "Abbé" Breuil. Much of my description of the Volp caves comes from the account provided by Breuil himself in *Four Hundred Centuries of Cave Art*, 153–77.

12. For more on Paleolithic "instruments," see Ian Tattersall, *Becoming Human*, 13–14, 213. According to Randall White, "There is accumulating evidence that acoustics played some role in the choice of painting locations within caves. Michel Dauvois in a study of three caves (Fontanet, Le Portal, and Niaux) has shown . . . a strong correspondence between zones of high-quality acoustics and density of paintings and engravings. This kind of research is in its infancy, but it is easy to imagine that sound quality was taken into consideration, especially if activities in the caves involved flute or lithophone music, singing, or chanting." Randall White, *Prehistoric Art*, 16.

13. Lewis-Williams argues that the dots are a record of visions (i.e., strange, otherworldly images that a shaman sees when he enters the other world) that prehistoric humans were "nailing down" after being in an "altered state of consciousness." By contrast, Leroi-Gourhan and Michelson have argued that the geometric patterns are representative of sexual organs: "[The patterns are] composed of male and female figures; genital representations; signs of very varied types which divide into two series: the first are 'full' signs (ovals, triangles, rectangles), the second are 'thin' signs (lines which are straight, hooked, or branched, and series of dots); and, finally, there are imprints of hands placed upon the wall and outlined in color. Comparison of the subjects of each series of signs leads us to see them as multiple variants of sexual symbols, masculine for the thin ones and female for the full ones." David Lewis-Williams, "Debating Rock Art: Myth and Ritual, Theories and Facts," *South African Archaeological Bulletin* 61/183 (2006): 105–11, and *The Mind in the Cave: Consciousness and the Origins of Art* (London: Thames and Hudson, 2004), and Leroi-Gourhan, "The Religion of the Caves," 12–13.

14. Ilga Zagorska writes about the symbolism of red ochre in Stone Age burial rites. "The colour red is reminiscent of natural substances sharing the same colour, such as blood. The presence of the colour red in burials is regarded as being connected with the concept of death and with the preservation of the energy of life, providing magical force for the route to the world beyond. In a wider sense, the use of ochre has been connected with the human spiritual world and the

broadening of knowledge, and in the burial context it has been related to the beginnings of symbolic thinking. . . . However, researchers have also emphasised that ochre has not been used in the same ways across space and time, and its presence or absence is not always comprehensible or interpretable." Ilga Zagorska, "The Use of Ochre in Stone Age Burials of the East Baltic," in *The Materiality of Death: Bodies, Burials, Beliefs,* ed. Fredrik Fahlander and Terje Oestigaard (Oxford: Archaeopress, 2008), 115.

Julien Riel-Salvatore and Geoffrey A. Clark note that the widespread use of ochre can be explained in functional rather than symbolic terms. "It could have provided better insulation against cold and humidity, produced smoother surfaces on ground and polished bone beads, served as an astringent or antiseptic, or even slowed down putrefaction. . . . Therefore its presence in graves may simply indicate knowledge of a useful substance that was gradually invested with aesthetic and/or ritual properties over the course of the Upper Paleolithic. Its occurrence in some of the Qafzeh burials shows that it was known (and probably used) in the Middle Paleolithic. This suggests that it may have come into widespread use only later, perhaps after 20,000 years B.P." Julien Riel-Salvatore and Geoffrey A. Clark, "Grave Markers: Middle and Early Upper Paleolithic Burials and the Use of Chronotypology in Contemporary Paleolithic Research," *Current Anthropology* 42/4 (2001): 449–79. See also Erella Hovers, Shimon Ilani, Ofer Bar-Yosef, and Bernard Vandermeersch, "An Early Case of Color Symbolism: Ochre Use by Modern Humans in Qafzeh Cave," *Current Anthropology* 44/4 (2003): 491–522.

15. One of the oldest forms of artistic expression in the Paleolithic period are the positive and negative handprints in red (most common), black, white, and yellow (least common) ochre. Whereas the positive handprints were made by placing a hand into wet pigment and pressing it against the wall of a cave, negative images were likely created by spraying pigment from the mouth around the hand, thereby creating a halo effect around the fingers, wrist, and back of the hand. A large number of caves from southern France, northern Spain, and Italy have yielded positive and negative handprints, but this particular form of expression was by no means limited to the caves of Western Europe.

The discovery of negative handprints in Indonesia that are con-

temporaneous with those of El Castillo and Altamira, not to mention
the discovery of figurative art that is as old as that of Chauvet, has
the potential to have wide-ranging consequences for our understanding of the origins and development of Upper Paleolithic art and its
meaning(s). See Paul Pettitt, A. Maximiano Castillejo, Pablo Arias,
Roberto Peredo, and Rebecca Harrison, "New Views on Old Hands:
The Context of Stencils in El Castillo and La Garma Caves (Cantabria, Spain)," *Antiquity* 88 (2014): 48; M. Aubert, A. Brumm, M.
Ramli, T. Sutikna, E. W. Saptomo, B. Hakim, M. J. Morwood, G. D.
van den Bergh, L. Kinsley, and A. Dosseto, "Pleistocene Cave Art
from Sulawesi, Indonesia," *Nature* (2014): 223–37; and Michel Lorblanchet, "Claw Marks and Ritual Traces in the Paleolithic Sanctuaries of the Quercy," in *An Enquiring Mind: Studies in Honour of
Alexander Marshack*, ed. Paul Bahn (Oxford: Oxbow Books, 2009),
165–70.

The majority of hand stencils are of the left hand rather than the
right. This would appear to have a relationship to the method that
was used to create the stencils (i.e., using the right hand to hold a
shell, container, or a strawlike device containing the pigment). Furthermore, there would appear to be a fairly strong relationship between the proximity of the handprints to cracks, depressions, and
bumps within the caves. Hand stencils, note Pettitt et al., "are found
in obvious association with natural features, notably fissures, convex
bosses and concave depressions. . . . In total 80% of observable stencils at La Garma and 74% at El Castillo have some kind of association, either with fissures or undulations on the caves' surfaces. As
areas of 'smooth' rock were easily accessible in each cave and within
close proximity to stencils, such associations cannot be entirely for-
tuitous. Some stencils seem to have been 'fitted' to subtle topographic features in the wall, and some were positioned on bosses in
the wall in such a manner that they appear to be 'gripping' the wall
in a similar way that explorers use their hands to steady themselves
when navigating the caves." Paul Pettitt et al., "New Views on Old
Hands," 53.

In two separate articles, Dean Snow has argued that women were
responsible for the majority of negative handprints dating to the UPP.
After analyzing 32 stencils from 8 caves in Spain and France, Snow

concluded that women were responsible for 24 of the 32 prehistoric handprints in his study (i.e., 75 percent). And in spite of the fact that Snow's algorithm was able to identify the sex of modern men and women from their handprints only 60 percent of the time, he claims that the sexual dimorphism of the earliest *Homo sapiens* was far more pronounced in the UPP than it is today. Snow's detractors aside, this new hypothesis raises some interesting questions about the art of the Upper Paleolithic Period. Namely, which of the two sexes, if either, was primarily responsible for the art of this period? And if women *were* primarily responsible for the creation of parietal art, then how might this affect the theories of Breuil and Lewis-Williams, who have argued that the paintings and images were related to "sympathetic magic" or the altered states of consciousness that were experienced by shamans? Finally, does the gender of the artist have any bearing whatsoever on the meaning, intentionality, or purpose of Upper Paleolithic art? See Dean Snow, "Sexual Dimorphism in Upper Palaeolithic Hand Stencils," *Antiquity* 80 (2006): 390–404, and "Sexual Dimorphism in European Upper Paleolithic Cave Art," *American Antiquity* 4 (2013): 746–61.

In the cave of Gargas (discovered in 1906), which is located in the Pyrenees region of southern France, more than 150 hand stencils dating to between 27,000 and 25,000 B.P. have been discovered. However, unlike the stencils from other Upper Paleolithic sites, a large number of the handprints from Gargas are missing fingers. Not surprisingly, these handprints have been the subject of much conjecture since Émile Cartailhac first mentioned them in print, and the various interpretations of these stencils can be boiled down to three hypotheses: (1) the "artist's" fingers were removed for sacrificial reasons (e.g., rites of passage, "sympathetic magic," or in-group/out-group identification); (2) the fingers were lost through accidental or natural means (e.g., frostbite, injury, disease, birth defect); (3) the fingers were intentionally bent so as to create different shapes and configurations (perhaps hunter/gatherer "sign language" for specific animals). Although the latter is probably the strongest of the three, none of the aforementioned hypotheses is particularly convincing.

To start with, if there were a sacrificial purpose behind the removal of digits, it stands to reason that we would be able to discern a standardized pattern to the mutilations in Gargas, yet no such pattern is visible. Similarly, if the mutilations were intentional, or if the fingers were purposefully bent so as to represent specific animals, then we would expect to see this practice represented in other caves, but comparable images are recorded in only two other caves. Furthermore, the purposeful removal of fingers is illogical in that it compromises both the safety and the productivity of the individual and his/her group, who depend upon all of their members in order to survive. Finally, several of the handprints from Gargas appear to have been made by the same person, yet different fingers are missing from one stencil to the next, which is suggestive of the bending of fingers, playfulness, or poor technique as opposed to the ritual mutilation or natural or accidental loss of fingers. See André Leroi-Gourhan, "The Hands of Gargas: Toward a General Study," *October* 37 (1986): 18–34; Ali Sahly, *Les Mains mutilées dans l'art préhistorique* (Toulouse: privately published, 1966); Breuil, *Four Hundred Centuries of Cave Art*, 246–57; and Émile Cartailhac, "Les mains inscrites de rouge ou de noir de Gargas," *L'anthropologie* 17 (1906): 624–25.

16. Regarding the symbolic nature of UPP art, Lewis-Williams notes that "the images are therefore not pictures of animals seen outside the cave, as is often supposed: there is never any painted suggestion of a ground surface . . . nor of grass, trees, rivers or indeed anything in the natural world. Rather the fixed divisions often blended with the form of the rock, a natural nodule for instance, being used as an animal's eye. Others appear to be entering or leaving the rock surface sometimes via cracks or fissures while still others are only partially drawn, the rest of the image being created by shadow when one's light is held in a certain position." David Lewis-Williams, *Inside the Neolithic Mind* (London: Thames and Hudson, 2009), 83–84.

17. Archaeological evidence from the UPP indicates there is little to no correlation between the animals featured in UPP cave art and the primary diet of *Homo sapiens*. Concerning the species of animals depicted in the art of the UPP, Leroi-Gourhan notes that "statistically speaking, the number of species represented [in the art of the UPP] is much lower than the number of species known to have existed at the time. Palaeolithic artists did not portray just any animal, but animals of certain species, and these did not necessarily play an important part their daily life." André Leroi-Gourhan, *The Dawn of European*

Art: An Introduction to Palaeolithic Cave Painting (Cambridge: Cambridge University Press, 1982), 45.

In a second publication, Leroi-Gourhan returns to this topic yet again: "This listing, in comparison with the animals most represented in the form of bone remains on the majority of settlement sites, raises questions of the representative nature of lists of animals in art. At the start one can examine a possible parallel with the traditions of the whole of Europe, with the lion and the eagle, rare and mediocre forms of food, nevertheless much more commonly represented in western heraldic art than the calf or the pig. We shall return to this question, but there are good reasons to suppose that the drawings of Paleolithic animals constituted a bestiary rather than a collection of edible species." André Leroi-Gourhan, *Treasures of Prehistoric Art* (New York: Harry Abrams, 1967), 111.

Finally, Margaret Conkey observes that "the frequency of certain animal depictions often contrasted sharply with the availability of those animals as well as how often they are found among excavated food debris. One conclusion, also suggested by Patricia Vinnicombe's *People of the Eland,* an elegant study of the rock art of the Kung of South Africa, might be the same as Lévi-Strauss's observation that certain natural species were selected in these cases as the subject of rock art not because they were 'good to eat' but because they were 'good to think.'" Margaret W. Conkey, "A Century of Palaeolithic Cave Art," *Archaeology* 34/4 (1981): 23. See also Patricia Vinnicombe, *People of Eland: Rock Paintings of the Drakensburg Bushmen as a Reflection of Their Life and Thought,* 2nd ed. (Johannesburg: Wits University Press, 2009). Lévi-Strauss's quote is from *Totemism,* trans. Rodney Needham (London: Merlin Press, 1991), 89.

As White has noted: "Another observation that would seem to refute hunting magic as an explanation for deep cave paintings (and portable representations as well) is that animals are almost never seen in postures of pain and suffering. Indeed, there is an almost total absence of violence and clear acts of hunting. When it occurs, it is truly the exception, such as the disemboweled bison in the well at Lascaux and the bow-hunting scene on a pierced baton from La Vache." Randall White, *Prehistoric Art,* 119.

18. "The cave itself," posits Leroi-Gourhan, "is integrated into the infrastructural schema, since its natural accidents are used by the artist.

These accidents are of two kinds. The first are natural reliefs which have lent their shape to the back, the neck, or the thigh of an animal which is completed by the painter, while others are fissures or galleries whose assimilation to female symbolism is demonstrated by the addition of thin signs or dots. The cave was thus 'an active participant.'" Leroi-Gourhan, "The Religion of the Caves," 16.

19. Breuil's description of the Sorcerer is particularly compelling: "First of all, the 'God' first called the 'Sorcerer' by Count Bégouën and me, the only figure painted in black of all those engravings in the Sanctuary, four meters above the floor in an apparently inaccessible position, only to be reached by a secret corridor climbing upwards in a spiral. Evidently, he presides over all the animals, collected there in incredible numbers and often in a terribly tangled mass. He is 75 cms high and 50 cms wide, he is entirely engraved, but the painting is unequally distributed: on the head there are only a few traces, on the eyes, nose, forehead and the right ear. This head is full face with round eyes with pupils; between the eyes runs a line for the nose, ending in a little arch. The pricked ears are those of a Stag. From a black painted band across the forehead rise two big thick antlers with no frontal tines but with a single short tine, fairly high above the base of each branch, bending outwards and dividing again to the right or left. This figure has no mouth, but a very long beard cut in lines and falling on the chest. The forearms, which are raised and joined horizontally, end in two hands close together, the short fingers outstretched; they are colourless and almost invisible. A wide black band outlines the whole body, growing narrower at the lumbar region, and spreading out round the legs which are bent. A spot marks the left knee-joint. The feet and big toes are rather carefully made and show a movement similar to steps in a 'Cakewalk' dance. The male sex, emphasized but not erect, pointing backwards but well developed, is inserted under the bushy tail of a Wolf or Horse, with a little tuft at the end. Such is the Magdalenian figure considered to be the most important in the cavern and which, after much thought, we consider to be the Spirit controlling the multiplication of game and hunting expeditions." Breuil, *Four Hundred Centuries of Cave Art*, 176–77.

20. This relationship with animals gives the shaman a certain power over them. He can see through the animal's eyes. They guide him in solving problems, in reading omens, or in healing the sick. According to

Jose Antonio Lasheras: "The communication which is established between different distinct levels of reality requires a celebrant, intercessor, shaman or priest, who connects with the small spirits which give life to everything, and who intervenes in or influences the apparent reality, that which is all around us and which we see all the time. It would be the celebrant-artist or the shaman who would discover in the reliefs of the ceiling the bison, the deer and the horses of Altamira, who would connect them to the things they represented. Palaeolithic art had a particular bestiary linked to an oral tradition, to particular common stories—myths—that explain their coherence and presence in the vast European landscape throughout the millennia." Jose Antonio Lasheras, "The Cave of Altamira: 22,000 Years of History," *Andoranten* (2009): 32.

21. The image at Lascaux of the so-called Bird-Headed Man depicts a human figure falling backward or lying prostrate in front of a charging bison. The attacking animal, whose horns are lowered in the direction of the man's chest, appears to have been struck in the stomach by a barbed shaft or spear. To the right of the man is an image of a stick or staff that has been adorned with a bird. Below the bison, at the point where the shaft has penetrated its body, a circular protrusion can be seen emanating from the animal's belly. Given the similarities between the facial features of the man and the bird on the staff, some have interpreted this iconic image as evidence of shamanism. See Matt Rossano, "Ritual Behaviour and the Origins of Modern Cognition," *Cambridge Archaeological Journal* 19/2 (2009): 249–50; Jean Clottes and David Lewis-Williams, *The Shamans of Prehistory: Trance and Magic in the Painted Caves* (New York: Harry Abrams, 1998), 94–95; Noel Smith, *An Analysis of Ice Age Art: Its Psychology and Belief System,* American University Studies, Series XX, "Fine Arts," vol. 15, book 15 (New York: Peter Lang, 1992); Henri Breuil and Raymond Lantier, *The Men of the Old Stone Age* (New York: St. Martin's Press, 1965), 263–64; and Jacquetta Hawkes and Sir Leonard Woolley, *Prehistory and the Beginnings of Civilization* (New York: Harper and Row, 1963), 204–205.

Perhaps the most famous human-animal hybrid from the Paleolithic era is the *Löwenmensch,* or Lion-Human, a 30,000-year-old ivory statue depicting a long-limbed man with an elaborately carved lion's head that was found in a cave in the Lone River valley region of southwestern Germany. The 28 cm statue is missing its right arm and foot; all along the left arm and around its ears are evenly spaced notches whose significance is a mystery. The *Löwenmensch* is not just one of the earliest and most famous therianthropic images we have, it is also one of the oldest examples of mobiliary, or portable, art. See Joachim Hahn, *Kraft und Aggression: Die Botschaft der Eiszeitkunst in Aurignacien Suddeutschlands?* (Tübingen: Verlag Archaeologica Venatoria, 1986), and Thomas Wynn, Frederick Coolidge, and Martha Bright, "Hohlenstein-Stadel and the Evolution of Human Conceptual Thought," *Cambridge Archaeological Journal* 19/1 (2009), 73–84.

22. Breuil argued that by inscribing the images of animals on the walls and ceilings of caves, Paleolithic humans were attempting to guarantee a successful hunt and safeguard their hunters from injury. According to Breuil, this theory explains both the arbitrariness of the images in the caves, which is merely a reflection of their randomness in nature, and the occasional incisions or marks on the images themselves, which seem to have been made with sharpened implements and are suggestive of pantomime or magical hunts. Breuil's theories regarding the parietal art of the Paleolithic period and "sympathetic magic" were the consensus position up to the 1960s, and they can still be found in many primers on prehistoric art.

   Since the 1960s, however, numerous criticisms have been leveled against Breuil. Notably, some have observed that the cave paintings could not have been used for sympathetic magic as many of the animals depicted were not a part of the diet for Paleolithic humans. Others have argued that Breuil was predisposed to see the caves as sacred spaces because he was a French priest with "high-church" sensibilities and that his work was hampered by methodological problems, such as his reliance upon overly simplistic ethnographic interpretations of the San bushmen of South Africa. In addition to these charges, Breuil has also been criticized for perpetuating a Eurocentric and colonialist understanding of cave art, which privileges parietal art over mobiliary art by referring to these forms of expression as "high art" and "low art" respectively.

   Even Breuil's tracings have been the subject of criticism, such as when Ronald Hutton questioned the addition of antlers in Breuil's representation of the Sorcerer from Les Trois-Frères. Yet in spite of these negative assessments, and the fact that mistakes have been found in some of Breuil's drawings, Jean Clottes (one of the few individuals to have been granted access to Les Trois-Frères) has repeatedly vouched for the authenticity of the Sorcerer image and the accuracy of Breuil's tracing. For more, see Oscar Moro Abadia and Manuel R. Gonzalez Morales, "Paleolithic Art: A Cultural History," *Journal of Archaeological Research* 21 (2013): 269–306; Margaret Conkey, "A Century of Palaeolithic Cave Art," *Archaeology* 43/4 (1981): 20–28; Paul Bahn, *The Cambridge Illustrated History of Prehistoric Art* (Cambridge: Cambridge University Press, 1998), 62–63; Ronald Hutton, *Witches, Druids, and King Arthur* (New York: Bloomsbury Academic, 2003), 33–35; Peter Ucko, "Subjectivity and the Recording of Palaeolithic Cave Art," in *The Limitations of Archaeological Knowledge,* ed. T. Shay and J. Clottes (Liege: University of Liege Press, 1992), 141–80; Robert Bégouën and Jean Clottes, "Les Trois-Frères After Breuil," *Antiquity* 61 (1987): 180–87; and Jean Clottes and David Lewis-Williams, *The Shamans of Prehistory: Trance Magic and the Painted Caves* (New York: Abrams, 1998).

2. THE LORD OF BEASTS

1. According to Alberto C. Blanc, "The engraved and painted figures of the so-called 'sorcerer' of the Cave of the Trois Frères in Ariège, described originally by Abbé Breuil as the figure of a sorcerer, bearing a sort of costume composed of parts of different animals—the horns of a deer, the paws of a bear, the eyes of an owl, the tail of a wolf or of a horse[—is] obviously the figure of a god or genius of the hunting people. Abbé Breuil was the first to reverse his previous opinion and as early as 1931 clearly pointed out that what he had called a 'sorcerer' must rather have represented a mythic supernatural being, furnished with the attributes of the animals that were the object of the hunts of the tribe. . . . Other so-called 'masked figures' in Upper Paleolithic art are likely to represent similar gods or geniuses." Alberto C. Blanc, "Some Evidence for the Ideologies of Early Man," in *Social Life of Early Man,* ed. Sherwood Washburn, rev. ed. (London: Routledge, 2004), 121.

"Initially, this figure had been interpreted as representing a dancing sorcerer. After further reflection, Breuil concluded that it was not a sorcerer but a god, a representation of what one today calls the master of animals. . . . But the name of 'sorcerer' had already stuck to this figure and was never replaced by that of the 'horned god' in the literature. It should be noted that for Breuil, the figure of this god was 'decked out with the same symbols of magical power (mask) as his human ministers' (Bégouën and Breuil 1958:54). It was therefore a masked god." Henry Pernet, *Ritual Masks: Deceptions and Revelations* (Eugene, Ore.: Wipf and Stock, 1992), 26.

Alby Stone concurs with Breuil's change of heart regarding the Lord of Beasts: "The sorcerer of Les Trois Frères might well depict someone in a ritual animal costume, though it could equally have been intended to portray a god or a powerful spirit. It might even have been intended as a metaphorical portrait of an esteemed or powerful individual." Alby Stone, *Explore Shamanism* (Loughborough, U.K.: Explore Books, 2003), 130. See also Morris-Kay, "The Evolution of Human Artistic Creativity," 169.

Bettina Arnold and Derek Counts describe the Lord of Beasts as a "Master of Animals, with powers that extend from divine control over both wild (e.g., lions and boars) and domestic (e.g., mules, cows, and sheep) animals to guardianship over the hunt." Bettina Arnold and Derek Counts, eds., *The Master of Animals in Old World Iconography* (Budapest: Archaeolingua Alapítvány, 2010), 9.

According to Jacquetta Hawkes and Sir Leonard Woolley, there is "no doubt that cave art, and to a lesser extent the home art as well, served the animal cult, part magical and part truly religious. . . . The status of the individuals and the life of the tribe were wholly dependent on the multiplication of the game herds and success in hunting them, and art responded to the urgency of these two great needs. Utilitarian in themselves, they cannot be separated from a religious impulse towards a form of communion with animals and nature, a participation mystique." Jacquetta Hawkes and Sir Leonard Woolley, *Prehistory and the Beginnings of Civilization* (New York: Harper and Row, 1963), 204–205.

For more on the Lord of Beasts/Master of Animals, see Jacqueline Chittenden, "The Master of Animals," *Hesperia: The Journal of the American School of Classical Studies at Athens* 16/2 (1947): 89–114, and Nanno Marinatos, *The Goddess and the Warrior: The Naked*

Goddess and Mistress of the Animals in Early Greek Religion (London: Routledge, 2000), 11–12.

2. Recent U-series results from nine caves on the island of Sulawesi in Indonesia indicate that negative handprints were being made in the caves of that region as early as 39,900 B.P., making them the oldest negative handprints in the world. Moreover, U-series tests of two pieces of figurative art from the Indonesian caves of Leang Timpuseng I and II (a female babirusa or "pig-deer" and an indeterminate piglike animal) have yielded results of 35,400 and 35,700 B.P. respectively. For more on the discovery and dating of the painted caves of Sulawesi, Indonesia, see M. Aubert, A. Brumm, M. Ramli, T. Sutikna, E. W. Saptomo, B. Hakim, M. J. Morwood, G. D. van den Bergh, L. Kinsley and A. Dosseto, "Pleistocene Cave Art from Sulawesi, Indonesia," *Nature* 514 (2014): 223–27.

   As Aubert et al. have noted: "Our dating results from Sulawesi suggest that figurative art was already part of the cultural repertoire of the first modern human populations to reach this region more than 40kyr ago. It is possible that rock art emerged independently at around the same time and at roughly both ends of the spatial distribution of early modern humans. An alternative scenario however, is that cave painting was widely practiced by the first *H. sapiens* to leave Africa tens of thousands of years earlier, and thus that naturalistic animal art from Leang Timpuseng and Leang Barugayya 2, as well as Chauvet Cave in France, may well have much deeper origins outside both western Europe and Sulawesi. If so, we can expect future discoveries of depictions of human hands, figurative art and other forms of image-making dating to the earliest period of the global dispersal of our species." Maxime Aubert et al., "Pleistocene Cave Art from Sulawesi, Indonesia," 226.

3. For more on the caves in Malaga, see Alistair Pike et al., "U-Series Dating of Paleolithic Art in 11 Caves in Spain," *Science* 336 (2012): 1409–13. For more on the Aveyron discovery, see Jacques Jaubert et al., "Early Neanderthal Constructions Deep in Bruniquel Cave in Southwestern France," *Nature* 534 (2016): 111–127.

4. For a discussion of *Homo erectus* skulls discovered at the Zhoukoudian cave system in Beijing (the so-called Peking Man), see Brian M. Fagan and Charlotte Beck, eds., *The Oxford Companion to Archaeology* (London: Oxford University Press, 1996), 774. Dates for

the Zhoukoudian bones range anywhere from 700,000 to 200,000 B.C.E., but the consensus is that it could not have been much later than 500,000 years ago. See Peter Peregrine and Melvin Ember, eds., *Encyclopedia of Prehistory*, vol. 3: *East Asia and Oceania* (New York: Springer, 2001), 352. For a discussion of *Homo erectus* burial practices discovered at the Zhoukoudian cave system in Beijing (the so-called Peking Man), see Brian M. Fagan and Charlotte Beck, eds., *The Oxford Companion to Archaeology* (New York: Oxford University Press, 1996), 774, and Peter Peregrine and Melvin Ember, eds., *Encyclopedia of Prehistory*, vol. 3: *East Asia and Oceania* (New York: Springer, 2001), 352.

5. "What the doctrine of the soul is among the lower races," argues Tylor, "may be explained in stating the animistic theory of its development. It seems as though thinking men, as yet at a low level of culture, were deeply impressed by two groups of biological problems. In the first place, what is it that makes the difference between a living body and a dead one; what causes waking, sleep, trance, disease, and death? In the second place, what are those human shapes which appear in dreams and visions? . . . [T]he ancient savage philosophers probably made their first step by the obvious inference that every man has two things belonging to him, namely, a life and a phantom." Edward Burnett Tylor, *Primitive Culture* (London: J. Murray, 1889), 428.

6. For Max Müller and the "encounter with nature," see *Introduction to the Science of Religion* (London: Longmans, Green, 1873), and *Comparative Mythology* (London: Routledge and Sons, 1909). It should be mentioned that Marett's book, which posits what he calls a theory of *preanimism,* was written as a critique of Tylor's theory of animism. See also Robert Ranulph Marett, *The Threshold of Religion* (London: Methuen and Co., 1914), 14.

7. The argument that ritual practice can elicit certain feelings that can provide an adaptive advantage can be found in Walter Burkert, *Creation of the Sacred: Tracks of Biology in Early Religions* (Cambridge, Mass.: Harvard University Press, 1996), 177.

8. The very term *transcendence,* it can be argued, implies a Western philosophical perspective that may not be applicable to the so-called religions of the East. Nevertheless, in defining transcendence as "that which lies beyond," we find that, for example, the concept of nirvana

as ultimate release from the cycle of rebirth, as well as the concept of the moksha as freedom from the bondage of karma and the illusion of reality (*maya*), both affirm similar notions of transcendence. Likewise, the concept of the Void (*sunyata*), in so far as it is a "concerted effort to grasp the meaning" underlying reality, also implies transcendence, particularly if we consider Nagarjuna's claim that there is no "non-Void entity." In this way, whatever can be said about the Transcendent Reality can also be said about the Void. See J. G. Arapura, "Transcendent Brahman or Transcendent Void: Which Is Ultimately Real? Transcendence and the Sacred," in *Transcendence and the Sacred,* ed. A. M. Olson and L. S. Rouner (Notre Dame, Ind.: University of Notre Dame Press, 1981), 83–99.

9. Émile Durkheim, *The Elementary Forms of Religious Life* (New York: Free Press, 1995), 227. See also W. Robertson Smith, *Lectures on the Religion of the Semites: The Fundamental Institutions* (New York: Ktav Publishers, 1969).

10. One hears echoes of Durkheim's theory today among his intellectual inheritors. The sociologist Peter Burger, for instance, argues that in providing cosmic significance to human activities, religion not only creates meaning and purpose for societies, it *legitimizes* societies. Religion, Burger writes, "is the establishment, through human activity, of an all-embracing sacred order, that is, of a sacred cosmos that will be capable of maintaining itself in the ever-present face of chaos." Peter Burger, *The Sacred Canopy: Elements of a Sociological Theory of Religion* (New York: Doubleday, 1967), 51.

11. For Freud's views on religion, see *Totem and Taboo: Resemblances Between the Psychic Lives of Savages and Neurotics,* trans. Abraham Arden Brill (New York: Moffat, 1918), and *The Future of an Illusion,* trans. W. D. Robson-Scott (London: Hogarth Press, 1928).

12. David Hume, *Four Dissertations* (London: A. and H. Bradlaugh Bonner, 1757), 94, and Ludwig Feuerbach, *The Essence of Christianity,* trans. Marian Evans (New York: Calvin Blanchard, 1855), 105. See also Feuerbach's *Lectures on the Essence of Religion,* trans. Ralph Manheim (New York: Harper and Row, 1967).

Girard believed that violence was caused by mimetic rivalry, which occurs when our desires are "borrowed" from other people in our community. See René Girard, *Violence and the Sacred* (Baltimore, Md.: Johns Hopkins University Press, 1979).

    The promise of religion, writes the contemporary German American scholar Martin Riesebrodt, is "to ward off misfortune, to help cope with crises, and to provide salvation." Martin Riesebrodt, *The Promise of Salvation: A Theory of Religion* (Chicago: University of Chicago Press, 2010), xiii.

13. Geertz defines religion by its purpose: to encourage and motivate people by making them believe in a meaningful and coherent universe. Clifford Geertz, *The Interpretation of Cultures* (New York: Basic Books, 1973), 87–125, 103. Similarly, as A. R. Radcliffe-Brown notes, "while one anthropological theory is that magic and religion give men confidence, it could equally well be argued that they give men fears and anxieties from which they would otherwise be free— the fear of black magic or of spirits, fear of God, of the Devil, of Hell." Alfred Reginald Radcliffe-Brown, "Taboo," in *Reader in Comparative Religion: An Anthropological Approach,* ed. William A. Lessa and Evon Z. Vogt (New York: Harper and Row, 1979), 46–56.

14. Peter van Inwagen on the problem of explaining religion in evolutionary terms: "Supernaturalistic beliefs are not without their cost: they have an obvious tendency to lead to actions (i.e., rituals and prayer) that involve an expenditure of resources that might have been devoted to survival and reproduction. And it is a commonplace of evolutionary biology that any feature of a species that is costly in terms of energy and resources requires some sort of explanation, such as the colorful plumage of the males of many species of birds." Peter van Inwagen, "Explaining Belief in the Supernatural: Some Thoughts on Paul Bloom's 'Religious Belief as an Evolutionary Accident,'" in *The Believing Primate: Scientific, Philosophical, and Theological Reflections on the Origin of Religion,* ed. Jeffrey Schloss and Michael Murray (Oxford: Oxford University Press, 2009), 129.

15. According to Matt Rossano, "Religion's most ancient traits represent an extension of the human social world into the supernatural, thus reinforcing within-group cooperation by means of ever-vigilant spiritual monitors. Believing that the spirits were always watching may have helped reduce the number of noncooperators within a group while reinforcing group behavioral norms, thus allowing humanlike levels of cooperation to emerge." Matt Rossano, "Supernaturalizing Social Life: Religion and the Evolution of Human Cooperation," *Human Nature* 18/3 (2007): 272. See also Robert Boyd et al., "The

Evolution of Altruistic Punishment," *Proceedings of the National Academy of Sciences* 100/3 (2003): 3531–35.

16. Bloom points out an alternative view, in which "[r]eligion . . . is a constellation of behaviors and thoughts that have evolved to benefit groups, and, in particular, to help solve the problem of free-riders." In this perspective, religion functions to mitigate the social effects of selfish behavior among individuals in a group. However, this perspective has a hard time explaining how and why religions evolved in the first place. Some believe that religion can evolve through a process called "cultural group selection," by which religion, including religious rituals, may emerge and succeed initially in societies if it confers an advantage over other groups. That is to say, groups with religion were more competitive and more likely to survive. In this case, religion is not genetic but rather mimetic—a highly controversial means of knowledge transmission that is parallel in process to genetic transmission. However, Tim Ingold and Gisli Palsson have pushed back against this idea. They refute the use of Darwinian evolution to explain cultural process, seeing it as fundamentally circular in logic. This problem can come in conflict with more anthropological theories for the evolution of cooperation. These theories often rely on the notion of altruistic punishment, which is a costly action an individual will take to punish another individual who does not follow some moral or cooperative norm. Punishment in this sense serves to promote cooperation in small groups, and potentially also in large groups if the costs and frequency of punishment actions are low. See Paul Bloom, "Religion, Morality, Evolution," *Annual Review of Psychology* 63 (2012): 186, 196, and Tim Ingold and Gisli Palsson, eds., *Biosocial Becomings: Integrating Social and Biological Anthropology* (Cambridge: Cambridge University Press, 2013).

17. Some scholars and scientists continue to insist that there must be some adaptive advantage to holding religious beliefs—that it may make for more desirable mates, for instance, as proposed by Jesse M. Bering in "The Folk Psychology of Souls," *Behavioral and Brain Sciences* 29 (2006): 453–62, or that it somehow allows certain societies to outlast and outgrow others, as hypothesized by David Sloan Wilson in *Darwin's Cathedral: Evolution, Religion, and the Nature of Society* (Chicago: University of Chicago Press, 2002).

18. Scott Atran, *In Gods We Trust: The Evolutionary Landscape of Reli-

gion (New York: Oxford University Press, 2002), 43; Paul Bloom,
"Religious Belief as an Evolutionary Accident," in *The Believing Pri-
mate: Scientific, Philosophical, and Theological Reflections on the
Origin of Religion*, ed. J. Schloss and M. Murray (Oxford: Oxford
University Press, 2009), 118–127.

3. THE FACE IN THE TREE

1. Michael J. Murray, "Scientific Explanations of Religion and the Justification of Religious Belief," in *The Believing Primate: Scientific,
Philosophical, and Theological Reflections on the Origin of Religion*,
ed. J. Schloss and M. Murray (Oxford: Oxford University Press,
2009), 169.

To understand what is meant by religion as a neurological phenomenon, recall that whoever made the Sorcerer, and for whatever
reason, did so around 18,000 years ago. However, the brain required
to conceive of the Sorcerer developed hundreds of thousands of years
earlier. That brain had to be capable of symbolic thought. It needed
to possess the conceptual thinking necessary to dream up an abstract
creature not of this world. It had to have the ability to join separate
and distinct categories such as "man" and "animal" to create a new
and unreal category, deliberately and with conscious effort. These
mental tasks are the product of certain executive functions in the
frontal and parietal lobes of the brain that took millions of years to
develop.

Wynn, Coolidge, and Bright argue, in reference to another hybrid
figure—the aforementioned *Löwenmensch* or "Lion-Human"—that
the abstract concept underpinning such hybrids resulted initially
from an effortful and attentive linking of "animal" and "person"
concepts via the working memory network of the frontal and parietal
lobes. "These 'animal' and 'person' concepts themselves were largely
unconscious folk biological categories generated by a parietal network that had evolved earlier, probably by the time of the earliest
Homo sapiens. These in turn rest on even older, basic ontological
categories of 'animate' and 'manipulable' objects that are temporal
lobe networks, and which evolved much earlier still, perhaps with the
advent of *Homo erectus*." Thomas Wynn, Frederick Coolidge, and

Martha Bright, "Hohlenstein-Stadel and the Evolution of Human Conceptual Thought," *Cambridge Archaeological Journal* 19/1 (2009): 73.

2. For more on the Theory of Mind and its relation to animism, see Maurice Bloch, *In and Out of Each Other's Bodies: Theory of Mind, Evolution, Truth, and the Nature of the Social* (New York: Routledge, 2016), and Christine S. VanPool and Elizabeth Newsome, "The Spirit in the Material: A Case Study of Animism in the American Southwest," *American Antiquity* 77/2 (2012): 243–62.

3. Jean Piaget and other developmental psychologists have long noted the "tendency among children to consider things as living and conscious." Following in Piaget's footsteps, Justin Barrett has outlined the process whereby babies not only implant agency into inanimate things but also instinctively find design and purpose in the natural world. Furthermore, studies by Gergely Csibra and Deborah Kelemen have yielded empirical evidence that children unwittingly attribute goals to moving objects, even if they are self-propelled and without purposeful motion. Concerning the concept of mortality, Jesse Bering has provided evidence that some children can understand physical death, although they intuitively hold the belief that the mind survives the body. Therefore teleological thought is theorized to exist inherently and possibly without cultural inheritance. Teleological thought allows one to conceptualize an invisible designer to phenomena even if you cannot observe the designer but rather you infer it. Children are therefore "intuitive theorists." Jean Piaget, "Children's Philosophies," in *A Handbook of Child Psychology,* ed. C. Murchison (Worcester, Mass.: Clark University Press, 1933), 537; Justin L. Barrett, *Born Believers: The Science of Children's Religious Belief* (New York: Atria Books, 2012); Gergely Csibra et al., "Goal Attribution Without Agency Cues: The Perception of 'Pure Reason' in Infancy," *Cognition* 72/3 (1999): 237–67; Deborah Kelemen, "Are Children Intuitive Theists? Reasoning About Purpose and Design in Nature," *Psychological Science* 15/5 (2004): 295–301; Deborah Kelemen and Cara DiYanni, "Intuitions About Origins: Purpose and Intelligent Design in Children's Reasoning About Nature," *Journal of Cognition and Development* 6/1 (2005): 3–31; and Jesse Bering, "Intuitive Conceptions of Dead Agents' Minds: The Natural Foundations of Afterlife Beliefs as Phenomenological Boundary," *Journal of*

Cognition and Culture 2/4 (2002): 263–308. See also Alfred Irving Hallowell's fascinating case study on nonhuman actors, the notion of self, and the cosmos in human culture as understood by the Ojibwa tribes of North America: Alfred Irving Hallowell, "Ojibwa Ontology, Behavior, and World View," in *Culture in History: Essays in Honor of Paul Radin,* ed. S. Diamond (New York: Columbia University Press, 1960), 20–52.

4. Pascal Boyer's most accessible books laying out his theories on how religious belief is transmitted include *Religion Explained: The Evolutionary Origins of Religious Thought* (New York: Basic Books, 2001) and *The Naturalness of Religious Ideas: A Cognitive Theory of Religion* (Berkeley and Los Angeles: University of California Press, 1994).

5. The term "minimally counterintuitive concept" was coined by Justin Barrett, who has worked with Boyer on many of his experiments demonstrating the impact of anomalous ideas. See Justin L. Barrett, *Why Would Anyone Believe in God?* (Lanham, Md.: Altamira Press, 2004) and *Born Believers: The Science of Children's Religious Belief* (New York: Atria Books, 2012).

6. An old but useful compendium of tree myths is *Cultus Arborum: A Descriptive Account of Phallic Tree Worship, with Illustrative Legends, Superstitions, Usages, &c., Exhibiting Its Origin and Development Amongst the Eastern & Western Nations of the World, from the Earliest to Modern Times; with a Bibliography of Works Upon and Referring to the Phallic Cultus,* which was privately printed in London in 1890 and is available at Archive.org. Many of the myths about talking trees were taken from this compendium.

We don't know much about either the Oak of Moreh or the Oaks of Mamre. Nahum Sarna discusses them briefly in his commentary on Genesis: "The Terebinth of Moreh, in Hebrew *'elon moreh*, was undoubtedly some mighty tree with sacred associations. Moreh must mean 'teacher, oracle giver.' This tree (or a cluster of such trees) was so conspicuous and so famous that it served as a landmark to identify other sites in the area. The phenomenon of a sacred tree, particularly one associated with a sacred site, is well known in a variety of cultures. A distinguished tree, especially one of great antiquity, might be looked upon as the 'tree of life' or as being 'cosmic,' its stump symbolizing the 'navel of the earth' and its top representing heaven. In this sense, it is a bridge between the human and the divine spheres, and it becomes an arena of divine-human encounter, an ideal medium of oracles and revelation. Trees may have also symbolized the protection or fertility the worshiper hoped to receive from a deity. Fertility cults flourished in connection with such trees, and this form of paganism proved attractive to many Israelites." Nahum M. Sarna, *The JPS Torah Commentary: Genesis* (Philadelphia: Jewish Publication Society of America, 1989), 91. Note also the prophetess Deborah, who sits beneath the "palm of Deborah" when dispensing oracles (Judges 4:5).

7. Note what the serpent tells Eve in Eden regarding the Tree of Knowledge of Good and Evil: "For God knows that when you eat of it your eyes will be opened, and *you will be like God,* knowing good and evil" (Genesis 3:5). More on this in the Conclusion.

8. Justin Barrett shows how HADD and Theory of Mind can reinforce but not create belief with the following analogies: "Suppose a woman walking alone through a deep gorge rounds a bend in the trail and rocks tumble down the steep wall and nearly hit her. HADD might reflexively search for the responsible agent. A man hiking through an unfamiliar forest hears something behind a nearby shrub. HADD screams, 'Agent!' If, after detecting agency in these sorts of cases, a candidate superhuman agent concept is offered and seems consistent with the event, belief could be encouraged. Similarly, when a god concept is already available as a good candidate, events that HADD might have overlooked become significant. For instance, a child in California prays for snow in May and a blizzard drops two feet of snow the next day. The context suggests agency. Or a man in New York is told by doctors that he is dying but he feels a tingling all over his body and a sense of peace that all will be well. The man recovers and attributes the miraculous healing to God. Because the agency detection device is so eager to find agency when other intuitive explanatory systems (such as Naive Physics or Naive Biology) fail, many different events may be attached to superhuman agency. These events then support belief." Barrett, "Cognitive Science, Religion and Theology," 86.

9. Jesse M. Bering has attempted to provide a cognitive answer to the problem of our intuitive knowledge of the soul, insofar as it pertains to the inborn belief in life after death. Bering argues that "because it

is epistemologically impossible to know what it is like to be dead, individuals will be most likely to attribute to dead agents those types of mental states that they cannot imagine being without. Such a model argues that it is natural to believe in life after death and social transmission serves principally to conceptually enrich (or degrade) intuitive conceptions of the afterlife." Bering, "Intuitive Conceptions of Dead Agents' Minds," 263.

4. SPEARS INTO PLOWS

1. Concerning the relationship between religion and the production of food, Gilbert Murray notes that agriculture was once "entirely a question of religion; now it is almost entirely a question of science. In antiquity, if a field was barren, the owner of it would probably assume that the barrenness was due to 'pollution,' of offence somewhere. He would run through all his own possible offences, or at any rate those of his neighbours and ancestors, and when he eventually decided the cause of the trouble, the steps that he would take would all be of a kind calculated not to affect the chemical constitution of the soil, but to satisfy his own emotions of guilt and terror, or the imaginary emotions of the imaginary being he had offended. A modern man in the same predicament," continues Murray, "would probably not think of religion at all, at any rate in the earlier stages; he would say it was a case for deeper ploughing or for basic slag. Later on, if disaster followed disaster till he began to feel himself a marked man, even the average modern would, I think, begin instinctively to reflect upon his sins. A third characteristic flows from the first. The uncharted region surrounds us on every side and is apparently infinite; consequently, when once the things of the uncharted region are admitted as factors in our ordinary conduct of life they are apt to be infinite factors, overruling and swamping all others. The thing that religion forbids is a thing never to be done; not all the inducements that this life can offer weigh at all in the balance. Indeed there is no balance. The man who makes terms with his conscience is essentially non-religious; the religious man knows that it will profit him nothing if he gain all this finite world and lose his stake in the infinite and eternal." Gilbert Murray, *Five Stages of Greek Religion* (New York: Anchor Books, 1955), 5–6.

2. Mircea Eliade, *From the Stone Age to the Eleusinian Mysteries,* vol. 1 of *History of Religious Ideas,* trans. Willard Trask (Chicago: University of Chicago Press, 1978), 29–55.

3. During the first half of the twentieth century, the prevailing opinion regarding prehistoric humans and their attitudes toward the acquisition of foodstuffs was that farming was more desirable than foraging. In the 1960s, however, this interpretation started to lose ground. As Jacob Weisdorf notes: "Evidence started to appear which suggested that early agriculture had cost farmers more trouble than it saved. Studies of present-day primitive societies indicated that farming was in fact back breaking, time consuming, and labour intensive, a view that would later gather strong support. . . . A picture began to emerge that showed that foraging communities were able to remain in equilibrium at carrying capacity when undisturbed and that new cultural forms would only result from non-equilibrium conditions. In the light of the fact that climatic changes did not seem to have led to significant crises and that foragers, reluctant to take up farming, decided to adopt it nevertheless the idea that agriculture resulted from necessity again began to take hold." In consonance with Weisdorf, Michael Guenevere and Hillard Kaplan have convincingly shown that the life expectancy of hunter-gatherers is far higher than once assumed. Jacob L. Weisdorf, "From Foraging to Farming: Explaining the Neolithic Revolution," *Journal of Economic Surveys* 19/4 (2005): 565–66; Michael Guenevere and Hillard Kaplan, "Longevity Among Hunter-Gatherers: A Cross-Cultural Examination," *Population and Development Review* 33/2 (2007): 321–65.

4. The transition from foraging to farming, argues Harari, was just a "faithfulness calculation" in that Neolithic man was incapable of fathoming the full consequences of his decision to farm instead of forage—"they did not foresee that by increasing their dependence on a single source of food, they were actually exposing themselves even more to the depredations of drought. Nor did the farmers foresee that in good years their bulging granaries would tempt thieves and enemies, compelling them to start building walls and doing guard duty." Yuval Noah Harari, *Sapiens: A Brief History of Humankind* (New York: HarperCollins, 2015), 87.

5. According to Childe, the "Neolithic Revolution" was the result of climatic changes resulting in the emergence of several geographical

oases where agriculture and food production were easily accomplished. Subsequent scholars, such as Robert Braidwood, found no evidence for the presence of such climatic crises and argued that the rise of agriculture was driven by social and cultural issues, such as technological advances that enabled people to inhabit areas that were adjacent to the Fertile Crescent for longer periods of time. By contrast, Lewis Binford argued that humans adapted to environmental changes through the development of material culture. Moreover, rising sea levels pushed people to marginal zones where they would have brought cereals and animals from other regions. In a dramatic departure from his predecessors, Jacques Cauvin has argued that the beginnings of the agricultural revolution can be found in the Holocene period (c. 9000 B.P.)—a time of extreme abundance, suggesting that climatic and environmental issues were not to blame for the shift from hunting and gathering to agricultural activities. More important, Cauvin has posited that the evolution of symbolic activity, such as that which is evidenced at Göbekli Tepe, preceded the rise of the agricultural economy by nearly a millennium, thereby indicating that a cognitive development among *Homo sapiens* with regard to the production of symbols occurred well before the emergence of sedentary life. See Vere Gordon Childe, *Man Makes Himself*, 3rd ed. (London: Watts and Company, 1936); Robert J. Braidwood, "The Agricultural Revolution," *Scientific American* 203 (1960): 130–41; Braidwood, *Prehistoric Men*, 6th ed. (Chicago: Chicago Natural History Museum, 1963); Lewis R. Binford, "Post-Pleistocene Adaptations," in *New Perspectives in Archaeology*, ed. L. R. Binford and S. R. Binford (Chicago: Aldine, 1968), 313–42; and Jacques Cauvin, *The Birth of the Gods and the Origins of Agriculture* (Cambridge: Cambridge University Press, 2007).

6. The consensus among scholars regarding the rise of agriculture and the factors that might have contributed to its development is that there is no consensus. "There seems to be widespread agreement that no single model so far proposed is entirely satisfactory," observes Weisdorf, "and for the theorist interested in rationalizing the transition from foraging to farming, new evidence is constantly appearing. For instance, there is evidence that indicates that sedentism occurred prior to and independent of the transition to agriculture and that tools for agricultural production were already available to the forag-

ers who eventually took up farming. Evidence also suggests that agriculture appeared in relatively complex, affluent societies, where a wide variety of foods were available and that these societies were circumscribed by other societies whose environmental zones were poorer in resources. It also appears that the egalitarian nature of foraging societies was replaced by hierarchical social structures among agriculturalists and that bands of hunters and gatherers had a communal organizational structure, whereas household level organization prevailed among farmers." Weisdorf, "From Foraging to Farming," 581–82.

7. As Allan Simmons has remarked: "Many but not all researchers agree that initial domestication of primary animal species occurred in the northern Levant and southeastern Turkey, rather than in the southern Levant." In support of this observation, and the argument that "animal domestication should be perceived as an end result of sedentism [not its catalyst]," Simmons cites archaeological evidence from Göbekli Tepe and other Neolithic sites across southeastern Turkey. In consonance with Simmons, Joris Peters has argued that animal domestication occurred well after humans had abandoned the life of the hunter-gatherer and embraced a more settled lifestyle. According to Peters: "Morphometrical as well as circumstantial evidence indicate that the domestication of sheep and probably also goat took place in the southern Taurus piedmont during the Early Pre-Pottery Neolithic B period [c. 7600–6000 B.C.E.]. . . . Thus the incorporation of sheep and goats into the economy of these early sites is less 'revolutionary' than the term 'Neolithic revolution' might suggest . . . According to archaeozoological and palaeobotanical evidence, large scale climatic change and/or landscape deterioration now seem unlikely, reinforcing the idea that socio-cultural factors were primarily responsible for this shift in the pattern of animal exploitation." Allan Simmons, *The Neolithic Revolution in the Near East: Transforming the Human Landscape* (Tucson: University of Arizona Press, 2007), 141–42; Joris Peters et al., "Early Animal Husbandry in the Northern Levant," *Paléorient* 25/2 (1999): 27–48, 27.

8. Cauvin, *Birth of the Gods*. See also LeRon Shults, "Spiritual Entanglement: Transforming Religious Symbols at Çatalhöyük," in *Religion in the Emergence of Civilization: Çatalhöyük as a Case Study*, ed. Ian Hodder (Cambridge: Cambridge University Press, 2010), 73–98, and

Ian Hodder, "Symbolism and the Origins of Agriculture in the Near East," *Cambridge Archaeological Journal* 11/1 (2001): 108.

Ian Hodder is right to note that "rather than religion or new forms of agency being prime causes in the domestication of plants and animals and the emergence of settled villages, religion and the symbolic were thoroughly engrained within the interstices of the new way of life. Religion played a primary role, allowing new forms of agency, setting up a symbolic world of violence through which new longer-term social and economic relations could be produced, but there is not good evidence that it was an independent cause of the changes." Ian Hodder, "The Role of Religion in the Neolithic of the Middle East and Anatolia with Particular Reference to Çatalhöyük," *Paléorient* 37/1, (2011): 111–22, 121. See also Hodder, "Symbolism and the Origins of Agriculture in the Near East," 108.

5. LOFTY PERSONS

1. There are numerous versions of the Sumerian flood legend but they basically come in three incarnations: the *Sumerian Flood Story,* written in Sumerian; the *Atrahasis Epic,* written in Akkadian and dated to around 1700 B.C.E.; and Tablet XI of the *Epic of Gilgamesh,* also written in Akkadian and dated to roughly the twelfth century B.C.E. We should add to this the recently discovered *Ark Tablet,* which its translator, Irving Finkel, dates to about 1750 B.C.E. My version of the Sumerian flood story is an amalgamation of two translations of the *Atrahasis Epic*—the first (and best) by Stephanie Dalley, *Myths from Mesopotamia;* the second by Benjamin R. Foster, *Before the Muses: An Anthology of Akkadian Literature* (Bethesda: University of Maryland Press, 2005)—sprinkled with material from the *Ark Tablet,* translated by Irving Finkel in *The Ark Before Noah: Decoding the Story of the Flood* (New York: Doubleday, 2014), and, for good measure, the Babylonian version recounted in the *Epic of Gilgamesh,* also translated by Dalley (with a few literary flourishes of my own).

2. The Sumerians' first attempt at writing amounted to little more than *pictographs,* each symbol an image corresponding to a physical object. For example, the image of a jug represented the word "beer." Eventually these images took phonetic values to create particular

sounds such as *bar, la,* or *am.* By connecting and crisscrossing the wedged lines, the Sumerians were able to create a kind of alphabet of around six hundred characters.

Interestingly, the earliest written texts were not myths about the creation of the world or grand epics recounting the exploits of gods and heroes. They were the ancient equivalent of tax documents, lists of incomes and expenditures, tallies of sheep, goats, and cattle, accounting records meticulously charting who owed what to whom. Indeed, writing arose solely for the purpose of facilitating accounting. Only much later did these numerical texts begin to combine numbers and nouns to craft complex sentences; and it was much later than that when these sentences were finally strung together to create the sprawling, unforgettable myths that defined the religions of Mesopotamia for thousands of years.

At this early stage in Mesopotamian development, it should be noted that religion had almost nothing to do with doctrine and everything to do with tending to the god's estate. Daniel T. Potts, professor of Ancient Near Eastern archaeology at NYU, has done a marvelous analysis of nearly four thousand so-called archaic texts, the earliest examples of proto-cuneiform from Mesopotamia, found in trash deposits in the Eanna precinct, in the temple complex of Inana, who was the sitting goddess of Uruk. His conclusion that these texts were like archived tax documents, indicating that writing was invented to facilitate accounting and record keeping, is difficult to dispute. I was honored to hear him present his findings at the Engelsberg Seminar in Sweden, the proceedings of which were published by the Axel and Margaret Ax:son Johnson Foundation. Professor Potts's article is titled "Accounting for Religion: Uruk and the Origins of the Sacred Economy," in *Religion: Perspectives from the Engelsberg Seminar 2014* (Stockholm: Axel and Margaret Ax:son Johnson Foundation, 2014), 17–23.

3. According to Michael Wise, "Aramaic became the common language in Palestine largely as a reflex of political realities. Aramaic was used as the language of political administration in the Near East for centuries before the Judean exile, beginning with the Neo-Assyrian Empire; the Neo-Babylonians and Persians continued to use it as the lingua franca." See also Fitzmyer: "The Aramaic documents of the Jewish military colony of the fifth century B.C. Elephantine have

been known since the early part of this century and have given us a good picture of the Official Aramaic which was in use at the time from southern Egypt across the Fertile Crescent even to the Indus Valley. It was used during five centuries, until the international means of communication switched to Greek, only after the conquest of Alexander." This would mean that Aramaic may have displaced Akkadian as the spoken language of the elites and political class even earlier than the first century B.C.E. Michael Wise, *Language and Literacy in Roman Judaea: A Study of the Bar Kochba Documents* (New Haven: Yale University Press, 2015), 9, 279; see also Joseph Fitzmyer, "The Aramaic Language and the Study of the New Testament," *Journal of Biblical Literature* 99/1 (1980): 5–21, 9.

4. Admittedly, the etymology of *ilu, el* (or Elohim), and *ilah* (whence we get the word *al-ilah,* or *Allah*) is far from clear. The best work done on the subject is by Marvin H. Pope, *El in the Ugaritic Texts* (Leiden: Brill, 1955).

5. No one knows exactly how many gods existed in the Mesopotamian pantheon. Jean Bottéro notes that the most complete count ever done by Babylonian scholars came up with almost two thousand names. However, Antonius Damiel, in his *Pantheon Babylonicum,* counted three thousand three hundred names. See Jean Bottéro, *Religion in Ancient Mesopotamia,* trans. Teresa Lavender Fagen (Chicago: University of Chicago Press, 2004), and Antonius Damiel, *Pantheon Babylonicum: Nomina Deorum e Textibus Cuneiformibus Excerpta et Ordine Alphabetico Distributa* (Rome: Sumptibus Pontificii Instituti Biblici, 1914).

   Ironically, while Mesopotamian stories of gods and goddesses shed enormous light on the religions of Mesopotamia, there was in actuality no Sumerian word for "religion." That is because religion was not considered a separate category of life in Mesopotamia. Religion *was* life. The existence of a god could not be separated from the god's function. In other words, neither An nor Shamash had any existence apart from, outside of, or beyond the natural functioning of the sky or the sun. Simply put, the gods are as the gods do. If a god failed to perform his or her function, or if the purpose for the god's existence ceased to be of relevance to the community, that god simply faded out of existence.

6. Kenyon's research on the skulls at Jericho can be found in *Digging up*

Jericho (New York: Praeger, 1957). Hodder points out that the sepa-
ration of heads from bodies and the subsequent plastering and pre-
sentation of skulls in the Neolithic, notably at Jericho and Çatalhöyük,
is not necessarily representative of religious activity: "The removal of
heads from corpses is shown clearly in the art, and in both the excavated examples there are reasons to consider the people so treated as
special. They may have been important elders or ritual leaders. The
retrieval of skulls suggests an emphasis on ancestors, with animals
also either representing ancestors or interceding with ancestors.
There is no need to introduce 'gods' here. Certainly there is a concern
with the past, with ancestors, with myth and perhaps ritual elders or
shamans. But nothing is suggested beyond a domestic cult and a concern with lineage continuity." Ian Hodder, "Symbolism and the Origins of Agriculture in the Near East," Cambridge Archaeological
Journal 11/1 (2001): 111. I respectfully disagree.

7. According to Stephen Bertman, "The term *ziggurat* derives from the
   Akkadian word *zigguratu,* which means a 'peak' or 'high place.'"
   Stephen Bertman, *Handbook to Life in Ancient Mesopotamia* (New
   York: Facts on File, 2003), 194, 197.

   However, it is not exactly clear whether the ziggurat was connected to a temple or was itself the temple. Herodotus, one of the
   earliest sources we have about the purpose and function of the ziggurat, described a ziggurat in the following way: "In the midmost of
   one division of the city stands the royal palace, surrounded by a high
   and strong wall; and in the midmost of the other is still to this day the
   sacred enclosure of Zeus Belus, a square of two furlongs each way,
   with gates of bronze. In the centre of this enclosure a solid tower has
   been built, of one furlong's length and breadth; a second tower rises
   from this, and from it yet another, till at last there are eight. The way
   up to them mounts spirally outside all the towers; about halfway in
   the ascent is a halting place, with seats for repose, where those who
   ascend sit down and rest. In the last tower there is a great shrine; and
   in it a great and well-covered couch is laid, and a golden table set hard
   by. But no image has been set up in the shrine, nor does any human
   creature lie therein for the night, except one native woman, chosen
   from all women by the god, as say the Chaldeans, who are priests of
   this god. The same Chaldeans say, that the god himself is wont to
   visit the shrine and rest upon the couch, even as in Thebes of Egypt . . .

for there too a woman sleeps in the temple of Theban Zeus and neither the Egyptian nor the Babylonian woman, it is said, has intercourse with men." Herodotus 1.181–82. Unfortunately, no Mesopotamian sources have been found that verify Herodotus's allusion to a divine sex rite.

John H. Walton writes that "the ziggurat does not play a part in any of the rituals that are known to us from Mesopotamia. If known literature were our only guide we would have to conclude that common people did not use the ziggurat for anything. The ziggurat was sacred space, and would have been strictly off-limits to profane use. Though the structure at the top was designed to accommodate the god, it was not a temple where people would go to worship. There was no image or any other representation of the deity there. The ziggurat was typically accompanied by an adjoining temple near its base where the image was housed and where worship took place . . . the ziggurat was a structure that was built to support the stairway [between heaven and earth]. This stairway was a visual representation of that which was believed to be used by the gods to travel from one realm to another. It was solely for the convenience of the gods and was maintained in order to provide the deity with the amenities that would refresh him/her along the way. At the top of the ziggurat was the gate of the gods, the entrance into their heavenly abode. At the bottom was the temple, where the people hoped the god would descend to receive gifts and worship of his/her people." John H. Walton, *Ancient Near Eastern Thought and the Old Testament: Introducing the Conceptual World of the Hebrew Bible* (Grand Rapids: Baker, 2006), 120–22.

It is interesting to note that, technically, every citizen was an employee of the temple, because the temple owned all the land. The farms, the vineyards, the grassy meadows where the cattle grazed, the winding rivers where the fish swarmed—all of these were the personal property of the god. The farmer who tilled the land did so on the god's behalf. He would bring his harvest to the god as an offering; there it would be carefully tallied and registered by the temple priests, and he would receive a portion of it back as "payment" for his labor. The same was true for the fishermen who fished the god's rivers, the sheep and cattle herders who grazed the god's meadows, the vintners who crushed and pressed the god's grapes, and so on. In this early

phase of Mesopotamian history, religion was little more than organized labor in the service of a particular god and under the strict supervision of a bureaucracy of professional priests. The laity's
relationship with the temple was purely transactional. See Potts, *Religion: Perspectives from the Engelsberg Seminar 2014.*

8. These idols are referred to collectively as the "Venus figurines"—an
unfortunate umbrella term coined by the Europeans who discovered
them (the figurines have no connection with the Roman goddess
Venus). These include the aforementioned Berekhat Ram Venus,
which, at around 300,000 years old, is not just the oldest statue ever
found, it is likely the very first cult object in history, and the Double
Venus found in Grimaldi, Italy, which is by far the most extraordinary, and most obviously ritualistic, of these statues. Affectionately
known as Beauty and the Beast, the Double Venus is a perfectly polished, pale green statue that actually consists of two bodies carved
back to back and joined at the head, shoulders, and thighs. One of
the bodies is of a lithe woman, pregnant and arching her back. The
other body is not human. No one knows what it is. It is sinuous and
serpentine, almost reptilian, with the face of some kind of mythical,
possibly horned beast. The idol has a hole at the top so that it could
be worn as an amulet.

It is difficult to dispute the ritual function that these statues must
have had in the spiritual lives of our ancestors. The Venus of Dolni
Vestonice, which is about 29,000 years old, has clearly defined holes
dug into the top of its head which may have held incense, herbs, or
flowers. The Venus of Willendorf, carved out of limestone some
30,000 years ago, has what appears to be either a woven veil or braided
hair covering its face. The Venus of Hohle Fels (c. 45,000–35,000 B.P.)
has a hook or loop where its head should be. In fact, a large number
of Venus figurines have been discovered with their heads obscured or
their faces left uncarved, as though they were meant to symbolize not
any particular woman, but womanhood. You can see a catalog of all
the so-called Venus Figurines in alphabetical order at Don's Maps,
http://donsmaps.com/venus.html; for a rundown of theories about
the meaning of the Venus figurines, see R. Dale Guthrie, *The Nature
of Paleolithic Art* (Chicago: University of Chicago Press, 2005).

9. "A cultic statue was never solely a religious picture, but was always an
image imbued with a god, and, as such, it possessed the character of

both earthly reality and divine presence." Angelika Berlejung, "Washing the Mouth: The Consecration of Divine Images in Mesopotamia," in *The Image and the Book: Iconic Cults, Aniconism, and the Rise of the Book Religion in Israel and the Ancient Near East,* ed. K. van der Toorn (Leuven: Peeters, 1997), 46.

"The statues," according to Jan Assman, "we are told, have two natures, one divine and one material, one above and the other below humankind. As creators of these statues, humans are reminded of their own divine origin, and by piously tending and worshiping them, they make the divine at home on earth." Assman continues: "The statue is not the image of the deity's body, but the body itself. It does not represent his form, but rather gives him form. The deity takes form in the statue just as in an animal or a natural phenomenon. The statues were not made, but were 'born.' . . . The Egyptians never blurred the distinction between image and deity, but they took it in a different direction and to a different level from that to which we are accustomed." Jan Assman, *The Search for God in Ancient Egypt,* trans. David Lorton (Ithaca and London: Cornell University Press, 2001), 41, 46.

10. Although it is a hotly debated subject, many scholars believe that the invention of Egyptian hieroglyphs was directly influenced by Sumerian cuneiform, or that, at the very least, the idea of putting thoughts into words came to Egypt from Mesopotamia. See Geoffrey Sampson, *Writing Systems: A Linguistic Introduction* (Palo Alto: Stanford University Press, 1990).

11. The gods of Egypt could take multiple forms, or they could change forms altogether. Sometimes two gods would merge to create one composite god who then reflected both divine powers within itself. That is what happened with the god Amun-Re (see chapter 6).

On the dual aspects of the gods (cosmic and active/abstract), Assman notes: "In the framework of our inquiry into the cosmic dimension of the divine as a heuristic model, the essence of Thoth, god of writing and calculation, bureaucratic punctiliousness, exactitude, supervision, and knowledge reveals itself as 'moon-ness,' as the religious interpretation of the moon and as such part of the comprehensive religious interpretation of the cosmos, that which we are calling Egyptian polytheism. . . . What we have learned from these examples and can extend to the Egyptian concept of the divine generally is that the cosmic dimension of the divine was not confined to the sheer materiality of cosmic elements such as earth, air, water, and so forth, or to celestial bodies such as the sun and the moon, but rather that it referred to specific complexes of actions, traits, attitudes, and qualities that were interpreted as cosmic phenomena 'in action' and in which humankind also participated." Assman, *Search for God in Ancient Egypt,* 81.

12. For linguistic evidence of Indo-European migrations, see James Patrick Mallory, *In Search of the Indo-Europeans: Language, Archaeology and Myth* (New York: Thames and Hudson, 1989). For more on Indo-European religiosity, see Hans F. K. Gunther, *The Religious Attitudes of the Indo-Europeans,* trans. Vivian Bird (London: Clare Press, 1967); Gerald James Larson, ed., *Myth in Indo-European Antiquity* (Berkeley: University of California Press, 1974); and J. P. Mallory and D. Q. Adams, eds., *The Encyclopedia of Indo-European Culture* (London and Chicago: Fitzroy Dearborn Publishers, 1997).

13. Even Soma, who was nothing more than a plant treasured by the Indo-Europeans for its mind-altering properties and so was never humanized in the same way as his cohorts, eventually takes on the body of Chandra, the Hindu god of the moon, to become a seated deity who holds a cup of the intoxicating drink in one of his four hands.

14. The Mycenaean script is known by the rather prosaic name of Linear B. As Edith Hall notes, Mycenaean sites have been excavated in Thebes, Tiryns, Therapne, Pylos, Crete, and of course Mycenae itself. Hall does a splendid job of outlining the influence of Mycenaean culture on the ancient Greeks in *Introducing the Ancient Greeks: From Bronze Age Seafarers to Navigators of the Western Mind* (New York: W. W. Norton, 2015), 29–49.

15. Barbara Graziosi, *The Gods of Olympus: A History* (New York: Picador, 2014), 12.

16. Barbara Graziosi notes that despite Phidias's famous statue of the virgin Athena erected in the Parthenon, the Athenians continued to revere the olive wood as Athena, and that in fact during the festival in honor of the goddess, it was the piece of wood and not Phidias's statue that would receive the ceremonial offering. *Gods of Olympus,* 47. For a description of Phidias's *Athena Parthenos,* see Pausanias, *Description of Greece* trans. W.H.S. Jones (Cambridge, Mass.: Harvard University Press, 1935) 5.1–15.

17. For Athena as the solar deity, see Miriam Robbins Dexter, "Proto-Indo-European Sun Maidens and Gods of the Moon," *Mankind Quarterly* 55 (1984): 137–44. On Hera's representation, see Walter Burkert, *Greek Religion,* trans. John Raffan (Cambridge, Mass.: Harvard University Press, 1985), 31.

18. As James Lesher notes in his outstanding translation and commentary of Xenophanes's work: "Fragment 15 generalizes . . . that various kinds of animals would depict their gods as similar to themselves, if they could, each assigning to the gods bodies like the ones they themselves had. . . . At least superficially, these are comments on the diversity of belief and on a certain propensity of believers to attribute to gods qualities which the believers themselves possess. We are not told [by Xenophanes] whether these considerations should serve to *undermine* these beliefs, either by having proved them false or having subjected them to ridicule, although they are commonly read in this way." James H. Lesher, *Xenophanes of Colophon: Fragments; A Text and Translation with Commentary* (Toronto: University of Toronto Press, 1992), 89, 91.

   Interestingly, Xenophanes lived during the sixth and fifth centuries, which is precisely when the Greeks were starting to create more and more lifelike images of the gods in stone and bronze.

19. Xenophanes is quoted in Catherine Osborne, *Presocratic Philosophy: A Very Short Introduction* (Oxford: Oxford University Press, 2004). Thales is quoted in Cicero, *The Nature of the Gods* (Oxford: Oxford University Press, 2008). For more on Greek monotheism, see Laurel Schneider, *Beyond Monotheism: A Theology of Multiplicity* (London: Routledge, 2007). Martin West refers to this Greek concept of "one god" as a "mindless god," though it's difficult to say whether thinkers such as Plato would agree with that definition. Consider this synopsis of Plato's *Timaeus* from the *Oxford Companion to Classical Literature:* "In the beginning God existed, and, being good, created the universe in as perfect a form as possible, from two substances, the incorporeal substance of ideas, and the material elements. From these, mingled in various proportions, God formed the world, its soul, the lower gods, the stars. The lower gods in turn created man and the animals, according to certain geometrical formulae. The origin of sensations and diseases is then traced, the three kinds of soul that inhabit man described, and the fate of man after death briefly

indicated." Paul Harvey, ed., *The Oxford Companion to Classical Literature* (Oxford: Clarendon Press, 1951), 431. Martin West is quoted in "Towards Monotheism," *Pagan Monotheism in Late Antiquity,* ed. Polymnia Athanassiadi and Michael Frede (Oxford: Oxford University Press, 1999), 21–40.

6. THE HIGH GOD

1. As Rita Freed has observed: "[Akhenaten was] depicted in a manner that can only have been shocking to the ancient viewer accustomed to the traditional rendering of the human figure." Numerous congenital diseases have been proposed to explain the unusual depictions of Akhenaten in Egyptian statuary and carvings, including Marfan's syndrome, but DNA evidence has more or less disproved these hypotheses. Based on this evidence, it has been suggested that Akhenaten's unusual physical features, and those of his family, including his wife Nefertiti and son Tutankhamen, were intentionally exaggerated by the artists of the Amarna period. Many Egyptologists, notes James Hoffmeier, have embraced the notion that the "unique Amarna style should be understood in some symbolic manner rather than being a naturalistic (or exaggerated) portrayal of the king's pathologies . . . there is a stream of thought that associates the male figure of the king with feminine characteristics as reflecting the universal nature of Aten as sole creator (i.e., no consort) who is father and mother." In consonance with Hoffmeier, Gay Robins has suggested that "since one of the functions of Egyptian art was to express religious ideas visually, it is highly probable that the change in the artistic representation of the king's figure was related to Amenhotep IV / Akhenaten's new religious ideas." See Rita Freed, "Art in the Service of Religion and the State," in *Pharaohs of the Sun: Akhenaten, Nefertiti, Tutankhamun* (Boston: Museum of Fine Arts in association with Bulfinch Press/Little, Brown, 1994), 112; James K. Hoffmeier, *Akhenaten and the Origins of Monotheism* (Oxford: Oxford University Press, 2015), 133; Ahad Eshraghian and Bart Loeys, "Loeys-Dietz Syndrome: A Possible Solution for Akhenaten's and His Family's Mystery Syndrome," *South African Medical Journal* 102/8 (2012): 661–64; and Gay Robins, "The Representation of Sexual

Characteristics in Amarna Art," *Journal of the Society for the Study of Egyptian Antiquities* 23 (1993): 36.

2. The Ennead consists of the creator god Atum, his children Shu and Tefnut, their children Nut and Geb, and their children Isi, Osiris, Seth, and Nephthys. See Rudolf Anthes, "Egyptian Theology in the Third Millennium B.C.," *Journal of Near Eastern Studies* 18/3 (1959): 169–212.

The sun was worshiped across multiple regions of Egypt by different names, such as Re, Khepri, Horus, and Atum, but by the fourteenth century these names had become incorporated into a national sun worship, and each one of these individual sun gods came to reflect different aspects of the sun. Early examples of this activity can be found in the *Pyramid Texts,* which were likely composed during the Fifth or Sixth Dynasties (2350–2175 B.C.E.): "I shine in the East like Re, I travel in the West like Khoperer [Khepri], I live on what Horus Lord of the sky lives on by the decree of Horus Lord of the sky" (PT 888). And in yet another section of the *Pyramid Texts:* "They will bring you into being like Re in this his name of Khoperer; you will draw near them like Re in his name of Re; you will turn aside from their faces like Re in his name of Atum" (PT 1693–95). Raymond O. Faulkner, *The Ancient Pyramid Texts* (Oxford: Clarendon Press, 1969), 156, 250–51.

3. Approximately two hundred years before Akhenaten was crowned, Ahmose I (c. 1539–1514 B.C.E.), the founder of the Eighteenth Dynasty, solidified the association between Amun and Re—the patron deities of the northern capital, Thebes, and the southern capital, Heliopolis, respectively. The conflation of these deities is evidenced on a stele of Ahmose I recovered from Karnak by Georges Legrain in 1901, which reads: "Horus: Great of appearances . . . Gold Horus: Who unites the Two Lands, the king of Upper and Lower Egypt, lord of the Two Lands: Nebpehtire, Son of Re, his beloved: Ahmose (may he live forever!), son of Amun-Re, of his body, his beloved, his heir, to whom his throne was given, a truly good god, mighty of arms, in whom there is no falsehood, a ruler equal of Re . . ." In this stele, argues Hoffmeier, we have concrete evidence that the names Amun and Re were used by Ahmose I "in synonymous parallelism, thereby equating the two deities." The merging of the Theban dynastic house with the solar cult of Heliopolis was a clever bit of political maneu-

vering on the part of Ahmose I, who was keen to promote the unification of Upper and Lower Egypt under one ruler after centuries of
division and strife. As Hoffmeier notes, "The ideology of the univer-
sally ruling pharaoh required a universal deity, and Amun-Re, the fu-
sion of sky and sun, was well suited for this role." Mark-Jan Nederhof,
"Karnak Stela of Ahmose," n.p. [cited 24 April 2014], mjn.host.cs
.st-andrews.ac.uk/egyptian/texts/corpus/pdf/urkIV-005.pdf; Georges
Legrain, "Second Rapport sur les travaux exécutés à Karnak du 31
octobre 1901 au 15 mai 1902," *Annales du Service des Antiquités de
L'Égypte* 4 (1903): 27–29; James Breasted, *Ancient Records of Egypt,*
vol. 2 (Chicago: University of Chicago Press, 1906), 13–14; and Hoffmeier, *Akhenaten and the Origins of Monotheism,* 50, 59.

4. It is not entirely clear whether Akhenaten visited Heliopolis during
his formative years or how much he knew of the Lower Kingdom's
theology. Most Egyptologists agree that the future king Akhenaten
was likely raised in Memphis, the city which had been liberated from
the Hyksos by Ahmose I nearly two centuries earlier. But even if
Akhenaten never set foot in Heliopolis, he would likely have come in
contact with the solar cult and its teachings. As Donald Redford has
argued, "The sun god and his theology so permeated the Egyptian
cultus that it would have been hard to insulate a young prince from
solar influence wherever he might have been brought up." Donald
Redford, *Akhenaten the Heretic King* (Princeton: Princeton University Press, 1984), 59.

5. Akhenaten quoted in Maj Sandman, *Texts from the Time of
Akhenaten* (Bruxelles: Édition de la Fondation Égyptologique Reine
Élisabeth, 1938), 7.

The Sun Disc of Aten was an important symbol during the rule of
Akhenaten's father, Amenhotep III, thereby indicating that there was
already a focus on a "solar religion" at the start of the fourteenth
century B.C.E. After the death of Amenhotep III, the king was deified
and became synonymous with the solar deity. According to Raymond
Johnson, the experience of losing his father, combined with his father's deification as Aten, had a profound effect on Akhenaten's religious sensibilities. Specifically, Johnson argues that Akhenaten's
actions after ascending to the throne were neither monotheistic nor
radical. Rather, Akhenaten was simply engaging in an elaborate form
of ancestor worship, whereby the deified father was the central focus

of his son's religious practices and aspirations. Johnson's view is not accepted by the majority of Egyptologists. See Raymond Johnson, "Monuments and Monumental Art Under Amenhotep III: Evolution and Meaning," in *Amenhotep III: Perspectives on His Reign,* ed. David O'Connor and Eric H. Cline (Ann Arbor: University of Michigan Press, 2001): 63–94; Donald B. Redford, "The Sun-Disc in Akhenaten's Program: Its Worship and Antecedents, I," *Journal of the American Research Center in Egypt* 13 (1976): 47–61; and Erin Sobat, "The Pharaoh's Sun-Disc: The Religious Reforms of Akhenaten and the Cult of the Aten," *Hirundo: The McGill Journal of Classical Studies* 12 (2013–2014): 70–75, 73.

6. It is unclear exactly when Zarathustra preached his faith. Dates range from the purely mythical (8000 B.C.E.) to the eve of the Iranian kingdom (seventh century B.C.E.). I believe the most logical date for the birth of Zoroastrianism is c. 1100–1000 B.C.E., and I explain why in my article "Thus Sprang Zarathustra: A Brief Historiography on the Date of the Prophet of Zoroastrianism," *Jusur* 14 (1998–99): 21–34.

7. The gods of ancient Iran had a function and task, but their influence was global, not local. For instance, Mithra was the deification of "covenant," but became associated with the sun because the sun sees everything. Nevertheless, as Boyce notes, "like most other Indo-Iranian divinities, Mithra was conceived in human shape, even if greater than any mortal king." The gods are themselves abstract, claims Boyce, "in that there was no natural object which one could look at and see as their regular physical embodiment; for although the association of Mithra and Vauruna Apam Napat with fire and water evidently existed already in Indo-Iranian times, it was not an identification, nor essential to their being. There existed, however, another group of gods who represented physical phenomena and who might be said actually to *be* those phenomena." For instance, Atar the god of fire, Anahita the goddess of waters, and Asman the sky god. Mary Boyce, *A History of Zoroastrianism,* vol. 1: *The Early Traditions* (Leiden: Brill, 1975), 24, 31, 68–69.

8. Zoroastrians are known by a range of terms. In Iran they are called Zartushti, though they mostly refer to themselves as Beh-Din. In South Asia they are known as Parsees. The Greeks called them Magis.

     Although there are those—Boyce included—who do not believe that Zarathustra viewed Ahura Mazda as the sole god in the universe, the fact remains that no other god exists in the Gathas. Composed in Old Avestan and meant to be sung aloud, the Gathas are a collection of seventeen hymns, purportedly written by Zarathustra himself. See Herman Lommell, *Die Religion Zarathustras. Nach dem Awesta dargestellt* (Hildesheim: Olms, 1971).

In all likelihood, Ahura Mazda was a "proto-Varuna" and may have originated as a god whose name is now lost to us. In other words, we may only know this divine figure through his two main epithets: Ahura, which means "Lord," and Mazda, which means "Wise" or "Wisdom." For a discussion on the etymology of Ahura Mazda, see F.B.J. Kuiper, "Ahura 'Mazda' 'Lord Wisdom'?" *Indo-Iranian Journal* 18/1–2 (1976), 25–42.

9. These reflections, which are known to Zoroastrians as Amesha Spentas, or "Holy Immortals," manifest themselves as six distinct emanations: Vohu Manah ("good mind"), Asha Vahistah ("truth"), Khshatra Vairya ("love"), Spenta Armaity ("devotion"), Hurvatat ("health"), and Ameretat ("immortality"). These reflections are brought into existence by Ahura Mazda's divine will and are meant to personify the deity's major attributes. Considered by Zoroastrians to be worthy of worship, the veneration of the Amesha Spentas was limited to the act of communing with Ahura Mazda.

The first appearance of the Amesha Spentas is in the Gathas. Although the term "Amesha Spentas" does not appear in the Gathas themselves, the names of the six reflections do (see Yasna 47.1). In the later writings of the Avesta—the collection of literature of which the Gathas are the oldest part—the Amesha Spentas become gods themselves, serving Ahura Mazda in his heavenly court. Dinshaw J. Irani, *Understanding the Gathas: The Hymns of Zarathushtra* (Wolmsdorf, Pa.: Ahura Publishers, 1994).

10. As mentioned, not all scholars of Zoroastrianism agree that Zarathustra was monotheist, for instance Mary Boyce in her comprehensive *History of Zoroastrianism,* 3 vols. (Leiden: Brill, 1975–1991). For an opposing view, see Farhang Mehr, *The Zoroastrian Tradition: An Introduction to the Ancient Wisdom of Zarathustra* (Rockport, Mass.: Element, 1991).

11. Another thing to note is that the "divine determinative"—a symbol in Egyptian hieroglyphics connected to the written name of a god, thus identifying that name as belonging to a god—was never used for

the Aten's name. In Akhenaten's mind, there was no need to expressly identify the Aten as divine, as though he were one god among many. Erik Hornung, *Akhenaten and the Religion of Light,* trans. David Lorton (Ithaca and London: Cornell University Press, 1999), 85, 199.

12. Such exclusivist ideals carry with them certain political and economic consequences. After all, the negation of all other gods leads to the swift unemployment of their priests and attendants and confusion among the general populace. It is well known that Akhenaten's religious reforms greatly reduced the power and privilege of Amun-Re's priestly establishment, which, under the Eighteenth Dynasty, had grown enormously wealthy. Similarly, Zarathustra's religion threatened the power and authority of the Magi by replacing all of their deities with a god who had no need for their mantras and rituals. It should come as no surprise, therefore, that after the death of both men, it was the priestly establishments that strongly and, in the case of Egypt, violently reasserted the previous religious traditions.

13. Henotheism can also be understood as the belief in a singular ultimate reality that manifests itself in the guise of numerous gods and goddesses, each of whom, as avatars of ultimate reality, can be objects of legitimate worship.

14. The term "politicomorphism" was coined by Thorkild Jacobsen, and it is he who has written most eloquently about this process in ancient Mesopotamia. See *The Treasures of Darkness*: *A History of Mesopotamian Religion* (New Haven: Yale University Press, 1976), 73.

According to Jacobsen, "The Sumerians and Akkadians pictured their gods as human in form, governed by human emotions, and living in the same type of world as did men. In almost every particular the world of the gods is therefore a projection of the terrestrial conditions. . . . In similar fashion, we must explain the fact that the gods are organized politically along democratic lines, essentially different from the autocratic terrestrial states which we find in Mesopotamia in the historical periods. Thus in the domain of the gods we have a reflection of older forms, of the terrestrial Mesopotamian state as it was in prehistoric times."

Jacobsen again: "Our material seems to preserve indications that prehistoric Mesopotamia was organized politically along democratic lines, not, as was historic Mesopotamia, along autocratic. The indications which we have, point to a form of government in which the normal run of public affairs was handled by a council of elders but ultimate sovereignty resided in a general assembly comprising all members—or perhaps better, all adult free men—of the community." Thorkild Jacobsen, "Primitive Democracy in Ancient Mesopotamia," *Journal of Near Eastern Studies* 2/3 (1943): 167, 172.

15. My translation of the *Enuma Elish* comes from the anthology of Wilfred G. Lambert, *Babylonian Creation Myths* (Winona Lake, Ind.: Eisenbrauns, 2013). For more on the transformation of Marduk and the metaphor of god as king, see Jacobsen, *The Treasures of Darkness*.

16. The Assyrian god Ashur was alone among the gods of Mesopotamia in not having a particular function or power or attribute, or even a personality, for that matter. But that was because Ashur was understood to be not just the patron god of the Assyrian capital city that bore his name, *he was the city itself*. He was the city deified. As such he simply took on the characteristics of his citizens. Thus, when, around the thirteenth century B.C.E., the city of Ashur was transformed from a small pastoral town into the seat of an expansionist Assyrian Empire, the god Ashur was transformed, too—from a charmless, impersonal deity into the god of war and the master of heaven. As Wilfred Lambert states: "There seems to be no certain case of a city in southern Mesopotamia bearing the name of the local god. The one possible exception is Muru. This is attested as a name of Adad, and there was a city of the same name. But the ancient sources do not make Adad patron of this city, so the identity of name may be a coincidence." Wilfred G. Lambert, "The God Aššur," *Iraq* 45/1 (1983): 82–86, 84.

17. Scholars generally agree that Shiva was originally known by the name Rudra, or "The Howling One," and that the word *shiva* ("kind; auspicious") was used in the Vedic period as an adjective for Rudra. The terms become interchangeable, however, after the Vedic period when Rudra is used as a synonym for Shiva. Adding further fuel to the fire, Shiva is called by numerous other names, thereby indicating an even greater association with other deities (*Devendra*, "chief of the gods"; *Trilokinatha*, "lord of the three realms"; *Ghrneshwar*, "lord of compassion"; *Mahādeva*, "Great god"; *Maheśvara*, "Great Lord"; and *Parameshvara*, "Supreme Lord"). "Rudra," claims Mark Muesse, "had no friends among the other gods and preferred to dwell in wild

and terrifying places. . . . Aryans usually left their offerings to Rudra outside their villages and implored him to stay away. But, paradoxically, Rudra was also a healer. . . . Many scholars, in fact, believe that the Vedic *deva* Rudra may have provided a prototype for the god later known as Shiva."

Similarly, Doris Srinivasan observes: "An intensification of Rudra's appearance and an amplification of his domain occurs mainly in the post–Rig Vedic Samhitas. In those texts, Rudra is decidedly on his way to becoming the great god promulgated by the Svetas'vatara Upanishad [i.e., Rudra-Shiva]. In this process, Rudra's features and affiliations are no longer meant to convey mythic or literal images. Rather, the sum of his traits are meant to impart a theological statement on the absoluteness of the Supreme, experienced as God. Such a god encompasses everything, gives rise to everything and is Lord of everything. . . . The radical intensification of Rudra's appearance and actions may thus be viewed as speculative attempts within the Vedic tradition to define the nature of the all-encompassing Supreme God." Mark Muesse, *The Hindu Traditions: A Concise Introduction* (Minneapolis: Fortress Press, 2011), 47–48; and Doris Srinivasan, "Vedic Rudra-Śiva," *Journal of the American Oriental Society* 103/3 (1983): 544–45.

7. GOD IS ONE

1. By the time of the Babylonian invasion, the kingdom of Israel had already fractured in half, the northern kingdom having fallen to the Assyrian forces of Sargon II in 722/21 B.C.E. In the wake of the Assyrian crisis, the literati from the north may have traveled to the south at this time, taking their writings and narratives with them (most likely in oral rather than written form). If true, then the influence of the Elohist source may have started as early as the late eighth century B.C.E., a time of major crisis for both the northern and southern kingdoms.

Two major military campaigns against the kingdoms, both at the hands of the Assyrians (722/21, Sargon II, and 701 B.C.E., Sennacherib), not to mention regional tensions with neighboring groups (Syria, Moab, and others), resulted in the production of a number of prophetic oracles and books during this and the following century in an attempt to reconcile the situation with their understandings of god: First Isaiah (south), Amos (north), Hosea (north), Micah (south), Nahum (north), Zephaniah (south), Habakkuk (south), Joshua, Judges, Samuel, Kings, parts of Psalms, and parts of Deuteronomy.

From a theoretical standpoint, one could argue that the emphasis on worshiping Elohim as a distinct god (i.e., the northern perspective) ends after 722/21 B.C.E. with the destruction of the northern kingdom. The worship of Yahweh continues in the south until 586 B.C.E., but Yahweh's worship may have been altered/affected/supplemented by the northern stories focusing on Elohim (thus the rise of J/E). In other words, there may have already been a blending of J and E in the 135 years between the destruction of the north and the destruction of the south. But even if there wasn't a blending during this period, J and E are definitely combined, if only in name, by the Priestly writers during the sixth and fifth centuries B.C.E. The preeminence of the Yahweh material, its association with Moses, and the feeling that it is older than the Elohist, may come down to the fact that the southern kingdom survived longer than the north and that the god of the north (Elohim) was defeated by the god of the Assyrians (Ashur) in 722. Had the south been destroyed rather than the north, it's possible that the Elohist material would appear to be older than that of the Yahwist. As it is, however, the Elohist material feels more recent and less personal than the Yahwist. Then, after the Babylonian exile, the biases against the north begin to subside and there is an effort on the part of the Priestly writers and redactors to retain as many of their traditions and stories as possible, which, from Second Isaiah's perspective, necessitates the merging of the J and E into a single god.

2. As L. Köhler maintains: "God is the ruling Lord: that is the one fundamental statement in the theology of the Old Testament. . . . Everything else derives from it. Everything else leans upon it. Everything else can be understood with reference to it and only it." Ludwig Köhler, *Old Testament Theology,* trans. A. S. Todd (Philadelphia: Westminster Press, 1957), 30.

3. Technically speaking, *Yahweh* does not mean "I am." Although God responds to Moses's request to identify himself in Exodus 3:14 by

saying *ehyeh asher ehyeh*, or "I am what I am," the deity subsequently directs Moses to tell the Israelites that "The LORD [*Yahweh*], the God of your fathers, the God of Abraham, the God of Isaac, and the God of Jacob, has sent me to you" (Exodus 3:15). Unlike the word *ehyeh*, which is the first person singular form of the Hebrew verb of being *hyh* ("I am/will be"), *Yahweh*, which is God's proper name in the Hebrew Bible, is a variation of the third person singular form of the same verb ("He is/will be"). See Francis Brown, S. R. Driver, and Charles Briggs, *A Hebrew and English Lexicon of the Old Testament* (Oxford: Oxford University Press, 1951), 217–18, and Sigmund Mowinckel, "The Name of the God of Moses," *Hebrew Union College Annual* 32 (1961): 121–33.

4. Moses's name is Egyptian, and it contains the same root as the theophoric names Tuthmosis ("Thoth born; drawn out by Thoth") and Rameses ("Ra born; drawn out by Ra"). Moses, the Hebrew Bible tells us, was born to Hebrew parents, though they are left unnamed in the original story of his birth and are given names only much later in order to shore up his genealogy and strengthen his connection to his Israelite ancestors: "Amram took to wife Jochebed his father's sister and she bore him Aaron and Moses, the years of the life of Amram being one hundred and thirty-seven" (Exodus 6:20).

   Although we have no archaeological evidence for Moses's existence, it is possible that he may have been born in the New Kingdom, perhaps a generation or two after the earth-shattering though ultimately doomed monotheistic revolution of the heretic pharaoh Akhenaten. That has led some scholars to suggest that Moses was heavily influenced by Akhenaten's radical monotheism and that indeed, Israelite religion was a form of Atenism that survived the post-Akhenaten purge. See Donald B. Redford, *Akhenaten: The Heretic King* (Princeton: Princeton University Press, 1984); Jan Assman, *Of Gods and Gods: Egypt, Israel, and the Rise of Monotheism* (Madison: University of Wisconsin Press, 2008); and *From Akhenaten to Moses: Ancient Egypt and Religious Change* (Cairo: American University in Cairo, 2014).

5. Genesis indicates that the Midianites were descendants of Midian, one of Abraham's sons through his wife, Keturah (Genesis 25:1–2). However, this seems like an editorial attempt to connect Moses to Abraham and should not be taken at face value. It is perhaps best to

think of the Midianites not in terms of a single location but rather as a confederate tribe of non-Semitic desert-dwelling peoples who extended from the Sinai to Arabia. See William J. Dumbrell, "Midian: A Land or a League?" *Vetus Testamentum* 25/2 (1975): 323–37.

6. For the location of "the mountain of god" near Seir, see Deuteronomy 33:2 and Judges 5:4. The confusion and lack of consistency within the traditions relating to Moses runs deeper than just a matter of location. For example, Moses's father-in-law is given three different names in the Bible: Reuel (Exodus 2, Numbers 10), Jethro (Exodus 3, 4, and 18), and Hobab (Numbers 10, Judges 4). In some places the father-in-law is described as a Midianite (Exodus 2, 18, Numbers 10) and in others he is a Kenite (Judges 4). Part of the confusion seems to come from Judges 4:11, in which Hobab is called Moses's father-in-law, but this is countered by Numbers 10:29, in which Hobab is described as the son of Reuel (that is, Moses's brother-in-law or a member of the tribe of Reuel). Whatever the explanation, it is clear that multiple sources, written at different times by different authors, have been brought together to create a sustained narrative about Moses. See William Foxwell Albright, "Jethro, Hobab, and Reuel in Early Hebrew Tradition," *Catholic Biblical Quarterly* 25/1 (1963): 1–11.

7. Technically, anyone who labored in construction under the authority of the state was a slave to pharaoh; indeed priests were considered slaves to the temples they served. See Schafik Allam, "Slaves" in *The Oxford Encyclopedia of Ancient Egypt,* ed. D. Redford (Oxford: Oxford University Press, 2001), 293–96.

Exodus 12:37 tells us that the Israelites numbered "six hundred thousand men on foot, besides women and children" (cf. Exodus 38, Numbers 2). If accurate, then the Israelites would have numbered well over one million, which would have rivaled the size of the entire Egyptian population. That of course is absurd; it should not be taken seriously.

There is a wide range of dates for the Exodus story with some maintaining an early date, circa 1447 B.C.E., and others suggesting a much later one, perhaps as late as 1270 B.C.E. The oldest reference we have to "Israel" as a distinct group, or people, appears in the so-called Israel Stele (c. 1208 B.C.E.), which lists the military conquests of pharaoh Merneptah (third son of Rameses II, who ruled from 1213 to

1203 B.C.E.). In the twenty-seventh line of this stele, the text reads, "Israel is laid waste; his seed is no more," which would indicate that a people called "Israel" were already in existence by the end of the thirteenth century B.C.E. This is at odds with the biblical chronology for the Exodus event that many have argued took place around 1280 B.C.E. (+ 40 years in the wilderness = 1240 B.C.E. for the conquest of Canaan by Joshua). The problem is that the witness of the Bible suggests that a couple of centuries pass before Israelites become a unified nation of tribes (i.e., "Israel") under Saul and David—eleventh century B.C.E. (i.e., the books of Joshua, Judges, which covers a couple of centuries all by itself, and the early chapters of 1 Samuel).

Rameses II, the pharaoh typically identified as the king of the Exodus events (Exodus 1:8–11), reigned from 1279 to 1213 B.C.E., which doesn't seem to fit with the witness of the Israel Stele. Bear in mind, of course, that the Bible doesn't provide any dates for Joshua, and biblical scholars have used the Egyptian records as a way to date the Exodus event. See Michael G. Hasel, "Israel in the Merneptah Stela," *Bulletin of the American Schools of Oriental Research* 296 (1994): 45–61; Anson F. Rainey, "Israel in Merneptah's Inscription and Reliefs," *Israel Exploration Journal* 51/1 (2001): 57–75; Hans Goedicke, "Remarks on the 'Israel-Stela,' " *Wiener Zeitschrift für die Kunde des Morgenlandes* 94 (2004): 53–72; and Bryant Wood, "The Rise and Fall of the 13th-Century Exodus-Conquest Theory," *Journal of the Evangelical Theological Society* 48/3 (2005): 475–89.

8. A possible clue as to Yahweh's origins may be located in the enigmatic way he first introduces himself to Moses. "I am who I am," Yahweh declares (Exodus 3:13), which, as DeMoor notes, was the same phrase that the Egyptian sun god Re used to describe himself. Johannes C. De Moor, *The Rise of Yahwism: The Roots of Israelite Monotheism,* 2nd ed. (Leuven: Peeters, 1997). See also Walter Zimmerli, *Old Testament Theology in Outline* (Edinburgh: T&T Clark, 1978), 152; Michael C. Astour, "Yahweh in Egyptian Topographic Lists," in *Festschrift Elmar Edel* in *Agypten und Altes Testament,* ed. Manfred Görg (Bamberg, Germany: Görg, 1979), 17–19; Horst Dietrich Preuss, *Old Testament Theology* (Louisville: Westminster John Knox Press, 1995), 69.

The Midianite connection seems plausible as it is something of a blot on Moses's record and an issue that he is challenged on by his brother Aaron and his sister Miriam: "Miriam and Aaron spoke against Moses because of the Cushite woman whom he had married, for he had married a Cushite woman" (Numbers 12:1). Not unlike the different names used for Moses's father-in-law (see note above), the Hebrew Bible here refers to Moses's wife as a Cushite, yet Moses is never described as taking a second wife. This confusion notwithstanding, the Midianite connection is further strengthened by the story of Balaam, who was likely a Midianite, and, more important, a prophet of Yahweh (Numbers 22–24; Numbers 31:8). See L. Elliott Binns, "Midianite Elements in Hebrew Religion," *Journal of Theological Studies* 31/124 (1930): 337–54; George W. Coats, "Moses in Midian," *Journal of Biblical Literature* 92/1 (1973): 3–10; Karel van der Toorn, *Family Religion in Babylonia, Ugarit, and Israel: Continuity and Change in the Forms of Religious Life* (Leiden: Brill, 1996), 283.

9. The most common use of El's name in the Bible is in its plural form, Elohim, meaning quite literally "gods." When the Bible uses the name Elohim, it tends to use third person masculine singular verbs (e.g., "he said" or "he created"). In a handful of instances, however, the Bible presents Elohim as speaking in the first person plural—"Let *us* make humankind in *our* image" (Genesis 1:26). Since the King James translation of the Bible, composed at the dawn of the seventeenth century, English speakers have generally dismissed this as an example of the *Plural of Majesty,* ignoring the fact that there is no such thing as the majestic plural in the Hebrew language. The real explanation for why El uses the plural form of address in these biblical passages is because El is speaking to the other divine beings in its court (for instance, Genesis 35:7, 2 Samuel 7:23, and Psalms 58:11; see also Genesis 11:7 and Isaiah 6:7). In other words, El, according to the first chapter of Genesis, is not the sole god in the universe; El is merely the highest god in a henotheistic pantheon. See Frank Moore Cross, "Yahweh and the God of the Patriarchs," *Harvard Theological Review* 55/4 (1962): 225–59, and *Canaanite Myth and Hebrew Epic: Essays in the History of the Religion of Israel* (Cambridge, Mass.: Harvard University Press, 1997); Mark S. Smith, *The Early History of God: Yahweh and the Other Deities in Ancient Israel,* 2nd ed. (Grand Rapids: Eerdmans, 2002), 32–43; W. R. Garr, *In His Own Image and Likeness: Humanity, Divinity, and Monotheism* (Leiden: Brill, 2003);

and Samuel Sahviv, "The Polytheistic Origins of the Biblical Flood
Narrative," *Vetus Testamentum* 54/4 (2004): 527–48.

The goddess Asherah held a place of extreme honor within the
Canaanite religious tradition as both the consort of El and matriarch
of the divine family. And with the eventual conflation of El and Yahweh into a single deity by the Priestly writers, the worship of Asherah
as the wife of Yahweh appears to have continued for some time. As
William Dever has argued: "The 'silence' [in the Bible] regarding
Asherah as the consort of Yahweh, successor to Canaanite El, may
now be understood as the result of the near-total suppression of the
cult by the 8th–6th century reformers. As a result, references to 'Asherah,' while not actually expunged from [the Hebrew Bible] . . . were
misunderstood by later editors or reinterpreted to suggest merely the
shadowy image of the goddess. . . . Yet the very fact of the necessity
for reform in ancient Israel reminds us that worship of Asherah, the
'Mother Goddess,' sometimes personified as the consort of Yahweh,
was popular until the end of the Monarchy." William G. Dever, "Asherah, Consort of Yahweh? New Evidence from Kuntillet 'Ajrûd," *Bulletin of the American Schools of Oriental Research* 255 (1984): 31.
See also William G. Dever, *Did God Have A Wife? Archaeology and
Folk Religion in Ancient Israel* (Grand Rapids: Eerdmans, 2008). For
information on Asherah and other Canaanite deities, see Smith, *The
Early History of God;* Dennis Pardee, *Ritual and Cult at Ugarit* (Atlanta: Society of Biblical Literature, 2002); and John H. Walton, *Ancient Near Eastern Thought and the Old Testament: Introducing the
Conceptual World of the Hebrew Bible,* 3rd ed. (Grand Rapids:
Baker Academic, 2009).

The editorial activities of the Priestly writers are evident in numerous places in the Bible, such as when Yahweh explicitly identifies
itself as El: "When Abram was ninety-nine years old, Yahweh appeared to Abram, and said to him, 'I am El Shaddai; walk before me,
and be blameless'" (Genesis 17:1). As Bandstra notes: "The God of
Abraham goes by three different designations [in the Bible]—YHWH,
El Shaddai, and Elohim. From Creation until Abraham, the deity was
Elohim. Then he revealed himself to Abraham and the other ancestors as El Shaddai. The ancestors never knew his name to be YHWH.
Here, in one of its rare uses of the name YHWH, the Priestly tradition makes the identification between YHWH and El Shaddai ex-

plicit so that readers will not be confused. In the Priestly historical record, God did not clarify that he was both YHWH and El Shaddai until he spoke to Moses. In [Genesis] 17:3 the Priestly writer reverts to Elohim, which is his normal pre-Exodus designation for God." Barry Bandstra, *Reading the Old Testament: Introduction to the Hebrew Bible,* 4th ed. (Belmont, Calif.: Wadsworth, 2009), 86.

10. The names of various Canaanite gods and goddesses continue to appear as nondivine concepts in the Hebrew Bible long after they have been stripped of their divine connotations. For example, the Canaanite god of the sea, *Yam,* eventually becomes the word for "sea" in the Hebrew Bible. Similarly, the designations for other Canaanite gods, such as *Mot,* the god of death, *Baal,* the lord of storms, and *Shemesh,* the sun god, become the Hebrew words for "death," "lord," and "sun" respectively. Furthermore, the recovery of various archaeological artifacts and texts, such as the Ugarit archive and Mari letters, as well as the inscriptions from Deir 'Alla, Kuntillet 'Ajrûd, and Khirbet el-Qôm, have shed considerable light on the Canaanite religion and its relationship with the Israelite tradition. As Mark Smith has observed: "Despite the long-regnant model that the 'Canaanites' and Israelites were people of fundamentally different culture, archaeological data now cast doubt on this view. The material culture of the region exhibits numerous common points between the Israelites and the 'Canaanites' in the Iron I period (c. 1200–1000). The record would suggest that the Israelite culture largely overlapped with, and derived from, 'Canaanite' culture." Smith, *Early History of God,* 6.

11. A number of biblical scholars have come to embrace the notion that the Israelites were, at one point in time, Canaanites. According to this theory, first proposed by George Mendenhall and later refined by Norman Gottwald, there was no conquest of Canaan by an external force, as described in the book of Joshua. Rather, the tribes who would eventually come to be known as the Israelites were actually disaffected hill-dwelling Canaanite pastoralists who were wearied by the oppressive rule of their valley-dwelling urban brethren. Through a series of violent revolts against their city-state overlords, these rural Canaanites succeeded in forming a distinct identity as Israelites—an identity that remained deeply rooted in the culture, language, and religion from which they had emerged. See George E. Mendenhall, "The Hebrew Conquest of Palestine," *Biblical Archaeologist* 25/3

(1962): 65–87; Norman K. Gottwald, *The Tribes of Yahweh: A Sociology of the Religion of Liberated Israel, 1250–1050* B.C.E. (Maryknoll, N.Y.: Orbis Books, 1979); and George E. Mendenhall and G. A. Herion, *Ancient Israel's Faith and History: An Introduction to the Bible in Context* (Louisville: Westminster John Knox Press, 2001). For more on the similarities between Israelite and Canaanite culture, see Michael David Coogan, "Canaanite Origins and Lineage: Reflections on the Religion of Ancient Israel," in *Ancient Israelite Religion: Essays in Honor of Frank Moore Cross,* ed. Patrick D. Miller et al. (Philadelphia: Fortress Press, 1987), 115–84.

12. The Bible notes numerous occasions when images of Baal and Asherah were placed in the Temple of Jerusalem and altars made to them at "high places," where the Israelites offered them prayers and sacrifices (see, for instance, 2 Kings 21:1–7). For evidence of monolatry in the Bible, see Exodus 20:3 and Deuteronomy 5:7. For evidence of Israel worshiping gods of its neighbors, see Judges 10:6.

13. Although Genesis 17 opens with Abram receiving a vision from Yahweh, the deity in question refers to itself by another name: "When Abram was ninety-nine years old the LORD [Yahweh] appeared to Abram, and said to him, 'I am God Almighty [El Shaddai]; walk before me, and be blameless'" (Genesis 17:1–2). It is El, therefore, not Yahweh with whom Abram makes his exclusive agreement: "Then Abram fell on his face; and God [Elohim] said to him, 'Behold, my covenant is with you, and you shall be the father of a multitude of nations. No longer shall your name be Abram, but your name shall be Abraham'" (Genesis 17:3–5). As with the example of Exodus 6, here again we see the Priestly writers struggling to conflate the Yahwistic and Elohistic sources on Abram/Abraham into a cohesive narrative with a singular deity. In fact, the story of Abram/Abraham in Genesis, like the story of Moses in Exodus, is muddled by the explicit attempt in the later Priestly writer to stitch the older, conflicting Yahwist and Elohist strands of the story into a single semicohesive narrative. But if we look closely, we can see the original Elohist source material peeking through the Priestly rewrite of the Abram/Abraham story, such as when Abram moves from Ur to Haran with his barren wife, Sarai, and his nephew, Lot (Genesis 11:31, 12:4–5). Once in Haran, Abram was visited by a deity that the Priestly writer who composed this particular section of the story calls Yahweh (Genesis

12:1, 4), despite the fact that in Exodus Yahweh tells Moses that Abraham never knew him by that name: "I am Yahweh. I appeared to Abraham, Isaac, and Jacob as El Shaddai, but by my name Yahweh I did not make myself known to them" (Exodus 6:2–3). Regardless, this deity orders Abram to leave Haran for the "land of the Canaan" (Genesis 11:31, 12:5–6). Abram obeys, and in doing so he becomes the first person to be called a Hebrew, meaning "one who crosses over" (Genesis 14:13). He travels with his kin down to the city of Shechem, which was El's cultic center in the north of Canaan.

At Shechem Abram stops at a sacred tree called the Oak of Moreh, renowned for making oracles (a talking tree!), in order to build an altar to the god that had called him to this land. From Shechem, Abram journeys on to the hill country just east of Bethel, which is not a city but rather a temple dedicated to the god El ("I am El of Bethel," El declares in Genesis 31:13), and then down into the Negev, where he seems to have settled for some time before taking a brief and highly unlikely sojourn in Egypt, the entire purpose of which was to connect Abram/Abraham's story (and his god!) with that of Moses (Genesis 12:10–13:1). Finally, Abram and his kin settle permanently in the city of Hebron, near another sacred oracular tree, the Oaks of Mamre (Genesis 13:18). In Hebron, Abram lives a life of wealth and luxury, somehow managing to accumulate an enormous amount of livestock, gold, and silver as well as an untold number of slaves, servants, and trained fighting men under his employ—all symbolic of the blessing of his god. The fighting men would come in handy. After Mesopotamian invaders launched a surprise attack on the Canaanite city of Salem (Jerusalem), Abram sent these men to defend the city. In return, Salem's grateful priest/king, Melchizedek, offered Abram a blessing in the name of God Most High: *El Elyon* (Genesis 14:18–20).

14. This thesis finds further support in the incident of Jeroboam, who may have acted to reestablish the cult of Yahweh-El at Dan and Bethel via his "golden bulls." Alternatively, the Golden Calf may also be seen as an attempt on the part of the Israelites to reembrace their Egyptian religious beliefs by worshiping Hathor, the goddess of motherhood and love who was often depicted as a cow (the use of Egyptian jewelry to make the Golden Calf is particularly interesting in this regard—Exodus 32:4, "These are your gods, O Israel, who brought you up out of the land of Egypt!").

15. As Mark Smith has observed, "It also suggests that Yahweh, originally a warrior god from Sinai/Paran/Edom/Teiman, was known separately from El at an early point in early Israel. Perhaps due to trade with Edom/Midian, Yahweh entered secondarily into the Israelite highland religion. Passages such as Deuteronomy 32:8–9 suggest a literary vestige of the initial assimilation of Yahweh, the southern warrior god, into the larger highland pantheism, headed by El." Smith, *The Early History of God*, 32–33.

16. There are only a handful of passages in which we find the Yahweh-El designation: Genesis 14:2—Yahweh El Elyon; Genesis 21:33—Yahweh El Olam ("eternal God"); Psalms 10:12—Yahweh El; Psalms 31:6—Yahweh El Emet ("faithful God"); Psalms 94:1—Yahweh El Neqamot ("God of vengeance"); and Psalms 140:7—Yahweh Ely ("LORD my God").

17. "According to the Bible," notes Marco Treves, "the earliest Reign of God was the regime existing in the days of the Judges. Gideon refused to accept an invitation of the Israelites to become their king because he did not wish to deprive the Lord of His kingdom (Judges 8:22–23). When the elders of Israel asked Samuel to give them a king the prophet reproached them, because the accession implied the rejection of the Lord (1 Samuel 5:4–7, 10:18–19, 12:12). From these two episodes we may infer: a) that in the opinion of the authors of these passages a human monarchy and a divine monarchy were mutually exclusive; b) that according to tradition, God had been the King of Israel in the days of the Judges; c) with the anointing of Saul God's Reign came to an end." Similarly, Martin Cohen has observed that the "evidence in the Bible demonstrates that the monarchy, as had been planned, was subordinated ideologically to the Shilonite priesthood. In both accounts of the selection of the first monarch, it is Samuel the Shilonite priest who anoints the regent; he acts in the name of Yahweh and as an official interpreter of Yahweh's will. Likewise, it is Samuel the Shilonite who completely transforms the traditional attitude of the Yahwistic ideology toward monarchy. Whereas formerly the ideology insisted that Israel was to have no king because Yahweh was its king, now Yahweh sanctioned the monarchy under his aegis and, it goes without saying, under the aegis of his spokesmen, the priests. The old guard leadership hoped that by subordinating the monarchy to the priesthood, it might be kept weak, and that

if it should seek to increase its strength at their expense the priests might hear Yahweh's voice dismissing the king from office. This is exactly what happened in the case of Saul." Marco Treves, "The Reign of God in the O.T.," *Vetus Testamentum* 19/2 (1969): 230–31; Martin Cohen, "The Role of the Shilonite Priesthood in the United Monarchy of Ancient Israel," *Hebrew Union College Annual* 36 (1965): 59–98, 69.

"The monarchy," argues Mark Smith, "was equally a political and religious institution, and under royal influence, religion combined powerful expressions of state and religious ideology. When the prestige of the national deity was increased, the prestige of the dynasty in turn was enhanced. The special relationship between Yahweh and the Davidic dynasty assumed the form of a formal covenantal relationship, called in 2 Samuel 23:5 an 'eternal covenant.' . . . The religious-political conceptualization of the covenant reached its fullest expression in the Davidic dynastic theology. The nationalization of the covenantal form exalted Yahweh as the national deity of the united monarchy. The national hegemony of Yahweh was thereby established for ancient Israel."

Smith continues: "The innovative centralization of national worship was also part of the process leading to monotheistic Yahwism, as it encouraged a single national deity and devalued local manifestations of deity. The royal unification of national life—both political and religious—helped to achieve political and cultic centralization by concentrating and exhibiting power through the capital city and a relationship with the national deity residing in that city. This development was concomitant with the development of the monarchy itself. It began with the establishment of the capital city under David, continued in the religious importance of Jerusalem achieved under Solomon, and culminated in the religious programs of Hezekiah and Josiah. . . . The religious function was but one dimension in the effects of cultic centralization. This religious policy held political and economic benefits as well. The role of the monarchy was both innovative and conservative, reacting to the needs of the developing state." Smith, *Early History of God,* 185–87.

18. The principal voice of this new religious expression was the prophet Isaiah, or, more specifically, the prophet scholars refer to as Second Isaiah (the book of Isaiah in the Bible is actually three books merged:

First Isaiah—chapters 1–39—written pre-Exile, Second Isaiah—chapters 40–55—written either during or immediately after the Exile, and Third Isaiah—chapters 56–66—written much later).

19. The appearance in Ezekiel of the prophet's vision of God in "something that seemed like a human form" (Ezekiel 1:26), or Zechariah's vision of God presiding over a divine counsel (Zechariah 3:7), attest to the fact that the old mythic conceptions of a humanized god do not completely disappear in the postexilic literature of the Bible. However, they are significantly diminished. See Smith, *Early History of God,* 141–47.

8. GOD IS THREE

1. In fact, John explicitly identifies Jesus as Yahweh. In an extraordinary passage near the end of his gospel, a torch-wielding mob of Temple police and Roman soldiers come to arrest him in the Garden of Gethsemane. "Whom are you looking for?" Jesus asks the crowd. "Jesus of Nazareth," they answer. Jesus replies, "I am," or *ego eimi,* which is the Greek rendering of the name Yahweh in the Septuagint, the Greek translation of the Hebrew Bible. And just in case any of his readers might have missed the significance of this moment, John has the entire arresting mob immediately fall to the ground at the power of Jesus's words (John 18:1–8).

   As I have written elsewhere, the term "Son of God," which is frequently applied to Jesus in the Synoptics, is not a *description* of his nature, but a common *title:* Many people are called Son of God in the Bible, including Satan. For more on "Son of God" as title, not description, see my *Zealot: The Life and Times of Jesus of Nazareth* (New York: Random House, 2013).

2. Chris de Wet notes that for the Greeks, "the Logos also functions as the rational principle by which the universe is governed. They discerned between different types of logoi . . . namely: (a) the Logos *spermatikos,* indicating a germinal indwelling of the Logos within all human beings; (b) the Logos *endiathetos,* an unspoken thought in the mind of God . . . ; and (c) the Logos *prophorikos* is then the expression of the latter mentioned divine thought. Especially with the Stoics, the Logos is already associated with the notion of expression."

Chris de Wet, "Mystical Expression and the 'Logos' in the Writings of St. John of the Cross," *Neotestamentica* 42/1 (2008): 35–50, 39.

3. As Chalupa notes: "Roman emperors were gods or at least many of them were proclaimed as such after their death. As far as we know, in the period from 14 C.E. until 337 C.E., of the 60 emperors who ruled the Roman Empire, 36 were deified, together with 27 members of their families. They received a cult and had their own priesthoods and festivals. Altars and temples were consecrated to them. Whether they were seen as gods when still alive remains an open question and a subject of many scholarly controversies." Aleš Chalupa, "How Did Roman Emperors Become Gods? Various Concepts of Imperial Apotheosis," *Anodos—Studies of the Ancient World* 6–7 (2006–2007): 201.

4. The Greek historian Diodorus of Sicily tells us that Philip of Macedon was killed by a jilted bodyguard at the theater of Aegae in 336 B.C.E., the assassination occurring while Philip was overseeing the erection of a statue of himself alongside those of the twelve gods of Olympus. It isn't clear if Philip was understood to be a god during his lifetime, or if his act of self-deification at Aegae was partly to blame for his murder, but one thing is certain—Philip was treated as a divine individual after his death. As Arthur Boak has observed: "Formally, the attribution of divinity to a monarch was made possible by the fact that Greek theology and mythology had never drawn very sharp limits between the divine and the human spheres. The demigods and heroes formed a sort of easy transition from the human to the divine. Most of the great families of Greece traced their descent from some god or hero, just as the Macedonian royal house itself claimed Heracles as its ancestor. The Greek colonies regularly raised their *oikistes,* upon his death, to the dignity of a hero, honored by the state with suitable ceremonies of worship, and similar cults existed in many of the older cities of Greece. But yet it must be observed that strict religious tradition did not sanction the deification of a human being during his lifetime. Actually, however, such honors had been rendered to men of note in the Greek world, while they were still living, long before the time of Alexander the Great." Moreover, as Larry Kreitzer notes: "The Greeks had a long history of deifying their kings, a practice that is traceable in coinage at least as far back as the reign of Alexander the Great (336 to 323 B.C.E.). Some kings actively

promoted this policy during their reigns, perhaps the most famous
example being the Seleucid king Antiochus IV (175 to 164 B.C.E.), one
of Alexander's successors. This act eventually brought Antiochus
into direct conflict with his Jewish subjects and set the stage for the
ensuing Maccabean revolt." Arthur Edward Romilly Boak, "The
Theoretical Basis of the Deification of Rulers in Antiquity," *Classical
Journal* 11/5 (1916): 293–94; Larry Kreitzer, "Apotheosis of the
Roman Emperor," *Biblical Archaeologist* 53/4 (1990): 212.

5. It's not that the ancient Egyptians considered their living pharaohs to
literally *be* Horus. Rather, the pharaoh sat upon his throne *as* Horus.
Horus was thought to inhabit the pharaoh's body. While the Egyptian sources confirm the pharaoh's divine nature, they also clearly
depict him as human, possessing human qualities and human limitations. Of course, ascribing human attributes to the pharaoh would
not in itself preclude his divinity, considering that the gods were also
described in similarly human terms. However, there is a marked contrast in the descriptions between the power of the gods and the power
of the pharaoh, with the pharaoh clearly viewed as inferior. That has
led some Egyptologists to surmise that the pharaoh's divinity was
merely a metaphor or a propaganda tool that few Egyptians took
seriously. But it is difficult to imagine how the concept of divine kingship could have survived for so long unless it held significant meaning
for the population as a whole. The more likely explanation is that it
wasn't so much the *person* of the pharaoh that was considered divine
as it was the *office*.

The pharaoh was considered human until he or she (there were a
handful of female pharaohs) took the crown; deification occurred at
coronation, though as time went on it became common to consider
the pharaoh to have been predestined for the position before birth.
John Baines sums it up this way: "The king was a human mortal with
a divine role in an 'everlasting' office and institution." John Baines,
"Kingship, Definition of Culture, and Legitimation," in *Ancient
Egyptian Kingship*, ed. David O'Connor and David P. Silverman
(Leiden: Brill, 1995), 3–48, 6. See also Donald B. Redford, "The Sun-
Disc in Akhenaten's Program: Its Worship and Antecedents, II,"
Journal of the American Research Center in Egypt 17 (1980): 21–38;
Byron E. Shafer, ed., *Religion in Ancient Egypt: Gods, Myths and
Personal Practice* (Ithaca and London: Cornell University Press,

1991); David P. Silverman, "The Nature of Egyptian Kingship," in *Ancient Egyptian Kingship,* ed. David O'Connor and David P. Silverman (Leiden: Brill, 1995), 49–94.

6. For more on the concept of divine kingship in Mesopotamia, see Henri Frankfort, *Kingship and the Gods: A Study of Ancient Near Eastern Religion as the Integration of Society and Nature* (Chicago: University of Chicago Press, 1948); Gillian Feeley-Harnik, "Issues in Divine Kingship," *Annual Review of Anthropology* 14 (1985): 273–313; Gebhard Selz, "'The Holy Drum, the Spear, and the Harp': Towards an Understanding of the Problems of Deification in Third Millennium Mesopotamia," in *Sumerian Gods and Their Representations,* ed. I. J. Finkel and M. J. Geller (Groningen: Styx, 1997), 167–209; Nicole Brisch, "The Priestess and the King: The Divine Kingship of Šū-Sîn of Ur," *Journal of the American Oriental Society* 126/2 (2006): 161–76.

7. It should never be forgotten that Jesus's primary identity on earth was as the Messiah: "the King of the Jews," in Roman parlance. Jesus's kingly status was affirmed by both his Jewish and Roman followers. The very language that Christians used to talk about Jesus reflected the language that Romans used for the emperor. An inscription in the city of Ephesus made in the latter years of Julius Caesar's life dubbed him "God made manifest and common Savior of Mankind." The birthday of Caesar's successor, Augustus, was called "good news," the same term Christians used for the birth of Jesus (and to describe their gospels). And the emperor's arrival in the city was known as "the *parousia*," which is how Christians described the Second Coming of Christ.

8. Justin Martyr as quoted in *Dialogue with Trypho the Jew,* trans. Lukyn Williams (New York: Macmillan, 1930), 113; Paul of Samosata as quoted in Dennis C. Duling, *Jesus Christ Through History* (New York: Harcourt, 1979), 74.

9. Marcion was an adherent of what was known as Docetism (from the Greek word *dokein,* meaning "to seem"), meaning he believed that Jesus only *appeared* to be human; that, as God, he could not really have taken flesh or been born of a woman. His physical body was merely an illusion, a means of allowing people to interact with what was in reality a purely divine spirit. As David Salter Williams notes, "Marcion is also thought to have promoted a docetic Christology,

denying Jesus's corporeality." David Salter Williams, "Reconsidering
Marcion's Gospel," *Journal of Biblical Literature* 108/3 (1989): 477.

10. According to Gnostic teachings, the unknowable God of the universe
(the Father) was responsible for the creation of several lesser-known
deities. The last of these deities, Sophia, desired to know the unknowable God, and as a result the Demiurge was brought into existence.
As the second-century church father Irenaeus tells us: "These men
[the Gnostics] falsify the oracles of God, and prove themselves evil
interpreters of the good word of revelation. They also overthrow the
faith of many, by drawing them away, under a pretense of [superior]
knowledge, from Him who rounded and adorned the universe; as if,
forsooth, they had something more excellent and sublime to reveal,
than that God who created the heaven and the earth, and all things
that are therein. By means of specious and plausible words, they cun-
ningly allure the simple-minded to inquire into their system; but they
nevertheless clumsily destroy them, while they initiate them into their
blasphemous and impious opinions respecting the Demiurge; and
these simple ones are unable, even in such a matter, to distinguish
falsehood from truth. They affirm, therefore, that he [the Demiurge]
was constituted the Father and God of everything outside of the Ple-
roma, being the creator of all animal and material substances. For he
it was that discriminated these two kinds of existence hitherto confused, and made corporeal from incorporeal substances, fashioned
things heavenly and earthly, and became the Framer (Demiurge) of
things material and animal, of those on the right and those on the
left, of the light and of the heavy, and of those tending upwards as
well as of those tending downwards. He created also seven heavens,
above which they say that he, the Demiurge, exists. . . . They go on to
say that the Demiurge imagined that he created all these things of
himself, while he in reality made them in conjunction with the pro-
ductive power of Achamoth. He formed the heavens, yet was ignorant
of the heavens; he fashioned man, yet knew not man; he brought to
light the earth, yet had no acquaintance with the earth; and, in like
manner, they declare that he was ignorant of the forms of all that he
made, and knew not even of the existence of his own mother, but
imagined that he himself was all things" (Irenaeus, *Against Heresies*
1.2–3, 5.2–3).

On *The Secret Gospel of John,* see Frederik Wisse, "The Apocryphon of John," in *The Nag Hammadi Library in English,* ed. James M. Robinson (San Francisco: HarperSanFrancisco, 1978), 104–23.

11. Soren Giversen and Birger A. Pearson, "The Testimony of Truth," in *Nag Hammadi Library in English,* 448–59.

12. It is important to note that Marcion was writing only about fifty years after the Jewish revolt, which led to the destruction of Jerusalem at the hands of the Romans and the outlawing of Judaism as a religion. By severing themselves completely from Jesus's religion, these Christians were not only making a theological argument, they were trying to avoid the same fate as the Jews. On this point see *Zealot: The Life and Times of Jesus of Nazareth,* 57–70.

13. According to Tim Carter, "Marcion argued that the New Testament had been contaminated by the teachings by the followers of the creator god, and he set himself the task of purging the text from their accretions. Accordingly, of the four gospels he only accepted a truncated version of Luke, which started with Jesus's appearance in Capernaum in the fifteenth year of the principate of Tiberias; Marcion also accepted Paul's letters, though he removed the Pastoral Epistles and all Old Testament quotations and positive references to Judaism." Tim Carter, "Marcion's Christology and Its Possible Influence on Codex Bezae," *Journal of Theological Studies* 61/2 (2010): 551–52. See also Einar Thomassen, "Orthodoxy and Heresy in Second-Century Rome," *Harvard Theological Review* 97/3 (2004): 241–56; Bart D. Ehrman, *Lost Christianities: The Battle for Scripture and the Faiths We Never Knew* (New York: Oxford University Press, 2003), 104–109; Williston Walker, *A History of the Christian Church* (New York: Scribner, 1918), 67–69; and Williams, "Reconsidering Marcion's Gospel," 477–96.

14. Elaine Pagels, *The Gnostic Gospels* (New York: Random House, 1979), 35. See also Elaine Pagels, "The Demiurge and His Archons: A Gnostic View of the Bishop and Presbyters?" *Harvard Theological Review* 69/3–4 (1976): 301–24.

15. Constantine's mother, Helena, who was by all accounts a devout Christian, claims to have found the true cross on which Jesus was crucified during a pilgrimage to Jerusalem in 326 C.E. She is also credited with building or renovating several important churches in the Levant and returning to Rome with numerous relics, such as earth from the site of Golgotha. But regardless of the truth of these claims,

one thing is certain—Helena's status as a Christian indicates that by the beginning of the fourth century C.E., Christianity had made its way into the highest levels of Roman society.

In response to the proliferation of the Christian faith within the Empire, Constantine enacted the Edict of Milan (c. 313 C.E.), which made it licit to be a Christian in the Roman Empire. As its informal title suggests, the Edict of Tolerance allowed for religious pluralism within the Roman Empire and freedom from persecution for Christians. Christianity did not become the official religion of Rome, however, until 380 C.E. with the passing of the Edict of Thessalonica under Emperors Flavius Theodosius, Gratian, and Valentinian II.

16. Ironically, Constantine was one of the thirty-six emperors who were deified by the Roman Senate after his death (337 C.E.), which speaks to the diverse range of religious beliefs within Roman society. According to Arnaldo Momigliano, "What really minimized the importance of being 'divus' for a Christian emperor was the chance of becoming 'santus.' Constantine himself was treated in the East like a saint, indeed like one of the apostles, soon after his death." Arnaldo Momigliano, "How Roman Emperors Became Gods," *American Scholar* 55/2 (1986): 191.

17. Tertullian, *Apologetical Works,* and Minucius Felix, *Octavius,* trans. Rudolph Arbesmann, Sister Emily Joseph Daly, and Edwin A. Quain (Washington, D.C.: The Catholic University of America Pres, 1950), 63.

Tertullian believed that the three beings in the Trinity did not share equally in the divine substance: The Father contained the greatest amount of divinity, followed by the Son, and then the Holy Ghost. In other words, Jesus may have been "of one substance" with God, just not in the same measure as God.

The founder of Neoplatonism, Plotinus (250–270 C.E.), also spoke about God in a trinitarian way supposing that the divine force, which rose out of the Greek hatred for anthropomorphism, was reflected in three forms: the One ultimate form, Intelligence, and the Soul. As Diarmaid MacCulloch notes, "The first represented absolute perfection, the second was an image of the first but was capable of being known by our inferior senses, and the third was a spirit which infused the world and was therefore capable of being diverse, in contrast to the Platonic perfection of the One and of Intelligence." Diarmaid

MacCulloch, *Christian History: An Introduction to the Western Tradition* (London: SCM Press, 2012), 80.

18. The Modalists tried to settle the issue by accepting the one substance/three beings interpretation of Tertullian but arguing that this substance wasn't shared by the three beings *at the same time:* It first appeared as the Father, then as the Son, and then finally as the Holy Spirit.

19. What is remarkable about Augustine's statement is not just his willingness to ignore the logical fallacy of his own position. It is also that embedded in the concept of the Trinity is the firmly Hellenistic belief that God can be understood as a material substance that can be divided and shared and, in the case of Jesus, shaped into the form of a man. Indeed, the very notion of God as spiritual rather than material was virtually nonexistent in the fifth-century Church. Augustine himself viewed God as a very large man in heaven with "an immense shining body."

20. Chalcedon translation from R. V. Sellers, *Council of Chalcedon: A Historical and Doctrinal Survey* (London: SPCK, 1953), 210. See also Roland Teske, "The Aim of Augustine's Proof That God Truly Is," *International Philosophical Quarterly* 26 (1986): 253–68.

It is a wondrous coincidence of history that the Jews were liberated from their Babylonian exile by the armies of Cyrus the Great, the same Persian king who had helped revive Zoroastrianism in its dualistic form, making it the official religion of his world-conquering Achaemenid Empire. Cyrus's military success lay in his explicit rejection of the idea that war was a battle between gods, with the victorious god vanquishing the defeated. Instead, Cyrus established what is widely regarded as the first human rights charter in the world (the famed Cyrus Cylinder), outlining the freedom of conquered peoples to worship their own gods as they pleased. In every city he captured, he would rebuild the local temples, lavish wealth on the local priesthood, and heap praise upon the local deities. Thus, long before he sent his armies into Babylon, Cyrus sent his Zoroastrian priests—the Magi—with a message for the Babylonian people. The Persian king wanted it to be known that he had no intention of destroying Marduk. On the contrary, he claimed to have been sent by Marduk to free the Babylonians from their own feckless and impious king, Nabonidus. The Magi conveyed a similar message to all of Babylon's captive people, including the Jews. The ploy worked. In 538 B.C.E., nearly five decades after the Babylonian destruction of Jerusalem, Cyrus walked through Babylon's gates in peace, welcomed by both the Babylonians and their captives alike as a savior. Among Cyrus's first actions was to send the exiled Jews back to their homeland, personally paying for the reconstruction of the Temple of Yahweh from Babylon's own treasury. As a result, Cyrus the Great was dubbed "Yahweh's shepherd" (Isaiah 44:28) by the Jews, becoming one of only a handful of individuals in the entire Bible, and the only non-Jew, to be called Messiah (Isaiah 45:1).

9. GOD IS ALL

1. According to the Prophet Muhammad's biographer, Tafsir al-Tabari, Muhammad sent letters inviting submission to Islam to Heraclius and Khosrow and also to the negus of Ethiopia, the ruler of Egypt, the ruler of Bahrain, and the governor of Syria. Although most scholars accept the historicity of the letters, some, including Gabriel Said Reynolds, have cast doubt on the veracity of al-Tabari's claims. See *The Emergence of Islam: Classical Traditions in Contemporary Perspective* (Minneapolis: Fortress Press, 2012), 49.

2. The best account of the centuries-long battle between the Byzantine and Persian empires—going back to before the rise of Christianity—is the one recounted by the eminent historian David Levering Lewis in *God's Crucible: Islam and the Making of Europe, 570–1215* (New York: W. W. Norton, 2008).

3. Interestingly, Najmah Sayuti, referencing the fourteenth-century historian Ibn Khaldun notes that "those who could not afford a temple or adopt an idol would put a stone in front of the Ka'ba or in front of any other temple they might choose, and then venerate it in the same way they would venerate the Ka'ba itself. The pagan Arabs named these stones *ansab;* however, if they resembled a human being or a living creature they called them *asnam,* or *awthan.*" "The Concept of Allah as the Highest God in Pre-Islamic Arabia," MA thesis, McGill University, 1999, 39.

4. The argument that Islam actually began as a Jewish messianic move-

ment is generally known as Hagarism and was first introduced by the eminent historians Patricia Crone and Michael Cook in their book *Hagarism: The Making of the Islamic World* (Cambridge: Cambridge University Press, 1977). Cook and Crone rely on Syriac and Hebrew sources for the rise of Islam to argue that Muhammad was a Jew (based on the connections between Judaism and Islam recounted above) and that his followers were originally called Hagarenes, after Abraham's first wife, Hagar, from whom Muhammad traced his ancestry. Although Hagarism has been almost completely dismissed by scholars of Islam, its influence can still be seen in some modern treatments of Islamic history—for example, Tom Holland, *In the Shadow of the Sword: The Birth of Islam and the Rise of the Global Arab Empire* (New York: Doubleday, 2012).

It is important to note that Muhammad's knowledge of Judaism came not from the Torah but from his encounters with Arab Jews. Although the traditional perception of the Prophet Muhammad as illiterate is inaccurate (as a successful merchant living in the most cosmopolitan of all Arab cities, Muhammad very likely had a rudimentary ability to read and write, perhaps even in multiple languages), he would not have had access to the Hebrew scriptures for the simple reason that there were no copies of the Hebrew scriptures among the Jews of Arabia. I explain this in my book *No god but God: The Origins, Evolution, and Future of Islam* (New York: Random House, 2005), 97–100.

I have translated *Allah-u Samad* as "God is Unique," because that is the best definition of the difficult Arabic word *samad,* which is sometimes translated as "eternal." The word literally means "independent of anyone," and so here I follow the tradition passed down by Ali ibn Husain, who explained *samad* as "One Who has no partner and it is not difficult for Him to protect things, and nothing is hidden from Him."

5. It should be mentioned that while Jews in the Sassanian Empire fared better than their coreligionists in the Byzantine Empire—the Babylonian Talmud was composed under Iranian rule, and numerous Jewish schools of learning were established across the realm—even there, laws against proselytizing limited Jewish influence over the great theological debates taking place in the court.

6. See Arent Jan Wensinck, *The Two Creeds, Fikh Akbar II* in *The Nor-*

ton Anthology of World Religions, vol. 2, ed. Jack Miles (New York: W. W. Norton, 2015), 1553–59.

7. For al-Ashari, see Majid Fakhry, "Philosophy and Theology: From the Eighth Century C.E. to the Present," in *The Oxford History of Islam,* ed. John L. Esposito (New York: Oxford, 1999).

8. A popular translation of Rumi's poems is Colman Barks, *The Essential Rumi* (1995); see also the two-volume *Mystical Poems of Rumi* translated by A. J. Arberry (1968) and Reynold Nicholson's *Rumi: Poet and Mystic* (1950). For more on Rumi's life, see Annemarie Schimmel, *I Am Wind, You Are Fire: The Life and Works of Rumi* (1992) and the new biography by Brad Gooch, *Rumi's Secret* (New York: Harper, 2017). Later interpretation of the first meeting between Shams and Rumi has developed the conversation into a theological doctrine on the nature of the Prophet Muhammad. On this point see Omid Safi, "Did the Two Oceans Meet? Historical Connections and Disconnections Between Ibn ʿArabi and Rumi," *Journal of Muhyiddin Ibn ʿArabi Society,* 26 (1999): 55–88.

9. For more on the Drunken Sufis see Ahmet Karamustafa, *Sufism: The Formative Period* (Berkeley: University of California Press, 2007).

10. Born in the Spanish city of Murcia in 1165 C.E.—a century before Shams met Rumi—Ibn al-Arabi grew up in Seville, the capital of al-Andalus, in an era marked not only by remarkable advances in the arts and sciences and the widespread translation of Greek scientific and philosophical works into Arabic, but also by an unprecedented religious cross-pollination among Jews, Christians, and Muslims. The famed Jewish philosopher Maimonides lived in al-Andalus at this time, as did one of history's most influential thinkers, Ibn Rushd—known in the west as Averroës. For more on al-Andalus under Muslim rule, see María Rosa Menocal, *Ornament of the World: How Muslims, Jews, and Christians Created a Culture of Tolerance in Medieval Spain* (New York: Back Bay Books, 2003). The story of Ibn al-Arabi's epiphany and Ibn Rushd's response is taken from the introduction to William C. Chittick's excellent book *The Sufi Path of Knowledge: Ibn al-Arabi's Metaphysics of Imagination* (Albany: SUNY Press, 1989).

11. "There is only one Existence. That existence is, naturally, a state of Being. That being, then, is the One and Only, Infinite Being. It exists through its own existence irrespective of any other consideration."

Bulent Rauf, "Concerning the Universality of Ibn 'Arabi," *Journal of the Muhyiddin Ibn 'Arabi Society,* vol. 6, 1987. Ibn al-Arabi was relying on the great thinkers who had come before him. In some ways he was refining the thought of the great Islamic thinker Ibn Sina—Avicenna in the west—and his doctrine of Necessary Existence, which itself was based on the Neoplatonic understanding of God as "pure Being."

CONCLUSION: THE ONE

1. There are at least three stories in the early parts of Genesis in which humans strive to be like God or tinker with godlike abilities: the story of Eden; the fallen angels of Genesis 6; and the Tower of Babel story ("Come let us build ourselves a city, and a tower with its top in the heavens, and let us make a name for ourselves . . ." Genesis 11:4). In each instance the theologians of Genesis put humanity in its place for striving to be gods or godlike.

2. See Michael P. Levine, *Pantheism: A Non-Theistic Concept of Deity* (London: Routledge, 1994), 91.

   The *Stanford Encyclopedia of Philosophy* defines pantheism thus: "At its most general, pantheism may be understood positively as the view that God is identical with the cosmos, the view that there exists nothing which is outside of God, or else negatively as the rejection of any view that considers God as distinct from the universe."

   A distinction is made between pantheism and panentheism. The former asserts that the universe is God. The latter says that while God is present within the universe, he transcends it. As William Rowe writes, the difference between the two really boils down to how one views the universe: "According to panentheism, the universe is finite and within God, but God is truly infinite and so cannot be totally within or otherwise limited to the finite universe." In other words, the differences between pantheism and panentheism depend on whether one believes the universe is finite or not. In my view, the definition of the word "universe" is "everything that exists," and so there can be no substantive difference between pantheism and panentheism. In fact, to me, panentheism is simply another way of holding on to a humanized God, one with will and intention beyond the workings of the universe. See William Rowe, "Does Panentheism Reduce to Pantheism? A Response to Craig," *International Journal for Philosophy of Religion* 61/2 (2007): 65–67.

Schopenhauer ridiculed the idea that the world should be called God. "Taking an unprejudiced view of the world as it is, no one would dream of regarding it as a god. It must be a very ill-advised god who knows no better way of diverting himself than by turning into such a world as ours, such a mean, shabby world."

But as Levine explains, God and the world do not mean the same thing, nor do they necessarily refer to the same thing for the pantheist. However, pantheists do take the world and God to have identical sense and reference on a certain interpretation of each. God, the world, and the all-inclusive Divine Unity all allegedly refer to the same thing. So they believe things to be true of God and the world that nonpantheists do not. It is a question of disagreement not just over the properties of God and the world, but over their meanings. When pantheists claim that the world, or God, is an all-inclusive Divine Unity, they mean something different by God and the world than in the nonpantheistic usage of these terms. See Levine, *Pantheism*, 26–29. For more on pantheism, see H. P. Owen, *Concepts of Deity* (London: Macmillan, 1971); Alasdair MacIntyre, "Pantheism," *Encyclopedia of Philosophy* 6:31–35; and John Macquarrie, *In Search of Deity* (London: SCM Press, 1984).

3. "Thus all beings are God, if considered in their essential reality, but God is not these beings and this, not in the sense that His reality excludes them, but because in the face of His infinity their reality is nil." Titus Burckhardt, *Introduction to Sufism* (London: Thorsons, 1995), 29. The analogy of the light passing through the prism comes from Ibn al-Arabi himself, as noted by Mazheruddin Siddiqi, "A Historical Study of Iqbal's views on Sufism," *Islamic Studies* 5/4 (1966): 411–27.

4. The Vedanta quoted is from W. S. Urquhart, *Pantheism and the Value of Life with Special Reference to Indian Philosophy* (London: Epworth Press, 1919), 25. Timothy Sprigge clarifies Urquhart's analysis, noting that "the first of these [i.e., Nothing is which is not God] says that nothing really exists except the ineffably unitary Brahman and that the ordinary world with all its variety and multiplicity is an illusion. The second [God is everything which is] says that, although the

ordinary world is more than a mere illusion, it consists entirely of modifications of the one universal spirit. The first is the Advaita Vedanta of which Sankara is the great classic exponent, the second is the qualified Vedanta classically formulated by Ramanuja." T.L.S. Sprigge, "Pantheism," *Monist* 80/2 (1997): 199.

Radhakrishnan on pantheism in Vedanta philosophy: "The Vedanta system is supposed to be an acosmic pantheism, holding that the Absolute called Brahman alone is real and the finite manifestations are illusory. There is one absolute undifferentiated reality, the nature of which is constituted by knowledge. The entire empirical world, with its distinction of finite minds and the objects of their thought, is an illusion. Subjects and objects are like the fleeting images which encompass the dreaming soul and melt away into nothingness at the moment of waking. The term Maya signifies the illusory character of the finite world. Sankara explains the Maya conception by the analogies of the rope and the snake, the juggler and jugglery, the desert and the mirage, and the dreamer and the dream. The central features of the Vedanta philosophy, as it is conceived at the present day, are briefly explained in the lines: Brahman is the real, the universe is false, The Atman is Brahman. Nothing else." Sarvepalli Radhakrishnan, "The Vedanta Philosophy and the Doctrine of Maya," *International Journal of Ethics* 24/4 (1914): 431.

Dogen Zenji quoted in *Zen Ritual: Studies of Zen Buddhist Theory in Practice,* Steven Heine and Dale S. Wright, eds. (New York: Oxford, 2008). Chuang-Tze quoted in Rodney A. Cooper, *Tao Te Ching: Classic of the Way of Virtue—An English Version with Commentary* (Bloomington, Ind.: AuthorHouse, 2013), xv. Cooper notes that "Taoism is much more than pantheism. For Tao existed before the Universe was formed. If it is to be compared to another belief system, it is more akin to panentheism—a belief system which posits that the divine (be it a monotheistic God, polytheistic gods, or an eternal cosmic animating force), interpenetrates every part of Nature and timelessly extends beyond it. Panentheism differentiates itself from pantheism, which holds that the divine is synonymous with the Universe" (xvi).

5. The doctrine of *tzimtzum* is more specifically a panentheistic view though numerous thinkers have noted the contradiction in trying to separate God's self from God's creation if that creation is drawn

from God himself. As Rufus Jones puts it, "In order to have a world at all outside of God, He must withdraw into His own Being and concentrate as En-Sof, for how can there be an external world if God is everywhere and all in all?" Rufus M. Jones, "Jewish Mysticism," *Harvard Theological Review* 36/2 (1943): 161–62. See also Gloria Wiederkehr Pollack, "Eliezer Zvi Hacohen Zweifel: Forgotten Father of Modern Scholarship on Hasidism," *Proceedings of the American Academy for Jewish Research* 49 (1982): 87–115.

According to Winfried Corduan, Eckhart's view of God verges on pantheism. "And yet, as close as it may appear—a hair's breadth—there is an infinitely wide gap between pantheism and what Eckhart teaches. For it is not the created order by itself that is divine. It is the redemptive act of God that transforms fallenness into union with him. What cannot be found in nature and cannot be attained beyond nature can be received from God." See Winfried Corduan, "A Hair's Breadth from Pantheism: Meister Eckhart's God-Centered Spirituality," *Journal of the Evangelical Theological Society* 37/2 (1994): 274.

6. Spinoza's pantheism is often referred to as monism: "the view that there exists only one thing or kind of thing." It should be mentioned that Michael Levine makes a clear distinction between pantheism and the philosophical "monism" of Spinoza and others. He writes: "Any simple equation of monism to pantheism can also be ruled out on the grounds that monists may deny that divinity should be attributed to whatever 'One' their monism refers to" (86).

Other "pantheistic" philosophers include Plotinus, Lao Tsu, F.W.J. Schelling, and G.W.F. Hegel, to name a few. See Peter Forrest and Roman Majeran, "Pantheism," *Annals of Philosophy* 64/4 (2016): 67–91.

7. With regard to our natural propensity for "substance dualism," the cognitive scientist Paul Bloom argues that it is "a natural by-product of our possession of two distinct cognitive systems—one for dealing with material objects, the other for social entities." Paul Bloom, "Religious Belief as Evolutionary Accident," in *The Believing Primate: Scientific, Philosophical, and Theological Reflections on the Origin of Religion,* Jeffrey Schloss and Michael J. Murray, eds. (New York: Oxford University Press, 2009), 118–27. Bloom outlines the numerous experiments conducted with children that indicate the foundational belief in mind-body dualism in his book *Descartes' Baby: How*

the Science of Child Development Explains What Makes Us Human (New York: Basic Books, 2004).

Few cognitive theorists have done more experiments on this subject than Justin Barrett. His conclusion is that "a growing number of cognitive developmentalists believe that something about the way human minds develop appears to make us highly susceptible to believing that something in us persists after death and that something might continue to act in the present world. . . . Exactly why believing in souls or spirits that survived death is so natural for children (and adults) is an area of active research and debate. A consensus has emerged that children are born believers in some kind of afterlife, but not on why this is." See Justin L. Barrett, *Born Believers: The Science of Children's Religious Belief* (New York: Atria Books, 2012), 118, 120.

Jesse M. Bering has attempted to provide a cognitive answer to the problem of our intuitive knowledge of the soul, insofar as it pertains to the inborn belief in life after death. Bering argues that "because it is epistemologically impossible to know what it is like to be dead, individuals will be most likely to attribute to dead agents those types of mental states that they cannot imagine being without. Such a model argues that it is natural to believe in life after death and social transmission serves principally to conceptually enrich (or degrade) intuitive conceptions of the afterlife." See Jesse M. Bering, "Intuitive Conceptions of Dead Agents' Minds: The Natural Foundations of Afterlife Beliefs as Phenomenological Boundary," *Journal of Cognition and Culture* 2.4 (2002): 263–308; also "The Folk Psychology of Souls," *Behavioral and Brain Sciences* 29 (2006): 453–98.

Index

Page numbers in *italics* refer to illustrations.

About the Author

Reza Aslan is an internationally acclaimed writer, commentator, professor, producer and scholar of religions. His books include the international bestsellers *Zealot: The Life and Times of Jesus of Nazareth* and *No God But God: The Origins, Evolution and Future of Islam*, which was named as one of the hundred most important books of the last decade. Born in Iran, he lives in Los Angeles with his wife and three sons.

ABOUT THE TYPE

This book was set in Sabon, a typeface designed by the well-known German typographer Jan Tschichold (1902–74). Sabon's design is based upon the original letterforms of sixteenth-century French type designer Claude Garamond and was created specifically to be used for three sources: foundry type for hand composition, Linotype, and Monotype. Tschichold named his typeface for the famous Frankfurt typefounder Jacques Sabon (c. 1520–80).